NO-BRAINER'S GUIDE TO HOW CHRISTIANS LIVE

NO-BRAINER'S
GUIDE TO HOW CHRISTIANS
LIVE

CRAIG

WRITTEN BY **JAMES S. BELL, JR.** AND **STAN CAMPBELL**

 TYNDALE HOUSE PUBLISHERS, INC., WHEATON, ILLINOIS

Visit Tyndale's exciting Web site at www.tyndale.com

Library of Congress Cataloging-in-Publication Data

Bell, James S.
  No-brainer's guide to how Christians live / by James S. Bell and Stan
Campbell.
    p. cm.
  ISBN 0-8423-4007-6 (softcover)
  1. Christian life. I. Campbell, Stan. II. Title.
BV4501.3 .B45 2002
248.4—dc21   2001001899

Printed in the United States of America

06 05 04 03 02
6   5   4   3   2   1

CONTENTS

'The Christian ideal,' it is said,
'has not been tried and found wanting;
it has been found difficult and left untried.'
—G. K. Chesterton

CHAPTER ONE

"HURRY UP, GUYS. WE'RE LOSING HIM TO A SPIRITUAL SLUMP."

Defibrillating Your Spiritual Life

AN INTRODUCTION TO HOW CHRISTIANS LIVE

Meet the DiCiples, a rather average family. Fred is a programmer for a local accounting firm, and Wilma is a stay-at-home mom who does quite well selling cosmetics and kitchenware for traditional home-sales companies. They have a nine-year-old daughter named Mary and a 14-year-old son named Joshua, though for some reason he's asking to be called "Z-Roy" these days. They are a relatively happy and well-adjusted family, active in their church and community.

Today the DiCiples are getting new neighbors, George and Jane Seeker. Peering through the blinds as the moving van is being unloaded, Fred and Wilma can see no hint of children's toys or furniture. And from the Seekers' taste in lamps, sofas, and such, Wilma is guessing they are young and fairly well-to-do. She says a quick prayer that she and Fred will get along better with this couple than they did with the previous neighbors. Yikes! What a fiasco that was!

We'll leave the Seekers to settle in today, but don't forget about them. You'll be hearing a lot about the DiCiples and the Seekers as

SOME THINGS YOU'LL DISCOVER IN THIS CHAPTER

1. A few basic reasons for *why* to pursue the Christian life

2. A CLEAR acronym for *how* to pursue it

3. Two basic priorities to use as guidelines in the Christian life

1

we go through this book. We may discover a few of their faults and shortcomings, but they're all good people we think you'll want to know better.

Christian Living 101

In the meantime, let us welcome you to the *No-Brainer's Guide to How Christians Live.* If you've seen other books in this series you probably know what to expect. If not, that's okay. You've picked a good place to start. Our goal in writing this series is to attempt to deal with some religious-type topics without making them sound dry or churchy.

This is especially true about the Christian life. If you ask people on the street what it means to live a "Christian life," you're likely to hear a litany of things that are forbidden: "Well, Christians can't drink, or smoke, or cuss, or chew, or look at certain magazines or TV shows, or go to certain kinds of movies." The "forbidden list" goes on and on. Before you even get to the end, it seems that the Christian life actually isn't much of a life at all.

Many of us have come to see Christian life as dry, somber, guilt-ridden, busy, and legalistic. By the time we follow all those rules, avoid all those temptations, and fulfill our obligations to God and others, who has time for much of a life? But that's what Jesus wants from us, right?

Don't be so sure. Let's see what Jesus *says* He wants from us. He told His disciples He had come "to give life in all its fullness" (John 10:10). Other translations say He came to provide "abundant life."

Does a lifetime obsessed with attempting to walk a behavioral tightrope to avoid falling into the pit of hell sound like "life in all its fullness"? Doesn't the very concept of "fullness" suggest being able to do more and more things rather than fewer and fewer? Do you think Jesus expects us to approach the Christian life as a chore-like obligation akin to going to the dentist or paying taxes?

The authors don't think that's what Jesus had in mind. And while it's true that God has certain expectations of His people, the things He tells us to do are always for our own benefit. Centuries went by with the Jews' complicated religious system of required animal sac-rifices and legal obligations, all of which pointed to the coming of Jesus. But now that Jesus has come to be the final sacrifice and take the burden of sin off of us, He invites everyone to reap the benefits of the Christian life:

> Come to me, all of you who are weary and carry heavy burdens, and I will give you rest. Take my yoke upon you. Let me teach you, because I am humble and gentle, and you will find rest for your souls. For my yoke fits perfectly, and the burden I give you is light. (Matthew 11:28-30)

Christians are called to wear the "yoke" of obedience to Jesus, but it is a much lighter load than the burden of sin we would bear other-wise. For many people, the promise of rest given by a "humble and gentle" God is irresistible. No other source of so-called spiritual enlightenment can match it. And of course, there are numerous ways for people to muck up the intentions of Jesus as they go about the Christian life. But if we can learn to identify the problems and keep our eyes on the clear promises of Jesus, the Christian life takes on a whole new brilliance that never fades.

As we go through this book we will see that living for Jesus should be a freeing experience rather than a weighty one. It should be filled with joy and laughter rather than weeping and wailing. It should make us grin rather than make us grim.

The Christian life by definition begins with a personal relation-ship with Christ. Maybe you're reading this book only to under-stand the process, or to figure out what makes your Christian friends tick, which is fine. But if you're hoping to experience the Christian life without taking this first step, you're going to be in for a lot of frustration. Many of the things you are called to do will be impossible in your own power. If Jesus isn't your ever-present source of strength and help, you're in for certain failure.

And frankly, that first step is the easiest part of the process. Some people make the decision to place their faith in Jesus based on an overwhelming desire to respond to God's love. Some are motivated by a fear of hell. Some are burdened by problems or situations that are too much to bear alone. And others realize there must be more to life than the emptiness they feel and are eager to pursue a higher calling and challenge. But whatever motivates the person, it's a simple matter of confessing sins, professing faith in Jesus, and making the commitment to become one of His twenty-first-century disciples. Many believers like to follow this decision with a public announcement and/or baptism. All the other believers get really excited, and life is wonderful for a while.

But for most people, it doesn't take long for the newness to wear off. That's because the decision to become a Christian is merely the first step of the Christian life. Success will require continuing to put one foot in front of the other and making regular progress. This book is written in the hope that it might help you march onward in confidence.

Why Bother?

So Jesus Himself has made the invitation to pursue the Christian life. The promise of rest sounds worthwhile, but how about that burden of obedience? Some people resist it with all their might. Why do others eagerly strap on the "yoke"?

Some people keep in mind the *eternal rewards* promised those who follow Christ. Right now they may be poor in spirit, hungry and thirsty for justice, meek, mournful, and more—but one day, Jesus says, they will inherit the kingdom of heaven, see God, and receive ample reward (Matthew 5:1-12). Each faithful action adds to their heavenly IRA, and the interest is compounding daily (Matthew 6:19-21). Regardless of the burden one must bear throughout the Christian life, heaven awaits. And that's enough . . . for some people.

Other people maintain a more immediate perspective of *present rewards*. Yes, they anticipate all the glories of heaven and eternity with God, but even the here and now is elevated to a point beyond what is possible for their nonbelieving peers. They discover a Spirit-inspired infusion of love, joy, peace, patience, self-control, and more (Galatians 5:22-23). When faced with depressing or even devastating events, they find their level of hope never disappears (1 Thessalonians 4:13). Each day takes on a heightened sense of purpose and possibility. Even if heaven weren't just beyond the horizon of death, the presence of Jesus in this present life would be enough.

Still other people find a *deep level of satisfaction* in discovering the Christian life. The highway to hell is a wide expressway with no traffic jams. The path to heaven, in contrast, is a narrow uphill path—less traveled, but much more scenic and refreshing. Only the minority of people who discover it realize how truly special it is (Matthew 7:13-14).

Finally, some people devote themselves to the Christian life because they sense God's calling to do so. Past and present rewards for personal benefit aren't their main motivation. Rather, they relish *the opportunity to serve other people* as preachers, teachers, pray-ers, hosts and hostesses, church administrators, and maybe even good neighbors, as we will see. Because of their selfless devotion, they find fulfillment. In addition, other people—spouses, kids, friends, and acquaintances—discover that narrow road and join them on their journey.

These are reasons *why* some people choose the Christian life. Now let's turn our attention to *how*.

Clear!

Before we can begin to improve our Christian life, we have to start *thinking* about it. Perhaps the biggest problem for many people is that they never stop to give spiritual matters much thought. People not involved in church may get in a routine that seldom touches on spiritual things. And people active in church may get in a routine that puts them through their spiritual paces at such a rate that they seldom take time to think about what they're doing or why.

We want to help you establish a healthy rhythm for your Christian life. Your spiritual commitments should be at the heart of everything else you're doing, and the heart is pretty important.

Your heart has a distinct rhythm. If that rhythm gets a bit too fast, the doctors will recommend exercise or medication to slow it down a bit. If the rhythm gets too slow, you can die. And sometimes a heart will begin to fibrillate, which means the muscles start acting independently of one another rather than working together to achieve the appropriate rhythm. Heartbeat and pulse get disconnected from one another, and the body is at risk. When this happens, the doctors whip out the defibrillator, yell "Clear!" and zap that out-of-sync heart with enough energy to restore the appropriate rhythm.

When it comes to your spiritual life, it might help to think of the word CLEAR as an acronym. Each letter represents a step in the process of preparing yourself for something better that lies ahead.

Cool It!

Before you do anything, do nothing. Just sit there. The Christian life will require that changes take place *inside* before they take place *outside,* and that begins as you actively resist the urge to *do.* We're going to remind you of something several times throughout this book, and this is a good place to start: *You are not in control of the Christian life.* It is the *Christ*-ian life, the *Spirit*-ual life. The secret to a successful Christian life will not be to take control and exert every ounce of energy you have for God. Rather, it is a matter of *yielding* control and letting God work through you.

We're going to get around to planning, working, and doing. But the first and most vital step is to quiet your heart and mind and allow God to speak. It's just as much a problem to get ahead of Him as it is to lag behind.

So calm your mind. Cease and desist. "Center down," as the Quakers say.

Lighten Up

Next, stop gritting your teeth. Unclench your fists. This isn't going to be so bad. Yes, it's your spiritual life, and it should be taken seriously. But when lived appropriately, the Christian life isn't the miserable segment of an otherwise enjoyable life. Rather, the spiritual aspects should begin to permeate *all* areas of life. So if your eyes roll back in your head at any mention of spiritual growth, you need to change your attitude before reading on or your eyes will soon be spinning like the cherries in a casino slot machine.

The philosophy of this book is that it's okay to laugh and attempt to be spiritual at the same time. If you have a sense of humor, you can assume it is God-given, and therefore to be used for His glory. The last thing God wants for His kingdom on earth is a bunch of morbid, robotic disciples shuffling around like the cast of Fritz Lang's 1937 movie, *Metropolis*. Scowling Christians tend to prevent others from investigating the Christian life. A hearty laugh, on the other hand, is a sound of hope that attracts people seeking purpose in an otherwise bleak world.

Evaluate Your Life

Now you're ready to evaluate your life. First, look backward. What is your personal experience with how Christians live? Lots of people have had unpleasant encounters with boring preachers, pushy evangelists, way-too-aggressive strangers, and others who claim to represent Jesus. They think that if that's what lies ahead, forget it! They stop pursuing the Christian life as an option and seek enlightenment elsewhere.

Others have been immersed in the Christian life from day one. It is not unusual for Christian parents to pray for their children while they are in the womb, or even before they are conceived. As those children grow up, they are surrounded by "the Christian life." But the drawback in many such cases is that "the Christian life" is little more than a label. Until the individual makes it personal, he or she is likely to experience a lot of frustration with a "Christian life" in name only.

So look backward and try to recall your own experiences—both good and bad. Perhaps you made some kind of commitment years (or decades) ago but have never really followed up on it. Maybe you've only recently discovered the rewards and promises involved in a Christian commitment and lifestyle. Maybe you've just been waiting for the right time. Whatever your history, try to be honest about your current attitudes and expectations.

Then, look forward. What do you *want* from life? Do you suspect there should be more to the Christian life than what you've experienced so far? Can you truthfully say you're approaching "life in all its fullness"?

If you're not where you long to be, don't worry too much. Life is a spiritual journey from beginning to end. Sometimes we don't progress as quickly as we might like. Sometimes we get detoured, stalled out, or turned around. But as long as we have life, we have the opportunity to regroup, face forward, and/or pick up the pace. However, first we must do an objective evaluation of where we've been, where we are, and where we would like to go. It does little good to make great time if you're going in the wrong direction.

Adjust Your Thinking

Bad experiences in your past may have left you with an attitude of skepticism or even cynicism concerning the Christian life. You may have become content with simply drifting along as if your spiritual journey were the Lazy River at your local water park. Or at the other extreme, perhaps you're long past the burnout stage yet are still surging ahead in your own power to do, do, do for God. None of these mind-sets leads to the abundant life God desires for us.

But if you can identify some of these potential traps, you can avoid them from now on. Among other things, God is something of a coach for His "team." A good coach will adapt and change strategies based on the events taking place on the field. What worked early in the game might be forsaken later on. The best players are those who are versatile enough to adapt, adjust, and, most of all, listen to what the coach has to say. It's not enough for us to thoughtlessly run plays; the object is to score—to win! The Christian life is an ever-changing challenge. It's one thing to get in the game. It's another to stay there. If we aren't pulling our weight, there are a number of capable teammates ready to step in and get the job done.

Recommit Yourself to God

As we pursue the Christian life, we must never forget that God provides "whatever is good and perfect" (James 1:17). He is the source of courage, wisdom, peace, patience, vision, and more. It's useless to attempt a godly life without God at the center.

Suppose you're preparing for a daylong hike through the desert. While preparing your supplies, you discover your canteen packed with sand from the kids' last hike. Do you ignore the sand and fill the remaining space with water? No! You get rid of the sand, flush the canteen, and then replace the gritty sand with pure water.

Similarly, a commitment to the Christian life might require a mental "flush" to rid our minds of accumulated waste products and refill them with devotion to God. The purpose of confessing sins and receiving God's forgiveness is to keep flushing out the "dirt" that tends to accumulate. Only then can we be filled with the living water of God's Spirit (John 7:37-39). If we don't get rid of the dirt first, our insight can get pretty muddy.

God is not only our coach during this journey, He is also the guide. If we're not following Him, we stand to find ourselves in dark and unfamiliar territory.

If your spiritual life has been out of rhythm, start by going through the CLEAR process we have just described. But notice that you haven't done anything other than prepare for God to step in. You can clear your mind, clear your schedule, and clear your grudge list—all fine accomplishments. But unless God gets involved, your spiritual condition is still likely to flatline before it comes back to life.

Suppose you're on the table in the emergency room when the doctor yells "Clear!" Everyone jumps back and waits for the next step. But if he never charges the paddles and applies a jolt to your heart, it is likely to stop fibrillating as it stops altogether.

You can go through the steps of your CLEAR process and still come up short. So you also need to approach God with confidence (Hebrews 4:16) and ask Him to supply the power you need each day as you pursue the Christian life. You probably already know the frustrations of trying it without Him. So as we go through the rest of this book, we're going to try to stay focused on getting Him involved. When your heart feels the power He provides, you will never be the same.

Jesus promised "life in all its fullness." Why should you settle for less?

Back to Basics

In your pursuit of the abundant life that Jesus promises, perhaps you have felt overwhelmed by what God expects. Then again, you might not even be sure what is okay in the Christian life and what isn't. People generally want to please God but sometimes have trouble drawing the lines between black and white.

God has provided His Word to help us out, and the Bible is a wonderful book filled with truth and help. Yet it also happens to be thousands of pages long and a bit unwieldy for beginners. Isn't there some starting point that can simplify the process for those of us committed to improving our lives?

Jesus was once asked essentially this same question. A legal expert who was well-versed in Old Testament Scripture asked: "Of all the commandments, which is the most important?"

Jesus replied: "The most important commandment is this: 'Hear, O Israel! The Lord our God is the one and only Lord. And you must love the Lord your God with all your heart, all your soul, all your mind, and all your strength.' The second one is equally important: 'Love your neighbor as yourself.' No other commandment is greater than these" (Mark 12:28-31).

Jesus' insight here was even better than CliffsNotes. Everything in the Bible is summed up in the commands to (1) love God and (2) love others. It is interesting to note that these two instructions were considered to be a singular "commandment" in the opinion of Jesus. Indeed, further New Testament clarification explains that our love for God is proven by our love for other people. An expressed love for God that doesn't encompass one's friends, family, and neighbors is not genuine love for God (1 John 2:9-11).

So as we go through this book, we are going to try to respond to Jesus' stated priorities. First, we will try to see what we can do to love God with more of our hearts, more of our souls, more of our minds, and more of our strength. We will examine the things that He does for us to enable such worship and how we can properly respond to Him. Next, we will take a look at relationships through a filter of how they provide opportunities for us to show our love for God. We cannot live Christianly apart from each and every one of our human relationships. And finally, we'll see what it means to love our neighbors *as ourselves*. What does it mean to love oneself, and how do we go about it without pride and other problems getting in the way?

Love God. Love others. It's a pretty simple plan. But those who have tried it know it is much more challenging than it sounds. While God is constant and always loving and forgiving, those other people we deal with are often fickle and downright rude. But if the Christian life is truly "life in all its fullness," we're going to have to learn to cope with the people who are every bit as appealing as lemon juice in a paper cut.

Sidebar Tabs

Beginning in the next chapter, look for recurring sidebars to amplify the text material. These short insets should give you additional things to think about as you go through this book. The sidebars are as follows:

Well Said!

This sidebar will contain quotations pertinent to the topic of each chapter. Sometimes what is being said takes on more meaning if expressed in a different way. While the authors will maintain a no-brainer's approach to most of the topics, some of our "guest speakers" will offer deeper insights.

Do's and Don'ts

While we will find that we are given much freedom in the Christian life, we will also come across several specific commands and

prohibitions. This sidebar will spotlight the "for sure" things we should or shouldn't do in regard to our spiritual journeys.

For Example...

Believe it or not, you're not the first person to struggle with spiritual maturity and development. This sidebar will suggest biblical people who faced the same struggles. Some had tremendous faith and became shining examples. Others failed miserably. It is hoped that we can learn from *all* of these people.

One Small Step

It is said that a journey of a thousand miles begins with a single step. Even if you feel you have a long, long way to go in your spiritual journey, we will suggest some steps to get you started. Some will be itty-bitty baby steps. Others will be significant strides. You can try as few or as many as you wish. Don't feel pressured. Trust God to lead you at the best pace for you.

Remember: This is a no-brainer's guide to how Christians live. You're not going to need to be an expert in anything—least of all theology—to understand what we're saying. More important than your level of knowledge is your willingness to consider a few new ideas or changes to your lifestyle. For some readers, the first steps to renewing their Christian life might involve just a little more effort, or doing things just a bit differently. For other people it might require doing less so that God can step in and do more.

But for all of us, it will require a shift of perspective. No longer should we look for the worst so we can shrug our shoulders and mutter, "That's life." From now on we will be looking for life's noncoincidental special events that our loving God provides liberally, as well as all the splendor involved in everyday "ordinary" living. We need to be quicker to notice such things. And when we do, we need to remind ourselves: "That's life in all its fullness!"

Questions to Ponder and/or Discuss

1. How would you define "how Christians live" in 25 words or less?

2. On a scale of 1 (least) to 10 (most), how would you rate each of the following things:

   • Your current level of love for God (including heart, soul, mind, and strength)
   • Your current level of love for others
   • Your current level of love for yourself

3. What do you feel is the first thing you need to do before you see significant improvements in your Christian life?

CHAPTER TWO

Abundant Life: The Owner's Manual

BIBLE STUDY

"Wiiiiill-ma!"

Fred's voice came from the attic. That couldn't be good.

Wilma climbed the ladder and stuck her head into the steamy atmosphere. "You bellowed?"

"Have you seen my Salvation Station Kit? We need to meet our new neighbors and I want to get them started on the Sinner-Saver Tract Program."

Wilma grimaced. "Now Fred, you leave them alone for a while. I want to be able to have a normal relationship with *these* neighbors."

"What are you suggesting?"

"I'm suggesting you scared our last neighbors right out of our neighborhood. And I'm suggesting that you get to know these new ones before you start getting all evangelistic on me."

"Hey, I'm not that bad. I'm just trying to be a good Christian."

"Fred, our last neighbor broke his ankle hurrying to get back inside his house before you could thrust Tract #7 upon him while he was innocently trying to repair his furnace. What was it you yelled?

SOME THINGS YOU'LL DISCOVER IN THIS CHAPTER

1. Several analogies to help us understand the importance of the Bible

2. A few key biblical promises and commands

3. Some basic suggestions to make Bible study more meaningful

ONE SMALL STEP

Try to recall if you've ever had an embarrassing or regrettable experience because of someone who came on too strong with Bible teaching or maybe just pushed his or her faith a little too hard. As you get involved with the Christian life in general, and Bible study in particular, how might you avoid alienating others in the same way?

Oh yes, I remember: 'People in hell won't need to worry about central heating!'"

"Oh look, Wilma. I found a stack of love letters you wrote me in college. I treasure these things, you know."

"Fred, do I have your word that you'll wait a while before pestering our new neighbors?"

"Hey, Wilma, listen to this: 'Dear Fred, you are the most special guy I have ever known. When I'm with you, my life is complete.'"

"Fred, I'm trying to talk to you."

" 'You are everything to me. I love you with all my heart, you righteous stud.' You sure knew how to write back then, Wilma."

"Fred!"

"What is it, Cupcake?"

"The same person who wrote those letters is right here in person trying to get your attention."

"We'll talk after I find my Salvation Station Kit. Okay?"

"All right, I guess. But I'm serious about this."

Wilma went back down the ladder. She didn't like to keep secrets from Fred, but sometimes it was for his own good. It would be months before Fred would find that silly evangelistic tool. That would be plenty of time to practice keeping a straight face when Fred started wondering how in the world it got boxed up with the Christmas decorations.

The DiCiples are a good couple. They really are. But in trying to live the Christian life, Fred sometimes gets carried away. He's convinced it's his duty to infuse his Christian faith into every possible conversation. He actually has tactics to help him turn a conversation from sports to Christianity, from politics to Christianity, from family to Christianity, and from "How about this weather?" to Christianity. He's convinced he's doing the right thing, but he tries way too hard. Just ask his wife, kids, barber, mechanic, coworkers, parents, waitresses, flight attendants, traveling companions—you get the idea.

Wilma is just as devoted to the Christian life as Fred is, but she isn't nearly as pushy. She is more than willing to share her faith but has a more natural and laid-back approach. Yet she has no shortage of opportunities. In fact, last year she began a weekly women's Bible study in her home, which several neighbors now attend. (They meet when Fred isn't around.) Fred, bless his heart, just doesn't have her sensitivity or natural ability to talk about his faith, and he usually resorts to some kind of program or preplanned approach.

Thanks to Wilma, George and Jane Seeker have been spared for a while. But an eventual confrontation is inevitable.

The Bible Tells Me So?

We'll get back to Fred's questionable evangelistic technique in later chapters, but in this chapter we want to start with something more basic: the Bible. If you were to sit down and challenge Fred, he would quickly recite numerous passages that convince him he is doing the right thing. First on his list would be "the Great Commission" of Matthew 28:19-20: "Go and make disciples of all the nations, baptizing them in the name of the Father and the Son and the Holy Spirit. Teach these new disciples to obey all the commands I have given you. And be sure of this: I am with you always, even to the end of the age."

Fred can cite the writings of Paul, Peter, James, and others that motivate him to doggedly pursue new converts in the name of Christ. And if it's in the Bible, he should faithfully obey. Right?

Wilma would argue (if she could get a word in) that evangelism should be based on love for other people. If she is presenting the message of the greatest act of love in history—that Jesus Christ came to earth to die and save the entire world—she wants to try very hard to demonstrate His love to others as she talks about it. Therefore, she tries to get to know people before bringing up sensitive religious topics. She can support her approach with the Bible as well.

Who is more correct: Fred or Wilma? It's hard to say definitively. A good argument can be made for both viewpoints. But one thing is clear. The better we know the Bible—the entire Bible—the better we

ONE SMALL STEP

As we look at the ongoing saga of the DiCiples and the Seekers, we may face a great temptation to pass judgment or take sides. But as we get a fresh start in the Christian life, we need to resist any tendency toward being judgmental. One of the ongoing challenges we will face is to accept people who are different from us by better understanding them. If we begin with our two fictional couples, the process might come a bit easier in real life.

FOR EXAMPLE . . .

Philip and the Ethiopian
(Acts 8:26-39)

When God's Spirit is at work, we don't need to try so hard in our own power. This story tells of Philip, a Christian leader, who found a confused seeker trying to make sense of a passage from Isaiah. Rather than demeaning the man or immediately beginning a long exegesis of the passage, Philip asked, "Do you understand what you are reading?" The man responded to the question, and a conversation ensued, resulting in the salvation of the man. Many people believe this Ethiopian man is the one who first carried the gospel to Africa.

WELL SAID!

In all my perplexities and distresses, the Bible has never failed to give me light and strength. —*Robert E. Lee*

can apply its teachings to our lives. This is true of evangelism as well as any other area.

If you're somewhat new to the Christian life, you may not understand all the fuss people make about the Bible. Certainly it has proved itself to be a "Good Book" throughout history. But why do we give it more significance than any other book?

The Bible functions on many levels for believers in God. Let's take a look at a few of them.

The Bible Works Like a Lamp. (Psalm 119:105)

If Psalm 119:105 had been written today, the image used probably would have been a flashlight rather than a lamp. If you're outside in unfamiliar territory on a dark and moonless night, any number of things could happen. You could trip and break your neck. You could get lost. You could step into something you don't even want to think about or onto something that gets angry at being stepped on. But none of those things is likely to happen if you have a trustworthy source of light.

Sometimes life gets dark. The Bible is the illumination to see us through that darkness. It not only dispels the darkness from your path; it also lights up a dreary soul.

The Bible Works Like a Hammer. (Jeremiah 23:29)

When the obstacles of life pile up before us like boulders, the Word of God can smash them to little pieces. We all face personal dilemmas, spiritual mysteries, and difficult decisions. These are all "tough nuts to crack," so to speak. But the Bible repeatedly reminds us that God provides the power and insight to enable us to deal with any obstacle and keep moving forward.

The Teachings of the Bible Work Like Seeds. (Mark 4:1-20)

We don't immediately comprehend everything we read in the Bible. Some people don't even try. Just as a certain amount of seed is lost during planting, and another percentage never reaches maturity, some people don't provide adequate spiritual "soil" to nurture the seed of God's Word. But if we allow God's Word to take root, it will eventually pay off in big ways. Often patience and cultivation are required before we make sense of what the Bible has to tell us.

The Bible Works Like a Sword. (Ephesians 6:17; Hebrews 4:12)

As a surgeon deftly removes a tumor that is threatening healthy tissue, the Bible helps us slice away damaging influences that loom around us, leeching our energy and resources. Of course, some people misuse their "swords" by going around poking other people. But a much more effective application is to swing the sword of God's Word at the real enemy—any harmful influence affecting our thoughts, words, and/or activities. As Jesus said, first we need to get rid of the giant sequoia trunks in our own eyes before we try to remove specks of dust from other peoples' eyes (Matthew 7:3-5). The Bible helps us see clearly how to do so.

The Bible Works Like a Mirror. (James 1:22-25)

How many times has a mirror saved you from a potentially devastating embarrassment? To ignore the services of a mirror is to risk going through your day with crust in your eyes, spinach between your teeth, unattended pimples, your skirt tucked into your pantyhose, and hair that looks like a Slinky exploded inside your skull. And while such problems may not be on a par with famine, drought, or nuclear war, they are things you would fix if you knew about them. Your coworkers may choose not to say anything if you sit in something brown and sticky, but the mirror is never afraid to reflect the truth. Neither is the Bible.

People committed to the Christian life must go to the Bible regularly. On any given day we are likely to find something that needs adjusting in our lives before we become the people God knows we can be. And in the long run, it can prevent us a lot of embarrassment.

FOR EXAMPLE . . .

Jesus' Temptation (Matthew 4:1-11)

When the devil was doing his best to get Jesus to commit a sin, Jesus didn't use miraculous power or call for heavenly reinforcements. Rather, He simply quoted an applicable passage of Scripture in each case. It's a technique any of us can use as well (provided, of course, that we know what's *in* the Bible to begin with).

You Have God's Word

But more important than being seen as symbolic of these other things, the Bible is literally "the Word of God." We might read

DO'S AND DON'TS

You must commit yourselves whole-heartedly to these commands I am giving you today. Repeat them again and again to your children. Talk about them when you are at home and when you are away on a journey, when you are lying down and when you are getting up again. Tie them to your hands as a reminder, and wear them on your forehead. Write them on the doorposts of your house and on your gates. (Deuteronomy 6:6-9)

Shakespeare, Stephen King, or supermarket tabloids with a casual attitude–for enjoyment, to pass the time, or for any number of reasons. It's no big deal to skip portions or reach a different conclusion than the author intended. But to read the Bible so casually is to miss the point.

The Bible should be given serious attention, and it should be taken as a body of work rather than a random collection of stories. It's important to discover how the Old Testament connects with the New Testament. The poetry, the legal portions, the prophecies, the Gospels, and all the rest are interrelated. Different people have different favorites, which is to be expected. You don't need to be an expert in everything, but you at least need to know the differences. And more importantly, you need to see not just what it says, but what it says *to you*.

Let's examine a few passages and see what the Bible has to say about itself.

> Every word of God proves true. He defends all who come to him for protection. Do not add to his words, or he may rebuke you, and you will be found a liar. (Proverbs 30:5-6)

> "My thoughts are completely different from yours," says the Lord. "And my ways are far beyond anything you could imagine. For just as the heavens are higher than the earth, so are my ways higher than your ways and my thoughts higher than your thoughts. The rain and snow come down from the heavens and stay on the ground to water the earth. They cause the grain to grow, producing seed for the farmer and bread for the hungry. It is the same with my word. I send it out, and it always produces fruit. It will accomplish all I want it to, and it will prosper everywhere I send it." (Isaiah 55:8-11)

> All Scripture is inspired by God and is useful to teach us what is true and to make us realize what is wrong in our lives. It straightens us out and teaches us to do what is right. It is God's way of preparing us in every way, fully equipped

for every good thing God wants us to do. (2 Timothy 3:16-17)

For we were not making up clever stories when we told you about the power of our Lord Jesus Christ and his coming again. We have seen his majestic splendor with our own eyes. . . . Above all, you must understand that no prophecy in Scripture ever came from the prophets themselves or because they wanted to prophesy. It was the Holy Spirit who moved the prophets to speak from God. (2 Peter 1:16, 20-21)

I solemnly declare to everyone who hears the prophetic words of this book [Revelation]: If anyone adds anything to what is written here, God will add to that person the plagues described in this book. And if anyone removes any of the words of this prophetic book, God will remove that person's share in the tree of life and in the holy city that are described in this book. (Revelation 22:18-19)

WELL SAID!

There's no better book with which to defend the Bible than the Bible itself. —*D. L. Moody*

While a casual reading of Scripture can be informative and enlightening, the Christian life requires a more serious and devoted level of attention to what the Bible has to say. Reading more into what is there can be just as problematic as ignoring the sections we don't happen to agree with.

According to the Bible, anyone and everyone who becomes a Christian receives the Holy Spirit (Romans 8:9; 1 Corinthians 2:10-12). And as with any new acquisition (car, refrigerator, lawn mower, etc.) the accompanying paperwork is important. For any new Christian just beginning to experience the changes possible in a Spirit-controlled Christian life, the Bible is the owner's manual, instruction booklet, and warranty rolled into one.

It would be foolish to purchase a $2,000 stereo system with CD/DVD player, dual cassette decks, equalizers, timer/recorders, and dozens of other special features if you weren't willing to read the instruction manual to see how to operate it. Without the willingness to see what the system is capable of doing, you would essentially have a $2,000 radio. It's just as ludicrous to attempt to

WELL SAID!

Bible study is like eating peanuts. The more you eat, the more you want to eat.
—*Paul Little*

WELL SAID!

No one ever graduates from Bible study until he meets its Author face-to-face.
—*Everett Harris*

putter through the Christian life without consulting the Bible on a regular basis. The more you read and study, the more you realize what you're capable of doing.

But simply to compare the Bible to an instruction manual is a bit cold and unfeeling. Even more importantly, it is a love letter. God has performed a lot of marvelous actions that are recorded in the Bible to convince us that we can trust Him. He has motivated a lot of people who testify to His love, power, and presence. And at the heart of the Bible is the ultimate love story of how Jesus came to earth, lived, died for our sins, rose again, and then invited us all to join Him for eternity in heaven. We don't want to miss the major theme while digging around for the "subplots" about how to live.

So is it really important to know how many years Zimri was king of Israel? Or what kind of tree Zacchaeus climbed to see Jesus? Or whether it was Elijah or Elisha who went to heaven in a chariot of fire? Or why Jesus wept?

Yes and no. Each of those stories is there for a reason, and we need to take them seriously. Sure, a better-than-average knowledge of the Bible might help you score big on *Who Wants to Be a Millionaire?* some night. Yet it is quite shortsighted to satisfy oneself with a Bible trivia mentality.

In the opening story when Fred and Wilma were in the attic, she was desperately trying to get his attention, yet he was enamored with a bunch of old love letters she had written years ago. The Bible is the Word of God, but written words pale in comparison to literally being *with* the writer. We should never get so caught up in memorizing and spouting Bible quotations that we miss out on God attempting to speak those words directly *to us*. A growing knowledge of the Bible is intended to provide us with a better understanding of God. Love letters are great when the writer isn't around, but the person's presence should always be preferable to his or her writings.

We should not just skim through the Bible. We need to search for truth and meaning. If successful, we end up with much more than a collection of good stories and wise quotations. If we give the Scriptures adequate attention, they always point us to Jesus. The purpose of searching the Word of God is to relate more effectively to the person of God (John 5:39-40; Acts 17:10-12).

Study Seems to Be the Hardest Word

Alexander Pope wrote, "A little learning is a dangerous thing." He suggested that knowledge has the opposite effect of alcohol. A smattering of facts tends to "intoxicate the brain," while "drinking largely" of knowledge leads to sobriety.

This is certainly true in reference to the Bible. Listening to a racist group spout a few Bible verses to back up their tiny-minded thinking is like listening to an intoxicated person loudly expound on the mysteries of the universe. It would be comical if it weren't so sad and/or potentially dangerous.

People interested in the Christian life need to devote themselves to Bible study. The very word *study* may bring unpleasant flashbacks of high school or college. But this time no one is forcing you to do anything. No homework. No long papers. No oral reports. Simply a desire to devote yourself to understanding the Word of God.

The story is frequently told of the guy who prayed for God to give him a special revelation from the Bible. After praying, he closed his eyes, flipped the pages, and stuck his finger down on his "special" verse. It turned out to be Matthew 27:5: "Judas . . . went out and hanged himself." After a nervous laugh the guy decided he ought to try again. This time his finger landed at Luke 10:37: "Now go and do the same."

When it comes to Bible comprehension, attempted shortcuts never seem to work very well. It's going to take time—years, as a matter of fact. You'll never learn all there is to know. The more you read, the more questions you will raise. In addition to the theological aspects of Bible study, you will also confront history, geography, anthropology, sociology, language and translation, and more. Delve into the things that interest you most, and Bible study will become something you look forward to.

DO'S AND DON'TS

Work hard so God can approve you. Be a good worker, one who does not need to be ashamed and who correctly explains the word of truth. Avoid godless, foolish discussions that lead to more and more ungodliness. (2 Timothy 2:15-16)

FOR EXAMPLE . . .

Two Disciples on the Road to Emmaus (Luke 24:13-34)

When the reality of Scripture juxtaposes with the reality of your personal life, you will become emotionally charged. In this story where two followers first encountered the resurrection of Jesus beyond any doubt, they told of how their hearts felt "strangely warm" (v. 32). This sensation of knowing and responding to the Word of God is rather common among those who devote adequate time to Bible study.

ONE SMALL STEP

Try to make some kind of commitment to Bible study. It may be for only five minutes a day, or perhaps a chapter a day. But if you get in the habit, you are likely to be surprised how quickly you will accumulate information and how much effect Scripture will have on your real life. If you find it difficult to maintain a personal discipline of Bible study, consider finding or starting a small group where you can hold one another accountable.

Therefore, don't you dare feel stupid if you start reading and don't understand something. The smartest Bible scholars in the world sit around and scratch their heads over certain portions of Scripture. Some words and phrases are hard to translate properly. Sometimes symbolic language is used that creates more questions than answers. Sometimes good people disagree on various points. Don't get too hung up on those things—not at first, anyway.

There will be plenty you *can* understand. Much of God's Word will be crystal clear as it speaks to you. If you're just getting started, or if you're coming back to the Bible after a lengthy absence, don't be overly ambitious. Don't try to make up for lost time. Don't try to read the whole thing in a year. Don't even begin by attempting to read start to finish.

Rather, begin with one of the Gospels—Matthew, Mark, Luke, or John. (Mark is the shortest one.) Each of them will give you a wonderful picture of the life, death, and resurrection of Jesus. That's a much better starting point than trying to make sense of all the Old Testament laws that are no longer practiced by most people.

The book of James is a short and very practical book. Many of Paul's letters can be read easily in a single sitting (though many tend to get a bit theological). Acts is long but filled with good stories and is fascinating as a history of the church. When you're ready for a bit of Old Testament, the book of Genesis is mostly narrative and easy to read. Ruth, Esther, and Jonah are self-contained short stories with excellent lessons we can apply to our own lives. The wisdom of Proverbs and poetry of Psalms have much appeal to many people. (You need not read all 150 psalms or the entire book of Proverbs in a single stretch. Sample a few passages and then go back to others later on.)

By all means, have some fun as you rediscover your Bible. If your particular translation is causing you a lot of problems, you might want to hop down to your local bookstore to compare some other translations and paraphrases to see what appeals to you. If you're really serious about understanding what's in the Bible, try to find a study Bible that can provide you with footnotes, maps, life application questions, or whatever you're looking for. Numerous transla-

tions are available, and each has dozens of different kinds of study Bibles, so take your time as you choose what you think is best for you.

However, resist the temptation to immediately skip to what the "experts" have to say in the footnotes and other reference material. God is the only true expert, and He is the source of our wisdom. Start by simply reading His Word and thinking about it. Let it speak clearly to you. After you have read it a few times, tried to apply it to your own life, and listened to see what God might be trying to say specifically to you, then check to see what the reference material has to add.

You can find additional insights and suggestions for Bible study in another book in this series: The *No-Brainer's Guide to the Bible*. But since Bible study is only one of many aspects of the Christian life, we're going to move on.

Before you turn to the next chapter, however, we urge you to dust off your Bible (or acquire a new one) and begin to familiarize yourself with it. Before you even read a word, think of what had to take place before you could hold that book in your hands. Think of the wonders and miracles of God. Think of the betrayals and unthinkable sins that are recorded there. Think of the suffering and perseverance of most of the writers. Think of the inspiration of God that motivated the authors, and the faithful duplication and reproduction by godly people throughout the ages. Think of how, after more than 40 writers and 1,500 years in the making, it remains a single cohesive unit. Then start reading. Once you realize exactly what you're holding, the prospect of Bible study should never seem blasé again.

WELL SAID!

Each man marvels to find in the divine Scriptures truths which he himself thought out. —*St. Thomas Aquinas*

FOR EXAMPLE . . .

King Josiah Rediscovers the Book of the Law (2 Kings 22–23:28)

In the history of Judah, a bleak period of wicked, sinful kings had brought the nation to the brink of extinction. But Josiah was one good king after a long line of rotten ones. While having the temple repaired, the workers found a copy of the Scriptures that had long been forgotten. This passage describes the king's shock in seeing how far his nation had drifted away from God and how he responded after being faced with God's written Word. (Don't worry too much about the names; just follow the action and see what lessons you might learn.)

Questions to Ponder and/or Discuss

1. Which symbol for the Bible (lamp, hammer, seed, sword, mirror, etc.) do you find most accurate, based on your experience? Why?

2. Can you think of other symbols to add to the list?

3. What response to Bible study best defines your own feelings:

   - It's not all that important. I can take it or leave it.
   - I know enough. Leave me alone.
   - I wish I knew more, but it seems like an impossible goal.
   - I'm happy with the progress I'm making.
   - The more I learn, the more I realize I don't know.
   - Other: _____

4. If you wanted to get more committed to Bible study, who are three people who might help in some way (as teachers, people to hold you accountable, deep thinkers, fellow strugglers, etc.)?

CHAPTER THREE

"LET'S SAY YOU'RE WORKING ON THE ARK AND YOU GOT A QUESTION ABOUT DIMENSIONS . . . JUST PICK UP THE PHONE."

Going Straight to the Top

PRAYER

It was an early Saturday morning in the neighborhood, and unbeknownst to the people involved, there was a lot of praying going on. Fred DiCiple was in his small upstairs office, deep in his usual weekend prayer/Bible study routine. He tried to have a quiet time with God every day, but he set aside more time on weekends. He was praying for strength, boldness, and courage to approach his new neighbors with the good news about Jesus. He still hadn't met the new couple, but he wanted to be ready.

At the same time Wilma was tending her flower garden and praying for the women in her Bible study group. When she finished with specific requests for each person, she asked God to "temper Fred's passion for the gospel with patience, humility, and sensitivity." She prayed for a good relationship with their new neighbors and for good opportunities to set a Christlike example. And she finished with a request for rain to water her garden.

Meanwhile, George and Jane Seeker were praying for the first time in a long while. Although it felt quite awkward and

SOME THINGS YOU'LL DISCOVER IN THIS CHAPTER

1. The Lord's Prayer as a model for our own prayers

2. Potential problems with prayer

3. The importance of persistence in prayer

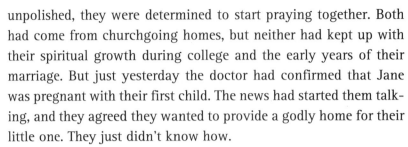

ONE SMALL STEP

Before continuing with this chapter, think about the history of prayer in your own life. What is your attitude toward prayer? At what times have you prayed with the most zeal? What has prompted long periods of time when prayer was absent or ineffective? How can you tell when your prayers are "on track"?

DO'S AND DON'TS

If my people who are called by my name will humble themselves and pray and seek my face and turn from their wicked ways, I will hear from heaven and will forgive their sins and heal their land. (2 Chronicles 7:14)

unpolished, they were determined to start praying together. Both had come from churchgoing homes, but neither had kept up with their spiritual growth during college and the early years of their marriage. But just yesterday the doctor had confirmed that Jane was pregnant with their first child. The news had started them talking, and they agreed they wanted to provide a godly home for their little one. They just didn't know how.

They took turns speaking their halting prayers out loud: seeking forgiveness for their long "sabbatical" away from the church, asking for help in raising a baby in a hostile world, thanking God for a new home, and asking for His help to find their way back to a close relationship with Him. And since this was the weekend of George's office picnic, they prayed that it wouldn't rain.

Now I Sit Me Down to Pray

Of all the aspects of the Christian life, perhaps prayer is the most varied and confusing. People have different styles and approaches to prayer, and what works best for one person might not work at all for another. Jesus was known to get up "long before daybreak" in order to have some time to Himself during which He could pray (Mark 1:35). If some people tried His approach, their attempts to pray would likely result in their sitting silent and spaced out in a semi-catatonic state until angels appeared and ministered to them with cups of strong coffee. But those same people might be able to pray fervently long into the night while other well-intended disciples would be falling asleep in spite of themselves.

Some people don't seem to validate prayer unless it is done in ecstatic tongues or unknown languages. Others are determined to keep their prayers plain and simple. Some people reserve "King James language" for their prayers, using Thees and Thous to address God as they learned from their families, churches, or Bible story heroes. Some have a favorite prayer position, such as kneeling, lifting their hands, or bowing their heads and closing their eyes. Others frequently pray while driving, jogging, or doing yard work. Some people have a regular "formula" for their prayers. Others prefer to keep their prayers informal and spontaneous.

So who is right? Which forms of prayer are "biblical"?

A Model Prayer

WELL SAID!

Certain thoughts are prayers. There are moments when, whatever be the attitude of the body, the soul is on its knees.
—*Victor Hugo*

When Jesus' disciples saw that He was someone special and that prayer seemed to be so effective and meaningful for Him, they asked Him to teach them to pray. After all, John the Baptist had tutored his disciples in prayer, and Jesus' disciples wanted similar lessons (Luke 11:1-4).

If you dared to ask a lot of today's pastors, priests, or other religious leaders the same thing, you might expect to take a 13-week class, be assigned a workbook/video series, or do any number of other assignments. But Jesus' reply was much simpler.

Pray like this:
Our Father in heaven, may your name be honored.
May your Kingdom come soon.
May your will be done here on earth, just as it is in heaven.
Give us our food for today, and forgive us our sins, just as we have forgiven those who have sinned against us.
And don't let us yield to temptation, but deliver us from the evil one. (Matthew 6:9-13)

Jesus also told a couple of stories to illustrate how God regards our prayers, and we will get to these in a moment. But first let us note the simplicity of this prayer. As translated here, it is five sentences—under 70 words total. The more traditional "Lord's Prayer" has more of a zinger ending ("For yours is the kingdom, and the power, and the glory forever") yet is still short and to the point. Many church congregations memorize it and say it in unison on a weekly basis.

So is Jesus telling us that if we repeat this prayer every day, we will fulfill the prayer portion of our Christian life? No, not really.

WELL SAID!

Prayer gives a man the opportunity of getting to know a gentleman he hardly ever meets. I do not mean his maker, but himself. —*William Inge*

Jesus' intent was not to provide us with a magical incantation, because He also warned us against becoming one of those people who "think their prayers are answered only by repeating their words over and over again" (Matthew 6:7). And even a cursory look at the life of Jesus shows that He was much more devoted to prayer than simply e-mailing heaven with a token 30-second message once a day.

Instead, the prayer He gave His disciples serves as a model for our prayers. Let's take a closer look at the Lord's Prayer, phrase by phrase.

"Our Father in heaven, may your name be honored."

To begin with, Jesus' model prayer is addressed to God. It is conversation rather than a mantra. It reminds us that God remains constant in heaven, no matter how our own situations may vary for better or worse. And before doing anything else, we remind ourselves that God deserves honor. We may be coming before Him to confess, complain, confer, request, or for any number of other valid reasons. God never minds when we express truthfully what's on our hearts, whether good or bad. He already knows! But before we start whining about all the stuff that we want God to improve, we need to remember to acknowledge His unique place in the universe.

"May your Kingdom come soon."

In a society where a lot of self-help resources encourage people to be their own "kings" if not "goddesses," Jesus reminds us that God's Kingdom is the only one that matters. It is the only one that will ultimately stand. By praying for God's Kingdom to come soon, we remind ourselves that our own little "kingdoms" are doomed to fall one day. If God's Kingdom is taking its rightful place, we must stand aside and yield to it.

"May your will be done here on earth, just as it is in heaven."

Even if we yield our own kingdoms to God, we might continue to live as rebels within His kingdom. So it is equally important to yield our wills to Him as well. As we go through the Christian life, we need to learn to submit each action, each decision, and even each thought to

the will of God. We are certain to continue to have sinful impulses. But if God's will is to be done, we cannot always act on our wills.

At work you might think, *I really hate my boss*—a sentiment perhaps not far from the truth. But in the Christian life, intense thoughts of hatred are on par with murder as far as God is concerned (Matthew 5:21-26); name-calling and insults are chargeable offenses; lust is equated with adultery (Matthew 5:27-30); what we consider harmless vows are more serious than we realize (Matthew 5:33-37); and so forth.

Sinful actions arise from sinful thoughts. In the Christian life, purity should begin on the inside and work its way out. It's no longer good enough to willfully seethe and simmer in a fit of ongoing emotional rage—even if you stop short of acting on your anger.

God's will in heaven is complete and total. Jesus tells us our goal should be to achieve the same on earth.

"Give us our food for today."

Think how different this prayer is from many of ours. Our prayers tend to reflect our financial strategies. We are rarely satisfied with just a small payoff. We want to strike it big. Therefore we pray for financial security, that our stocks will split, that we will hit the lottery. We want to be set for life.

The problem with being set for life is that we tend to neglect spiritual pursuits. Jesus teaches us to turn to God daily (at least) and seek His provision for that day. If we truly believe that He is an endless source of whatever we need, we shouldn't have a problem with that approach. Usually, however, the problem is with us. We know we tend to get a bit sloppy in our spiritual disciplines, so we would rather "stock up" enough security so we can turn to God only once in a while—usually when we need something. That's not how Jesus tells us to live.

"And forgive us our sins, just as we have forgiven those who have sinned against us."

As we realize that we may be trying to establish our own little kingdoms, acting on our own wills instead of God's, and yearning for more than the simple daily provisions that God provides for

FOR EXAMPLE . . .

Solomon (1 Kings 10:14–11:13)

If anyone was ever "set for life," it was Solomon. He had wisdom, riches, lands, peace, and everything his little heart desired. To begin with, even his prayers were right on target and pleased God (1 Kings 3:5-15). But in the luxury of his kingdom, he married 700 wives and took 300 concubines as well. Not all of his harem were devoted followers of God, and some turned his heart to false gods. As a result, God divided the kingdom after Solomon's death.

FOR EXAMPLE . . .

The Parable of the Unforgiving Debtor (Matthew 18:21-35)

This parable is a classic teaching on forgiveness. The story seems to speak for itself, but Jesus' closing words make the parable even more emphatic.

His faithful followers, what are we to do? God doesn't want us writhing in guilt and shame. We can never be comfortable in His presence in such a condition. So He offers forgiveness for all our sins, and our regular daily prayers should include an element of confession.

God already knows what we've done that's off course for the Christian life, but confessional prayer helps *us* remember. Otherwise, we're a bit too good at overlooking the "little" ways we've put down others or have gone our own ways instead of God's.

We also need to note that a few passages in Scripture suggest we determine, to some extent, the level of forgiveness we receive from God (Matthew 6:14-15; Mark 11:24-25). When we first place belief in Jesus, God's acceptance of us is complete and total. He no longer holds us accountable for the sins of the past. Anyone who enters the Christian life begins with a clean slate. However, we still struggle with sin and frequently get that slate good and dirty. New sins accumulate and need to be dealt with. And we quickly learn that God is gracious and merciful in forgiving us time and time again as we continue to struggle and make mistakes—erasing the slate again and again.

We're supposed to learn from His example and start doing the same when we are sinned against. Like a big forgiveness chain letter, God heaps His unconditional forgiveness upon us, and we're supposed to pass it along to our friends, who pass it along to *their* friends, and so on.

Why is forgiving others such a big deal? Perhaps one of the main reasons is that until you've tried to forgive someone who (in your opinion) doesn't deserve forgiveness, you cannot comprehend what God has so magnanimously done for you. Only after you discover how difficult it is can you even begin to understand what it means for God to forgive you. (We'll say more about this when we get to our chapters on relationships.)

"And don't let us yield to temptation, but deliver us from the evil one."

After confessing recent sins, striving to forgive those who have offended us, and having God erase the slate to give us another fresh start, we are left with this final phrase. At this point we need to consider a biblical fine line, but a clearly drawn line nevertheless: God never tempts anyone, but He allows His people to be *tested* from time to time.

Abraham's attempted sacrifice of Isaac was not a temptation to do evil, but a test of his faith and obedience to God (Genesis 22:1). God allowed Job's sufferings, but it was Satan who initiated them (Job 1–2). Similarly, Satan afflicted Paul with some kind of "thorn" that God chose not to remove because, He said, "My gracious favor is all you need. My power works best in your weakness" (2 Corinthians 12:6-10). We might not enjoy tests, but it's a terrific feeling to ace a difficult exam. God's tests allow for spiritual high points among His faithful people.

Temptations, on the other hand, arise from our own inner, evil desires. It's up to us to determine whether or not we allow those inner impulses to flower into evil actions (James 1:14-15).

Satan does plenty of tempting. In fact, one name occasionally used for him is Tempter (1 Thessalonians 3:5). The very name Satan means "adversary," and one of his primary roles is to accuse God's people (see Psalm 109:6; Zechariah 3:1). So your spiritual adversary uses all sorts of clever tactics to tempt you to do wrong, and when you do, he stands before God and accuses you of being weak and sinful. (Perhaps this sounds like someone you went to school with.)

So why doesn't God simply eliminate Satan's evil influence from the earth? According to the Bible, He will. But when He does, it's going to be Judgment Day for everyone, so God is waiting patiently for anyone to come to Him who is willing to do so (2 Peter 3:9-10). Until then, we humans find ourselves in the midst of a spiritual battle. Both sides are attempting to recruit us. God offers love, forgiveness, and eternal life to those who side with Him. Satan makes promises, twists the truth, and eventually drags all his followers to hell with him (Revelation 20:10-15).

As Jesus closes the Lord's Prayer, He tells us to acknowledge the reality of Satan's temptations and to ask God's deliverance from Satan's attempts to bring us down.

DO'S AND DON'TS

Remember, no one who wants to do wrong should ever say, "God is tempting me." God is never tempted to do wrong, and he never tempts anyone else either. (James 1:13)

ONE SMALL STEP

Consider using the Lord's Prayer or some other model to improve your prayer life this week. You might even want to design a model of your own. For example, you could focus on one segment of the Lord's Prayer each day. You could designate each day of the week to dwell on a different aspect of prayer. Or you could do any number of other things. The better you are able to keep your focus on God, the more likely your prayers will become more relevant and meaningful to you.

DO'S AND DON'TS

Keep on asking, and you will be given what you ask for. Keep on looking, and you will find. Keep on knocking, and the door will be opened. For everyone who asks, receives. Everyone who seeks, finds. And the door is opened to everyone who knocks. (Matthew 7:7-8)

"ACTS" of Prayer

So in summary, you can see that the apparent simplicity of the Lord's Prayer actually includes a lot of depth and variety. Even if you use the Lord's Prayer as an outline for each day's praying, your prayers can change quite dramatically depending on the specific situations you are facing. Good weeks may pass where you spend most of your prayer time acknowledging the glory of God and all He has done in your life. At other times you may feel a strong financial crunch and pray for your material needs. And all of us go through spiritual trials where we need to focus our attention on seeing God's will clearly enough to avoid yielding to strong temptations.

The Lord's Prayer isn't the only model to follow. Some people like to use the acronym ACTS to remind them to include Adoration, Confession, Thanksgiving, and Supplication (requests) in their prayers. And there are other models.

We should never get so caught up in models that our prayers become mechanical. But sometimes a model helps us realize the great variety of things we can discuss with God, and it gets us started toward discovering what works best for us.

The things we ask God to do must seem quite amusing to Him at times, although we would be frustrated beyond coping in the same situation. As in our opening example, one person might be praying for rain (for good reason) as the next-door neighbor prays for sunshine (for equally good reason). One person is praying for boldness as his spouse is praying that he will tone down his unfocused spiritual passion. So sometimes when your prayers aren't answered as you might wish, the reason may be quite simple. Perhaps God is responding to someone else's prayers that are in conflict with yours. Don't give up. It should only be a matter of time before you also receive an answer from God.

When our prayers continue to focus so strongly on what we want, God logically cannot answer every prayer as we wish. As we go through the Christian life, the challenge is to learn to pray that we can accept what *God* wants. And since God always wants what's best for us, that's never a bad idea (Matthew 7:9-11).

Prayers That Don't Get beyond the Ceiling

Prayer seems so simple, doesn't it? What could be easier than having regular conversations with the person in the universe who loves you most, sharing your innermost feelings and seeking all the positive qualities you lack? You might think that all you have to do is set aside blocks of time on a regular basis and let your prayer life flourish. Sometimes it's just that easy. Sometimes it isn't.

Let's look at some ways people tend to mess up the prayer aspect of the Christian life.

Praying without Faith

If we really believe we're talking to God, we should be convinced that He will hear and respond. However, some people tend to treat prayer only as a "backup plan" in cases of emergency. They'll take care of their own lives, thank you very much, but in severe circumstances or unexpected failures they want to be sure God is around as their Phone-a-Friend.

If we're certain God is with us, then we can face temptations, sufferings, major obstacles, and anything the world can throw at us. But if we're not sure, those situations suddenly become quite threatening. We need to learn to pray with faith and confidence, knowing that God will provide for us—no matter how He responds to our specific requests (James 1:5-8).

Prayer Becomes Merely a Routine

It has been said that "familiarity breeds contempt," and this can be true even in our prayer habits. We're supposed to pray to keep in touch with God, but sometimes people are so bound to the prayer habit that they tend to forget why they're doing it in the first place.

Small children get quite good at whipping through "Now I lay me down to sleep" or other short prayers. Similarly, adults might become so accustomed to "saying grace" before meals that any thought of God is only a frustrated concession in order to get to the roast beef. But if prayer is truly conversation with God, each conversation should be sincere. We would never treat our friends with the callous insincerity we sometimes put into our prayers.

FOR EXAMPLE . . .

Prayers from the Bible

The Lord's Prayer is only one of many listed in the Bible. Here are a few other examples you might want to look up:

- Abraham "negotiates" with God (Genesis 18:22-33).
- Jacob literally wrestles with God in seeking a blessing (Genesis 32:22-32).
- Moses intercedes on behalf of the sinful Israelites and saves a nation from immediate destruction (Numbers 14:5-25).
- God initiates a conversation with the young Samuel (1 Samuel 3).
- David confesses his sin with Bathsheba (Psalm 51).
- Elijah's short prayer calls fire from heaven (1 Kings 18:36-39).
- King Hezekiah's heartfelt prayer adds 15 years to his life (2 Kings 20:1-11).
- Daniel's prayers get him in—and out of—trouble (Daniel 6).
- Jonah prays in an unusual location (Jonah 2).
- Jesus prays for his followers (John 17).
- Stephen's prayer turns out to be his last words (Acts 7:54-60).

DO'S AND DON'TS

Always be joyful. Keep on praying. No matter what happens, always be thankful, for this is God's will for you who belong to Christ Jesus. (1 Thessalonians 5:16-18)

DO'S AND DON'TS

When you pray, don't be like the hypocrites who love to pray publicly on street corners and in the synagogues where everyone can see them. I assure you, that is all the reward they will ever get. But when you pray, go away by yourself, shut the door behind you, and pray to your Father secretly. Then your Father, who knows all secrets, will reward you. (Matthew 6:5-6)

Pride

Sometimes people get so good at prayer that they take pride in their praying ability. This sounds extreme, but Jesus told a parable that targeted this very problem (Luke 18:9-14). God is responding less to the words of the prayer than the sincere emotion of the person praying. Sometimes we aren't even able to form the right words, but God still understands us perfectly and responds to our anguish (Romans 8:26-27). As we listen to others pray, we can learn what to pray for, and even how to express ourselves. But public prayer is seldom as powerful as the inner, heartfelt prayer between a person and God. If it gets to a point where we start comparing our prayers to those of someone else, we may need to watch out for pride creeping into our spiritual lives.

Praying Rather Than Taking Action

We have said prayer is conversation with God, which means it should be a two-way dialogue. Too frequently we tend to shoot off a "shopping list" of the things we want without considering what God might want of us. Good prayers include times of silence with a quieted heart, so God's Spirit can speak to us. And when He does, we need to act on what He says. We might want to pray until we see the entirety of God's master plan laid out before us. But more often, He reveals one step at a time and we need to respond in faith.

After the Israelites were leaving Egypt and were getting ready to cross the Red Sea, they saw the entire Egyptian army barreling down on them. At that point God told Moses, "Why are you crying out to me? Tell the people to get moving!" (Exodus 14:15). When Nehemiah faced threats and opposition when rebuilding the walls of Jerusalem, his plan made sense: "We prayed to our God and guarded the city day and night to protect ourselves" (Nehemiah 4:9).

In any crisis, there is no substitute for prayer. Praying takes our eyes off the problem and puts them on God. But after God has spoken, continued prayer can become a stall tactic. We need to take action instead.

Forgetting to Pray

As we grow in our spiritual lives and get closer to God, sometimes we make assumptions or take things for granted. We become wiser and more experienced, and forget that God is even smarter than we are. Early in the process of spiritual growth, prayer is what keeps us wise. Later on, prayer is what keeps us humble.

A case in point comes from the saga of Joshua. After his incredible victory at Jericho and other military successes, everyone in the land feared him. Based on the direction he was moving, one of his next conquests was going to be a territory known as Gibeon. The Gibeonites, therefore, came up with a brilliant strategy. They put on their rattiest clothing, loaded up their animals with moldy bread and brittle wineskins, and rode toward Joshua's army. When the two groups met, the Gibeonites said they had come from a very distant country, hoping to ally with Joshua. The author of Joshua notes, "The Israelite leaders examined their bread, but they did not consult the Lord" (Joshua 9:14). So they signed a peace treaty. Three days later the Israelites found out they had been snookered, but they were bound by their oath.

We are likely to face many situations in life where we will examine the specific circumstances and draw our own conclusions. But we should never neglect to "consult the Lord" as well.

Misuse of Prayer

Sometimes our prayers get a bit brutal. When we've been mistreated, for example, we may want revenge on the person(s) who offended us. It's a positive step that we take our complaint to God rather than exacting our own vengeance, to be sure. But if we start praying for God to smite our enemies, have them break out in painful sores, or grow excessive hair on their backs, we may still not be to the point God wants us to be in our spiritual growth.

Indeed, Jesus teaches us to pray for our enemies (Matthew 5:44-48). This is probably one of the hardest challenges in the Christian life. It's very difficult to pray on behalf of a personal enemy and really mean it. But the underlying purpose of all the disciplines of the Christian life—Bible study, prayer, and all the rest—is

WELL SAID!

Pray to God but keep on rowing the boat ashore. —*Russian Proverb*

WELL SAID!

The best way to destroy your enemy is to make him your friend.
—*Abraham Lincoln*

to help us become more like God. More than simply "getting by," we should be trying to see our lives from His perspective. He loves each of our enemies no more and no less than He loves us. If we pray for harm to come to others, we're asking God to act in a way contrary to His nature. After all, your enemies may be praying against you as well, and you certainly don't want God to answer *those* prayers. (We'll say more about this topic in chapter 16.)

Prayerful Persistence

These are just a few ways we can get off base when it comes to praying. But if we remain faithful and sincere, our prayers will get better quickly with practice. We can sense God's presence and His response. Indeed, persistence in prayer was something Jesus stressed.

From a purely human standpoint, Jesus suggests, you can convince almost anyone to do anything if you pester him or her long enough. God, however, never feels pestered by our persistent prayers. Just as you might awaken a friend late at night to ask a favor, you can go to God at any time with any request. Because of the closeness of the relationship, He will be willing to help (Luke 11:5-13). And as even an unjust, selfish judge will make the correct ruling if someone comes before him time after time, God is eager to respond to our heartfelt requests (Luke 18:1-8).

If prayer seems like a burden or obligation, you're probably not doing it right. In the Christian life, prayer is a wonderful privilege. No longer do you need to slaughter a prime bull before going before God to make a request. No longer do you need to wait in line for the availability of a priest (though some denominations continue to use priests for intercessory prayer). Thanks to Jesus, God is now available to any Christian, anytime, anywhere. You go straight to the top, without busy signals, tenacious secretaries, voice mail, or other hindrances you might face trying to get to a corporate head.

And you are heard. The person in the universe who cares most about you hears you clearly. You're never alone. Just as the Bible becomes a love letter from God, prayer becomes a "phone call" to a loved one. If this becomes your perspective on the Christian life, then you'll no longer feel that prayer and Bible study are things you "have" to do. Instead, you'll be eager for each and every opportunity.

Questions to Ponder and/or Discuss

1. Asking God for things in prayer makes me feel like:

   - A child tugging on Dad's pants leg for a quarter
   - A street beggar
   - A pest who interferes in a busy person's schedule
   - A friend asking another friend for a favor
   - Other: _____

2. What aspect of prayer do you feel is most neglected in your life? Why?

   - Adoration/Praise
   - Confession
   - Thanksgiving
   - Supplication/Asking for Things

3. What are five things you could do this week to begin to improve your prayer life? (Change some attitudes? Join a prayer group? Talk to someone you consider a good pray-er?)

ONE SMALL STEP

Many people find that a prayer journal is a valuable tool in helping them pray more effectively. Not only can they list everything they want to pray for in one place, but they can also record when and how God answers each request. Journals can help with persistence in prayer, and looking back through them is usually a wonderful (and delightfully surprising) reminder of God's faithfulness over long periods of time.

"I HATE TO SEE A GOOD WORSHIP
SERVICE COME TO AN END."

CHAPTER FOUR

Father Knows Best

WORSHIP

Fred and Wilma DiCiple sat with George and Jane Seeker in the
Seekers' new living room. Most of the boxes had been put away, but
the bare walls and not-quite-right furniture arrangement revealed
the fact that George and Jane weren't completely settled in yet.
Wilma had taken over a couple of casseroles as an opportunity to
introduce herself—but only after she had Fred's strongest promise
that he wouldn't mention religion during this introductory meeting.

So far things were going well. Jane was glad to meet a friendly
person who could help her get to know the rest of the neighbors.
George and Fred had some common sports interests, and George's
loyalties to his former hometown would create some friendly rival-
ries that would make it fun to watch games together.

As Fred and Wilma were getting ready to leave, Jane was asking
about the best grocery, the nearest health club, recommendations
for new doctors and dentists, and other basics. After Wilma had
given all the help she could, she added, "And if you're looking for a
new church, we have friends in many of the different denominations and can probably recommend a good one."

SOME THINGS YOU'LL
DISCOVER IN THIS
CHAPTER

1. The simplicity and benefits of
personal worship

2. How to get beyond some
common barriers to worship

3. The crucial difference
between obedience and
sacrifice

ONE SMALL STEP

Perhaps you have already renewed your commitment to Bible study and prayer. This week, add an element of worship if you haven't already done so. Spend time doing nothing but specifically thinking about God: who He is, what He has done for you, how you have responded to Him in the past, and how you would like to respond to Him from now on.

At that point George spoke up and said, "Thanks for asking, and it's interesting that you should bring it up because we've just been talking about trying to get closer to God. But we're not really church people. I want my faith to be a personal thing, and I would much rather spend my Sunday mornings out in the country where God feels so much closer. I think we're going to try that for a while."

Immediately Fred raised his index finger and opened his mouth to rebut. Wilma read the warning signal and immediately said, "Well, it's been so nice to meet you two, and I'm sure we'll be seeing a lot of each other. Come on, Fred, I think I may have left the oven on and I want to check it."

Fred, of course, knew what she was doing and wasn't sure he wanted to give up that easily, but Wilma was right. Now that they had an "in" to their new neighbors, he would have other opportunities to share his "Ten Reasons Why Everyone Should Go to Church." As the DiCiples walked back across the lawn to their own home, both they and the Seekers noted: "What a nice couple!"

What's the Worship That Could Happen?

So far we've covered the importance of prayer and Bible study. But we did so with a warning that both these aspects of the Christian life can become routine and mechanical if we don't maintain the right attitude. In this chapter we want to examine the importance of worship. It too can be an action, but more importantly, it is a mind-set that anyone devoted to the Christian life ought to develop.

The purpose of prayer and Bible study is not to cause us to grit our teeth and learn to persevere in our spiritual disciplines in spite of knowing that we could be doing lots of other more interesting things instead. Rather, the purpose is to put us in contact with God. This isn't to say we won't fall short of that purpose quite frequently. But we should keep our eyes open as we scan the pages of God's Word and keep our ears open as we send up prayers. At any moment, God might appear with clarity through a newly understood passage or quiet inner voice in response to a request for wisdom.

So as we approach prayer and Bible study, we need to do so with an attitude of worship.

The word worship literally means "worth-ship." So we worship God to show that we feel He is worthy of our praise, thanks, and time. We ascribe worth to Him and acknowledge His premier spot in the hierarchy of the universe. It sounds easy but is frequently more complicated than it sounds.

Tuning In to the Right Frequency

Have you ever wanted to listen to a particular radio station, but were a bit too far away from the source of the signal? It's a frustrating feeling to keep trying to fine-tune the frequency and hear through all the static. And that's essentially the image of worship in the Christian life. God is sending out a clear signal that we need to hear. First let's see how to tune in (through worship) to the proper frequency. Then we'll take a look at how to eliminate the sources of static that prevent us from clearly hearing what He has to say.

We Need a Transformer.

In a literal sense, a transformer is a device that helps maintain a steady frequency of energy even though levels of voltage and current may be fluctuating. In any life, even a Christian one, we can expect variations in passions, desires, commitment, faith, and other "charges." We need a spiritual transformer to maintain a (mostly) steady level of energy to keep making progress.

But that's already taken care of. If we are willing, God serves as that transformer. All we need is the willingness to submit. Here's how Paul explained it to the Roman citizens who were pursuing the Christian life: "Don't copy the behavior and customs of this world, but let God transform you into a new person by changing the way you think. Then you will know what God wants you to do, and you will know how good and pleasing and perfect his will really is" (Romans 12:2).

In our own minds, we tend to jump quickly from frequency to

WELL SAID!

The one essential condition of human existence is that man should always be able to bow down before something infinitely great. If men are deprived of the infinitely great, they will not go on living and will die of despair. The Infinite and the Eternal are as essential for man as the little planet on which he dwells. — *Fyodor Dostoyevsky*

DO'S AND DON'TS

Come, let us worship and bow down. Let us kneel before the Lord our maker, for he is our God. We are the people he watches over, the sheep under his care. Oh, that you would listen to his voice today! (Psalm 95:6-7)

ONE SMALL STEP

Identify a situation you know will come up this week where you expect conflict, disappointment, or some other negative response. Ask God now to begin to transform your mind and prepare you to handle the situation appropriately.

frequency. But by submitting ourselves to God, He fine-tunes our thinking to His frequency. And lest we fear we won't enjoy the broadcast, we are promised that it is "good and pleasing and perfect."

Hand God the Remote Control.

In order to transform us, God needs total control of our lives, and that includes the remote control. After people become Christians, it's an almost universal tendency to revert to the "oldies" stations rather than staying tuned in to the new way of thinking God has in mind for us. Old habits. Old lifestyles. Old ways of thinking. They've grown comfortable and familiar, and we keep flipping back to those frequencies.

God has something better for us, of course, but we can't receive what He's offering until our hearts and hands are emptied of the oldies we've grown so attached to. He wants His Spirit to lead, guide, and provide us with "life in all its fullness." Ultimately, that's what we want too. It's just hard to switch to that new station and leave it on.

The old familiar ways are not the best ways. In chapter 7 we'll look at the specific characteristics inherent in "the desires of the sinful nature" listed in Galatians 5:19-21. At this point let's just say that new is definitely *improved* when it comes to the inner qualities of a person whom God has brought into His Kingdom. But the only way to make significant changes is to stay tuned to what God is urging us to do. As long as we cling to the remote control, we're likely to keep going back to our favorite sins. We need to let God take over instead. Worship helps us make *permanent* changes for the better rather than temporary ones.

Clearing the Static

After ensuring you're tuned to God's frequency for your life, you can still face problems with static. We all go through periods where God's voice seems remote or fuzzy. The noises that surround us can prevent us from hearing clearly, especially when the signal may be weak to begin with. But there are some things we can do to improve our reception and ensure that God continues to come through loud and clear.

Get Closer to the Signal.

Perhaps you've seen the bumper stickers: "If God seems distant, guess who moved?" It's not unusual in the Christian life to have a number of "mountaintop experiences" where God feels nearer than He has ever been, and where a response of devotion and commitment is automatic. But in time those feelings fade and we find that serving Him requires much faith and discipline. We may even begin to worship somewhat reluctantly. During such times it's easy to drift away from God altogether and get involved in things that are harmful.

This widespread tendency to drift away from God and eventually suffer the consequences is why Jesus' parable of the Prodigal Son has become so well loved. Many of us can relate to the son who left his home and his father seeking independence. And it didn't take long before independence became "wild living" (Luke 15:13). But not long afterward followed poverty, hunger, and servitude.

Jesus tells us the young man finally "came to his senses" (Luke 15:17) and returned to his father, who saw him coming while he was still a long way away and ran to meet him. God never deserts us. And when we stray from Him, He doesn't resent us for it. He eagerly yearns for our return, and when we come to our senses and decide to get closer to Him, He celebrates. That was the whole point of all three parables in Luke 15, culminating with this one.

You can tune in to the signal of the most powerful radio stations in the country, but if you face the opposite direction and go far enough, that signal will be replaced with static. If we want to remain tuned in to the proper spiritual frequency, we need to be facing God, not turned away from Him. And the closer we get, the stronger the signal will remain.

Raise the Antenna.

Whenever we begin to focus more on our own concerns than on God, it's like riding in a car with the antenna retracted. The range

FOR EXAMPLE . . .

Moses on Mount Sinai (Exodus 34:29-35)

Moses had a mountaintop experience—literally. When he came down from Mount Sinai with the Ten Commandments, his face was actually glowing from being in the presence of God. "Regular" people were afraid to go near him, and he finally had to resort to covering his head. We may never reach such extremes, but whenever you get very close to God for a period of time, other people will notice.

DO'S AND DON'TS

Since we have a great High Priest who rules over God's people, let us go right into the presence of God, with true hearts fully trusting him. For our evil consciences have been sprinkled with Christ's blood to make us clean, and our bodies have been washed with pure water. (Hebrews 10:21-22)

DO'S AND DON'TS

Let the words of Christ, in all their rich-ness, live in your hearts and make you wise. Use his words to teach and counsel each other. Sing psalms and hymns and spiritual songs to God with thankful hearts. (Colossians 3:16)

and clarity of anything coming in on your radio is severely impeded. But as soon as our spiritual antennas go up and point toward God rather than ourselves, the signal begins to come in loud and clear.

If God's signal seems distant, there are things we can do to extend the antenna and provide more of a clear channel. We've already discussed Bible study and prayer, which are two good start-ing points. God speaks clearly through the printed page of the Bible. He also makes His will known as we learn to communicate with Him through prayer. But worship can include different, less formal forms as well.

One vital element for many people's worship is music. Rather than automatically surrounding yourself with rock standards or country songs, give your heart and soul an opportunity to make music to honor God. Thoughts and meditations on God should prompt more from our musical repertoire than "Papa Was a Rolling Stone" or "All My Ex's Live in Texas." Focus on creation rather than billboards for a change. Think about heaven instead of your cubicle at work. And let worshipful music generate from deep within you. (If singing isn't your forte, listen for the "music" of children's laughter, mooing cattle, the wind through the treetops, etc.) Before long, you will experience a much deeper level of worship, and God's signal will start beaming in clearly once more.

Other people find newness in worship by giving to hurting people and charitable causes, or otherwise helping those in need. We will establish the connection later in this book to explain how helping such people is a valid form of worship to God.

Trust That the Signal Is There, Even When You Can't See or Hear It.
God's broadcast is a 24-hour signal. It may not always get through all the static, but it's always there.

If you know the frequency, keep the dial tuned to it and don't be too quick to switch stations. One of the temptations we face is to shift our attentions to something we can see and hear. If we adore our kids, we can pick them up and cuddle them in our arms. If we love our spouses we can give them a big hug and kiss. When we

worship God, however, we may be frustrated initially that we cannot find tangible ways to relate to Him.

The Bible says, "God is Spirit, so those who worship him must worship in spirit and in truth" (John 4:24). God is unseen, yet we are much more comfortable with things we can see, hear, touch, and smell.

Actually, it's a good thing God is spirit. It's what makes it possible for Him to be omnipresent—everywhere at once. If God were tangible *and* everywhere at once, it would be quite hard for us to get around.

Yet because God is Spirit, we need practice to worship Him properly. We're told not to run out and carve tangible idols, but we can respond in different ways as we attempt to worship a God of Spirit. When we sense His signal coming through, things are fine. But when we don't, we may tend to turn to other options. So if the signal gets quiet for a period, we need to be patient while doing what we can to strengthen it. We don't want to be bouncing all over the spiritual radio dial looking for alternative objects of our worship. No other station is worth listening to.

Check with Other People.

When your spiritual "radio" is on the fritz, it's usually good to consult with other Christians to see what messages you're missing. Worship can certainly be done on an individual basis, but it should never be limited to that. Many people have George Seeker's mentality of looking for God in creation, which can certainly be worthwhile and inspirational. Yet Scripture also makes it clear: "Let us not neglect our meeting together, as some people do, but encourage and warn each other, especially now that the day of [Jesus'] coming back again is drawing near" (Hebrews 10:25).

We'll come back to that verse in chapter 15 and discuss additional reasons why Christians should meet together. But the verse makes a couple of other points clearly. When we get with other believers, we are able to encourage one another to persevere and find God's will for our lives, and we can also warn each other about potentially harmful sins we might notice in ourselves or others.

FOR EXAMPLE . . .

The Golden Calf (Exodus 32)

When God called Moses to the top of Mount Sinai for a 40-day conversation, the Israelites lost physical touch with their human leader. Their subsequent demand for a golden calf was an attempt to have something—anything—on which to focus their attention and worship. It is ironic that while they were coming up with the brilliant plan to shape Almighty God into the form of a baby cow, God was giving Moses the Ten Commandments, which specifically forbade other gods, idols, or images of any kind. (Exodus 20:2-6)

WELL SAID!

One can be coerced to church, but not to worship. —*Georgia Harkness*

47

FOR EXAMPLE . . .

The Collective Work of the Psalmists (The Book of Psalms)

If you ever want a good example of how to worship, why to worship, or the value of worship, page through the psalms. They contain honest expressions of faith, doubt, and pondering, yet the underlying theme is the worthiness of God to oversee humanity and the rest of the natural world. Psalm 100 is a favorite worship psalm of many people (perhaps because it's short and easy to memorize).

WELL SAID!

In the New Testament sacrifice is not meant to be a conciliatory influence, putting an angry demon into a good mood. . . . Unlike the temple priests, Jesus offered not merely external, material gifts (fruits, animals), but himself: a voluntary, personal self-surrender in obedience to God's will and in love for men. —Hans Küng

Worshiping in private has certain benefits, but so does worshiping in public.

Sometimes when you aren't receiving God's signal clearly, someone else will be able to help you. Many times God chooses to work through other people to speak, heal, and minister in numerous ways.

Obedience vs. Sacrifice

Like prayer and Bible study, worship can be done in a mechanical way, without much thought or conviction. It can also be perceived as a spiritual obligation. But under such conditions it won't mean much either to the person or to God.

In the Christian life, it's very easy to establish a "comfort zone" where we're willing to bear the title of Christian, devote ourselves to God for the most part, and appear to the rest of the world to be completely "religious" or "spiritual." Yet while our level of faithfulness may be impressive to observers, it may not be total. God knows when we're holding back. He is fully aware of our comfort zones.

We will commit to serve God wholeheartedly by attending church services—except during NBA playoffs, Super Bowls, and the Sundays our favorite team plays at home. We will study His Word every day, but when it gets specific about sins that are a little too close to home, we'll simply skip ahead a little bit. We will make a valiant effort to show His love to every stranger we meet, yet we do nothing to resolve the years-long grudge held against a flesh-and-blood relative.

God isn't as impressed as other observers are at the good things we do—not if they are to compensate for things we know we *should* do but don't. If we're truly worshiping God, we are acknowledging that He knows better than we do, and we are placing ourselves at His complete disposal. A true act of worship is not doing the fifty nice things you would probably do anyway; it is doing the one thing you've been resisting even though you believe that's what God wants you to do.

One classic case in point took place with King Saul, the first king of Israel (1 Samuel 15). God had told him, through the prophet Samuel, to conquer the Amalekites and spare neither people nor animals. Saul did as he was instructed—sort of. He eradicated most of Israel's enemies, but he captured the enemy king alive and set aside many of the best sheep and cattle.

God let Samuel know what had happened. When Samuel first confronted Saul, the Israelite king quickly boasted that he had "carried out the Lord's command!" Samuel sarcastically replied, "Then what is all the bleating of sheep and lowing of cattle I hear?" Saul explained that he was planning on offering those prime animals to God as a sacrifice. When pressed by Samuel, Saul finally admitted he hadn't done exactly as God had instructed.

Samuel clarified God's opinion on the matter: "Obedience is far better than sacrifice." In other words, God would much prefer that His people actually obey Him rather than go through the ritual of sacrifice if their hearts aren't really in it. Too often our own worship habits reflect Saul's mentality. We may "sacrifice" something to God, but it is often more to make us feel better than to actually act in complete obedience to God.

DO'S AND DON'TS

"What should I do with you?" asks the Lord. "I want you to be merciful; I don't want your sacrifices. I want you to know God; that's more important than burnt offerings." (Hosea 6:4, 6)

Just Ask Bud and Kitten

Maybe you remember the old television program *Father Knows Best.* Maybe not. The concept was developed during a time when the viewing public would believe and endorse a wise and benevolent father overseeing his family, providing for his lovely wife, helping the kids solve their weekly problems, and setting a good example in his behavior.

Today many people would consider such a concept naïve, smarmy, and too "precious" to watch. We would rather relate to father figures who are beset by numerous faults and foibles. We much prefer to laugh at barely competent fathers rather than learn from positive male examples. And that's okay when it comes to *The Cosby Show, Home Improvement, Married with Children, The Simpsons,* or any number of other programs that poke fun at Dad.

ONE SMALL STEP

Test yourself. See how long you can maintain a worship mentality before your mind starts to drift or someone irritates you and breaks the mood. See if your "record" time is measured in days, hours, minutes, or seconds.

But when it comes to worship, we must deal with the reality that God has no faults or foibles. We can never "put one over on Him." He's never too strict. He never gets our actions confused with those of a sibling. He is perfect—perfectly loving, just, gracious, forgiving, and everything else a Father *should* be.

We're not accustomed to relating to anyone like that. We tend to have the attitude that "I'm not perfect, but then neither is the authority figure who wants my obedience." So we're accustomed to making excuses to validate our disobedience.

In the Christian life, complete and total obedience to God is the standard by which our worship will be measured. No matter how numerous or impressive our actions, without obedience to accompany them, worship is essentially meaningless.

The ironic twist to all this is that obedience to God is always to our advantage. Oh, we might encounter some short-term persecution, jeers, or other unpleasantness, but obedience always has a long-term payoff. When God told Abraham to move from his homeland to the land of Canaan, Abraham obeyed. It was only after he got there that God rewarded him with land, an heir, and numerous other blessings. Daniel refused to vary his worship habits to placate a self-centered king and was tossed into the lions' den as a result. But he came out without a scratch the next morning. Peter stepped out of the boat and onto the water at Jesus' command, and for a moment he experienced the power of God in a way no one else ever had.

If we're resisting total obedience to God because we're afraid we'll have to miss out on something better, we're on the wrong frequency. We need to get back to the "All God, All the Time" station. The daily rewards of obedience are terrific. The eternal ones are even better.

God transmits. We receive, and then we heartily endorse that reception. In a nutshell, that's what worship is all about.

Questions to Ponder and/or Discuss

1. What things have you tried in the past to draw closer to God? Which ones worked? Which ones didn't?

2. If you were to receive a report card reflecting the quality of your worship during the past six weeks, what grade would you expect? Which of the following comments might qualify your grade:

   - Excellent! Great job!
   - Needs improvement
   - Unsatisfactory
   - Doesn't work or play well with others
   - Mind doesn't seem to be focused on his/her assignments
   - Other: _____

3. During the past month or two, can you cite some truly authentic acts of worship where you were in complete obedience to God?

4. Can you recall other instances that felt more sacrificial and mechanical and not quite as genuine as they should be?

CHAPTER FIVE

The Way You Do
the Things You Do
OTHER SPIRITUAL DISCIPLINES

Fred plodded in from his morning jog and collapsed into a patio chair. Wilma saw him out the window and took him a glass of ice water. After downing half of it in two big gulps, Fred asked her, "Is it just me, or is the pull of gravity stronger these days than it used to be?"

Without cracking a smile she replied, "I believe the pull of gravity is the same, but the force may seem stronger because it's pulling on a larger mass."

Fred was too tired for a comeback, so Wilma continued, "What would you like for breakfast?"

"Nothing! Well, I'll take toast and juice. But I've got to start laying off the bacon and eggs for a while. And the doughnuts. And the Pop-Tarts. And the waffles. And the . . . ." Fred's voice trailed off as he went upstairs to shower and dress.

He returned to find his toast and juice waiting for him—along with fake butter, low-cal jam, and the newspaper turned to a large ad for an in-home exercise machine. He ran five miles almost every day, but he knew (as apparently did Wilma) that it wouldn't hurt for him to start supplementing his runs with some sit-ups. But he could do it! It was only a matter of discipline. This was the day he would start!

As he headed for the car, the doorbell rang. He paused long enough to see who it was. He heard Wilma say, "Oh, hi, Jane. Come in."

It was Jane Seeker. He waved hello and heard her tell Wilma, "I was testing out our new oven, and I wanted to thank you for the casseroles. These are one of my specialties—seven-layer cookies with chocolate, caramel, coconut, and some other surprises. I hope you enjoy them."

Fred rolled his eyes as he headed for his car. Maybe the diet could wait until next week. And if so, he had just enough time to get coffee and a bear claw at Drive-Thru Donuts on the way to work.

As we get older and wiser, we discover that the concept of "discipline" in any aspect of life quickly becomes multiple "disciplines." In the discipline of physical health, for example, Fred was intensely devoted to the exercise aspect—or one of them at least. But he was beginning to see a need for other exercises as well as adding a dietary discipline. If we commit to financial discipline (singular), it will affect spending, saving, investing, speculation, and numerous other disciplines (plural). And the same pattern is true when we consider spiritual "discipline."

We've already discussed Bible study, prayer, and worship, which are certainly essential to any regimen of spiritual health and growth. But as we progress with those primary disciplines, we may discover that we could benefit greatly by adding additional elements to our program. That's what we want to examine in this chapter. We'll start with a few disciplines that have a reasonably solid biblical basis, and then we'll look at a few others that are farther "out there" in regard to Christian tradition.

Why Do They Call It Fasting When the Time Goes So Slowly?

One of the more commonly known, but not commonly practiced, disciplines is *fasting*. The purpose of this discipline is to deprive oneself of food and/or drink for a period of time, during which our physical cravings should direct our attention to God. People have widely varying opinions as to how this discipline should be applied (or not) in a modern spiritual regimen.

Only one fast was required in the Mosaic law. Once a year, on the solemn Day of Atonement, when people were offering sacrifices and repenting of sins, they were to fast (Leviticus 16). It was a 24-hour fast, from sundown to sundown (Leviticus 23:32). Later, after the Israelites were taken into captivity, other annual fasts were added.

But voluntary fasting was practiced by numerous people in the Old Testament, and for various specific reasons. Fasting wasn't always a religious matter. For instance, it would frequently take place as part of the mourning process after the death of a loved one (1 Samuel 31:8-13; 2 Samuel 1:12).

At other times, fasting wasn't done to bring oneself closer to God, but because the person was already so close that apparently food didn't seem necessary. In a couple of exceptional instances, both Moses (Exodus 34:28) and Elijah (1 Kings 19:8) had 40-day fasts where God sustained their strength for special tasks.

In the New Testament, fasting was an established part of religious life. Jesus taught about fasting but apparently didn't practice it on a regular basis. His 40 days without food in the wilderness, where He was tempted by the devil, are a clear example of His willingness to fast (Matthew 4:1-11). But later He was criticized by the religious leaders who wanted to know why they and John's disciples fasted but Jesus and His disciples didn't. Jesus replied, "Do wedding guests fast while celebrating with the groom? Of course not. They can't fast while they are with the groom. But someday he will be taken away from them, and then they will fast" (Mark 2:18-20). Jesus went on to contrast old traditions with new ones, leading some people to believe fasting is no longer an expected spiritual discipline (Mark 2:21-22).

In fact, Jesus' lack of fasting caused Him to be labeled "a glutton and a drunkard" by the religious leaders of His time (Luke 7:31-35). Clearly, anyone who fasts to honor God and focus on Him will be

FOR EXAMPLE . . .

Fasting in the Old Testament

Here are a few other Old Testament fasters, but the list is by no means complete:

- Daniel's visions of the future led him to mourn and fast for three straight weeks (Daniel 10:1-3).
- After David's sin with Bathsheba, he fasted in hopes that God would retract the death sentence passed on the child she had conceived (2 Samuel 12:13-23).
- Wicked Queen Jezebel used fasting as part of a devious, hypocritical scheme to take land from someone who wouldn't sell it to her husband (1 Kings 21:1-16).
- After returning from exile and beginning to rebuild their homeland, the Israelites included fasting and confession in their initial ceremonies (Nehemiah 9:1-2).
- Even the vicious Ninevites fasted when they heard God was about to destroy their city (Jonah 3:6-10).

DO'S AND DON'TS

When you fast, don't make it obvious, as the hypocrites do, who try to look pale and disheveled so people will admire them for their fasting. I assure you, that is the only reward they will ever get. But when you fast, comb your hair and wash your face. Then no one will suspect you are fasting, except your Father, who knows what you do in secret. And your Father, who knows all secrets, will reward you. (Matthew 6:16-18)

WELL SAID!

Whoso will pray, he must fast and be clean,
　And fat his soul, and make his body lean. —*Chaucer*

commended by God. But those who do it as a type of spiritual one-upmanship are only fooling themselves if they think it somehow makes them superior to other Christians. If you are well aware that someone else fasts on a regular basis, he or she must not be doing it right because fasting should be a private matter between the person and God (with the exception of church-wide fasts for special purposes).

When Jesus referred in His parables to the practice of fasting by the Pharisees, it was to show that they were missing the point by performing religious acts but lacking a sincerity for God and other people (Luke 18:9-14). Certain people today continue to miss the point.

Who Says You Can't Take It with You?

Chapter 2 started our look at the specifics of how Christians live by delving into Bible study. But everything that could be said for reading and studying Scripture also applies to *memorizing* it. Scripture memory is an ongoing discipline that some people enjoy, others commit to, and still others have little regard for.

Some people might argue that it's enough to know what the Bible says and/or where to find it. The effort to memorize it verbatim requires time that could be spent in other beneficial ways.

Other people, however, find tremendous satisfaction in knowing large portions of Scripture word for word. They argue that if we want to be able to call appropriate Bible instructions to mind during our daily routines (as Jesus did during His temptation), what better way than to have them firmly implanted in our minds to begin with? And in discussions with other people who want to know more about the Bible, they are much more comfortable being able to quote chapter and verse rather than fumble around to find relevant answers.

We don't question the devotion of actors who memorize entire plays of Shakespeare or other writers in order to repeat those well-chosen words and inspire an audience. In fact, some people earn quite comfortable livings by merely repeating words they have memorized from a script. The Bible is more moving and inspiring (not to mention more inspired) than any other work of literature or modern screenplay.

The difference is that we don't memorize Scripture in order to sway a large audience. We do it in order to sway our own way of thinking. Just as an actor might request "Line!" when stumped about what to say, we can call on God's Spirit in our own struggles to cue us with an appropriate verse or passage we have committed to memory.

Memorized Scripture is like a backup generator when the electricity goes out. If you don't have a Bible handy as you find yourself with a spiritual seeker or trying to navigate a particularly treacherous temptation, the passages you have memorized serve as beacons to see you through. Taking God's Word with you in printed form is useful, but carrying God's Word with you in memorized form can have value all its own. Some Christians have entire Bible books committed to memory and keep adding to their "memory files" on a regular basis.

Are You Taking Your Meditations?

Eastern religions have placed such an emphasis on meditation that sometimes Christians are reluctant to discuss or consider it. But in the Christian life, meditation can play a valid part in spiritual growth. It's one thing to read the Bible. It's another to go the extra step and memorize it. Yet we can still do all that and never get personally involved with what God's Word is saying to us. Meditation is an even deeper level of Bible examination that gets us to the point of considering personal application of the material. Meditation addresses the "So what?" perspective many people have toward Scripture.

If you're taking a difficult college course that is crucial to your major and eventual graduation, you're likely to do much more than skim the textbook when final exams roll around. You will delve into the content, attempting to absorb and understand the material completely. You know the test will have questions that require you to assimilate and apply what you have learned and not simply parrot a few key facts.

Meditation on Scripture takes the same approach, except the

ONE SMALL STEP

If you've never attempted to memorize Scripture, you might want to give it a try. You can find some good organized programs at your local Christian bookstore, but you might want to start with a few of your favorite passages. Don't make yourself miserable. Start with a verse or two each week and add another couple of verses next week as you continue to review what you've already learned. You may be surprised at how quickly you'll accumulate a repertoire of memorized verses—and at how frequently they come to mind at appropriate times.

DO'S AND DON'TS

Study this Book of the Law continually. Meditate on it day and night so you may be sure to obey all that is written in it. Only then will you succeed. (Joshua 1:8)

FOR EXAMPLE . . .

Psalm 119

The longest of all the psalms, Psalm 119 remains focused from start to finish on the importance of paying close attention to God's Word. Along with the psalmist's repeated intent to read, reflect, and apply what he finds, he also professed the need to meditate on Scripture (Psalm 119:23, 27, 48, and other places).

"exam" is day-to-day living. When you first begin reading the Bible, you may pride yourself in reading a chapter or even an entire book at each sitting. It's helpful to see the big picture of Scripture and how various portions relate to one another. But in meditation you might spend the same amount of time on one verse. And you don't give up until you discover something that applies to your own life.

For example, at first you might read the Noah account in Genesis 6–9 and be impressed with what a guy Noah was. The flood, the devastation, the rainbow/promise, the animals, and all the rest makes for good drama. But as you start meditating, you get to the "so what?" question. Why is that story in the Bible? What can I learn from it?

Of all the people on earth, why did God choose Noah? What was significant about Noah building an altar as soon as the ark ran aground? Why are all these details included? What can I learn from them about obedience to God even if I feel conscientious and conspicuous? What can I learn from the positive examples of other people? What can I learn about God's protection during times of trial? And so forth.

Give till It Stops Hurting

Another spiritual discipline of the Christian life involves letting go of some of the money and possessions that come our way. This can be done in numerous ways.

One standard method of giving is through *tithing,* the habit of devoting one-tenth of one's goods as a religious offering or political tribute. This was an ancient cultural custom that existed in Babylon, Egypt, Persia, and even China, as well as being written into the Mosaic law. The tithes collected from the Israelites went to support the work of the priests and Levites. (The tribe of Levi was not given a chunk of territory in the Promised Land as were the other tribes. Instead, the Levites lived and ministered among the other tribes. And since they did the work of God instead of raising crops and such, they were dependent on the contributions of others to live and continue their work.)

The practice of tithing continued into the New Testament. And like most other elements of a godly life, people found ways to mess it up. The giving of tithes could become quite an elaborate ceremony, but Jesus denounced the showiness of it all.

In addition to cash, people would sometimes tithe other things: grain, flocks, crops, etc. Consequently, this practice was also something people could go overboard on. Some of the Pharisees would even tithe their seasonings—mint, dill, cumin, and such (Matthew 23:23; Luke 11:42, NIV). Yet after being so picky about their giving habits, they still didn't give their hearts to God, which was, and is, the underlying purpose of tithing.

As the church was formed, less emphasis was placed on the ritual of tithing than on the need for cheerful and selfless giving. Before the roster of Christians grew too large, it was simply a matter of giving anything you had to someone else who needed it. The mentality was that everything belonged to God, and everyone was "of one heart and mind" (Acts 4:32-35). People even sold houses and lands to provide for others.

Later, as the number of believers grew and the church spread from Jerusalem to other numerous cities and towns, the same principle was in effect to some extent. Local churches who were going strong would take collections to be sent to other churches that were experiencing severe poverty. As Paul traveled from place to place, he made frequent mention of churches that had given and where the money would be going.

Whether tithing, giving, sharing, or otherwise using your possessions to help others, the ultimate purpose should be to glorify God. We're not supposed to be in it for the tax write-offs or spiritual brownie points. If we have homes rather than homelessness, we ought to thank God and help the homeless. If we have large bank balances rather than enormous debts, we need to remember it's God who gave us the work ethic, the financial acumen, or the wealthy dead relative that provided such financial security. If we're hoarding what we have, there are other kinds of spiritual security we're probably missing out on.

FOR EXAMPLE . . .

Abraham and Melchizedek (Genesis 14)

Centuries before God gave the law to Moses, Abraham practiced tithing. After his nephew Lot was taken prisoner along with much of the wealth and food of Sodom, Abraham assembled an army, rescued Lot, and recovered the stolen goods. After his victory he met a man named Melchizedek, who was "the king of Salem [Jerusalem] and a priest of God Most High." Abraham offered Melchizedek a tenth of all the goods he had recovered.

DO'S AND DON'TS

Take care! Don't do your good deeds publicly, to be admired, because then you will lose the reward from your Father in heaven. When you give a gift to someone in need, don't shout about it as the hypocrites do—blowing trumpets in the synagogues and streets to call attention to their acts of charity! I assure you, they have received all the reward they will ever get. But when you give to someone, don't tell your left hand what your right hand is doing. Give your gifts in secret, and your Father, who knows all secrets, will reward you. (Matthew 6:1-4)

DO'S AND DON'TS

You must each make up your own mind as to how much you should give. Don't give reluctantly or in response to pressure. For God loves the person who gives cheerfully. And God will generously provide all you need. Then you will always have everything you need and plenty left over to share with others. (2 Corinthians 9:7-8)

The rules of giving aren't carved in stone anymore. But the guidelines are clear about what attitudes we should have and what actions we should take. As we will see later in the chapter, some people go to extremes in their attempts to keep from having more than anyone else.

Celibate Good Times, Come On!

While many people are more than willing to sacrifice food, money, or time in order to get closer to God, a few go yet another step and give up sexual gratification to live celibate lives. Those who are willing and able to channel all their passions into the Christian life rather than a physical relationship frequently find themselves with more time and freedom than those who opt for marriage.

Paul realized that he was able to do as much as he did for God because he wasn't responsible for a wife as well as his ministry. A wife might not have been as willing to endure the beatings, stonings, prison time, shipwrecks, and other adventures Paul experienced (2 Corinthians 11:22-33). Paul wanted others to consider committing to a lifestyle like his, yet he also realized that not everyone could turn off their sexual urges and remain celibate. His official word on the matter was, "It is better to marry than to burn with lust" (1 Corinthians 7:9). Jesus had made a similar comment: "Some are born as eunuchs, some have been made that way by others, and some choose not to marry for the sake of the Kingdom of Heaven. Let anyone who can, accept this statement" (Matthew 19:12).

Jesus had also said that our hearts and thoughts follow whatever we treasure in life (Matthew 6:19-21). We usually interpret His statement as a motivation to follow God rather than money or some less satisfying pursuit. But it's also true in regard to marriage. There is nothing wrong with deciding to "treasure" a spouse. But in doing so, we must realize that marriage and family, as rewarding as they can be, require time, energy, and resources that might otherwise go entirely to God. Happily married people can hardly comprehend life without a spouse. Happily celibate people can hardly imagine having a life partner to intrude into their personal ministry. God's plan varies from person to person. That's why Bible study, prayer, and worship are so important to keep His plan for you in perspective at all times.

The Aesthetics of the Ascetics

So far we have seen a number of options for additional spiritual disciplines, all of which have some degree of biblical basis. And the principle behind each one has been essentially the same: By giving up certain things for God, we receive a greater amount of God's blessing and insight. By giving up a little food from time to time, we divert our primary focus from ourselves to the One who so freely supplies that food. If we give up time to meditate on Scripture, we see more clearly how it applies to us than if we give it a cursory reading. By giving up our tithes and gifts, the wealth of the kingdom of God is more evenly distributed. By giving up sex and marriage, we create much more time to devote to the work of God.

These are all good options and opportunities for growth. Most of us are drawn to certain of these options more than others. And if the Christian life is new to you, perhaps you will want to experiment with some of these opportunities, adding them to Bible study, worship, and prayer when you feel the time is right.

The purpose of spiritual disciplines should be to bring us closer to Jesus, who in turn provides us with "life in all its fullness." Yet it should be said that, historically, most of these options (and others) have been taken to great extremes without any glimpse of abundant life. Let's take a few quick peeks at some ascetics throughout history.

If you want to define asceticism, think "Lifestyles of the Rich and Famous," and then go just as far in the opposite direction as you possibly can. Ascetics are people who deny their personal comforts to extremes in pursuit of a higher spiritual and/or moral state.

John the Baptist was something of an ascetic. He had a job to do for God, so he remained in the wilderness, preaching repentance and baptizing those who responded. While there, he wore clothes

FOR EXAMPLE . . .

Philip and His Daughters
(Acts 6:1-7; 8:4-8, 26-40; 21:8-9)

How people choose to devote themselves to God seems to be a matter of personal taste. Philip was one of the original seven overseers of the church who helped the apostles, and he did some powerful things for God. He apparently was married because he had four daughters. His daughters, however, remained celibate and served God through the gift of prophecy. Had they taken husbands in their culture, they likely would not have had the same freedom to exercise their God-given abilities.

WELL SAID!

God could have made all rich, or all men poor;

But why He did not, let me tell wherefore:

Had all been rich, where then had Patience been?

Had all been poor, who had His Bounty seen? —*Robert Herrick*

WELL SAID!

Self sacrifice which denies common sense is not a virtue. It's a spiritual dissipation. —*Margaret Deland*

made from camel hair with a leather belt. He ate locusts and wild honey. He lived simply and didn't waste a lot of energy worrying about diet or sartorial elegance (Matthew 3:4-5).

Perhaps a page from the John the Baptist fashion catalog caused the hair shirt craze of the early 1700s. As a self-imposed punishment or act of penance, ascetics would wear undershirts of coarse haircloth next to their skin. In the days before air conditioning, this habit not only inhibited the comfort level of the wearer but most likely that of anyone in the surrounding area as well.

Another common ascetic practice was living in "cells" (small rooms) without any conveniences. Taking this issue to further extremes were the Stylites (not to be confused with the Chi-Lites who performed "Have You Seen Her?" or the Stylistics who did "Betcha By Golly, Wow"). The Stylites were a group of Christians who would spend long periods of time atop a narrow pillar (*stylos*). Sometimes the person would construct a small hut or roof for protection against the elements but was otherwise out in the open for all to see. An ascetic named Saint Simeon Stylites climbed a column more than 100 feet high in A.D. 423 and didn't come down for 30 years. Another devoted pillar hermit of the sixth century was St. Alypius, who is said to have spent 67 years on his pillar without a break but had to spend the final 14 years lying down because he could no longer stand. Other people in this group even stood on one leg for lengthy periods of time.

Many ascetics saw wine as something to be shunned. To avoid any possibility of intoxication, some would even substitute milk or water for wine taken in the commemoration of the Lord's Supper. Some were of the belief that marriage was "of the devil" and remained single. A guy named Origen went to the point of castrating himself in order to remain pure.

In some cases even sleep and personal hygiene were perceived to be comforts to be avoided. People would sleep standing, tied to upright posts, or hanging from ropes tied around their abdomens. Some would prohibit washing, haircuts, changing clothes, clipping fingernails, or other such luxuries. (Is it beginning to make sense why so many of them lived in solitude?)

Taking the concept even further, other forms of asceticism (sometimes known as self-mortification) were created that literally produced pain. Simple forms included physically exhausting exercises or unnecessary exposure to cold or heat. Some early Hindu ascetics were known to stare at the sun until they went blind, or to hold their arms above their heads until their arms literally withered.

The pain-inflicting techniques evolved into more complex methods such as iron chains or bands worn under clothing that would continually rub against the neck, hands, feet, or more sensitive areas of the body. In addition to a castration here and there, other ascetics would practice flagellation, or whipping oneself until blood would gush.

We would be hard-pressed to find biblical teachings that endorse such extreme levels of asceticism. Fasting? Sure. Purity and self-denial? Good spiritual goals. But some people add other elements of more radical asceticism because they want to relate to the sufferings of Jesus.

Still others would argue that any Christian life committed fully to Jesus will contain adequate sufferings and challenges. We need not impose numerous additional restrictions on ourselves in the name of religion. Rather, we should learn to hurdle the spiritual obstacles that come our way while continuing to seek out the abundant life Jesus has promised His followers. Yes, we are told to take up our crosses and follow Him (Matthew 10:38-39). But He also adds that the burden He places on us is a light one (Matthew 11:28-30).

That Was Then; This Is Now

The scope of one's spiritual disciplines is a personal matter that varies from individual to individual. It is also a private matter between the person and God. Someone might feel led to reject most personal comforts and give everything to the poor. Others might feel equally led to use financial skills for the glory of God. A summer home in the country could be sold to finance a ministry,

FOR EXAMPLE . . .

The Recabites (2 Kings 10:15-29; Jeremiah 35)

After a reign of extreme wickedness and selfishness by King Ahab and Queen Jezebel, God determined it was time to put an end to their ongoing sin. God had chosen a warrior named Jehu to do some "housecleaning" by killing the queen, the entire royal family, and the idol-worshiping priests of Baal. (Ahab had recently met his prophesied death in battle [1 Kings 22:29-40].) Assisting Jehu was a man named Jehonadab, the son of a man named Recab.

Partially to protest the religious erosion of their nation, the Recabites had adopted a somewhat ascetic lifestyle—living in tents instead of homes, abstaining from wine, and refusing to sow crops. Two hundred years later they were still going strong, and God used them as a positive object lesson. But they weren't singled out so much for their different lifestyle as for the fact that they continued to uphold the instruction they had received from their forefathers (in direct contrast to how the Israelites were responding to God).

ONE SMALL STEP

Some churches celebrate Lent annually, giving up something for the 40 days before Easter with the intent of focusing more clearly on Jesus. If you've never tried this, you might want to give it a shot and see what happens. Of course, you need not wait until Easter, or even go for a full 40 days. Designate your own timetable and then see how well you do when it comes to sacrificing meat, morning lattes, chocolate, or whatever you choose in order to honor God.

but it might also be loaned out to lots of people who couldn't otherwise afford a week out amid the glory of God's creation. Only by staying in touch with God will the owner know which option to pursue. Numerous ministries depend on conscientious Christians who support them financially. People with money and generosity can be just as saintly as those who give away all they have and then make no further contribution to the church or community.

It is not the purpose of this chapter to sway you one way or the other. We simply want to lay out some of the options and allow you to see what other people have chosen. Personally, we would advise against the self-castration or flagellation options. We serve a loving and forgiving God, and there are much better ways to find His mercy and remain in His good graces.

But you might want to give up some time to meditate on God's Word a bit more than you've ever done before or to memorize Scripture. You might want to give up something small just to remind yourself of how many of God's blessings you take for granted each day and how much other people have willingly sacrificed to get closer to God. While maintaining your Bible study, prayer, and worship, you might discover someday that you're still a little on the flabby side (spiritually), and then you'll know that these other exercises are open to you.

The next section of this book will show what God is doing to help us through the Christian life. His resources will be essential in our ongoing spiritual journeys.

Questions to Ponder and/or Discuss

1. For each of the following spiritual disciplines, list any examples you have witnessed that demonstrate an appropriate practice of the discipline and/or what you would consider an inappropriate or too-extreme application.

SPIRITUAL DISCIPLINE	APPROPRIATE EXAMPLES	INAPPROPRIATE EXAMPLES
Fasting		
Bible Memorization		
Meditation		
Giving		
Celibacy		

2. What guidelines might you use to determine when a spiritual discipline has ceased to serve a practical purpose and is bordering on asceticism/fanaticism?

3. On the pie chart below, fill in all the spiritual disciplines you feel are important to an active Christian life. Determine the relative importance of each one based on the size of the "pie slice" you assign it.

Prayer
Bible Study
Worship
Fasting
Bible Memorization
Meditation
Giving
Celibacy
Other: _____

4. How well do your current spiritual disciplines match up to the ideal model you have created?

CHAPTER SIX

"IF WE HAD JUST A FEW MORE, WE'D REALLY BE HAPPY."

The Pursuit of Happiness
THE BEATITUDES

"I'm bored!"

"Yeah. Me too."

Two kids. A unanimous vote. Another typical summer day. Wilma (and every other mom in the world) had heard it all before.

"Josh, why don't you get out and get some exercise? If you're hoping to be a starter on the football team this fall, don't you need to be out running and training, or at least breaking a sweat every once in a while? And Mary, if you want to pick up that Summer Reading Award that you've been talking about, you need to get started. You've been out of school for a month, and I haven't seen a book in your hand. Why don't you walk down to the library, pick up a few books, and sit outside and read for a while? It's a beautiful day."

Neither Joshua nor Mary moved.

"Josh?"

"It's too hot, Mom."

"It's 72 degrees. You won't find more perfect weather."

"I'll go later." Josh reached for his latest video game.

SOME THINGS YOU'LL DISCOVER IN THIS CHAPTER

1. Eight unusual ways to seek happiness

2. Several paradoxical aspects of how Christians live

3. The connections between happiness, obedience, and persecution

"How about you, Mary?"

"The library's too far. Maybe you can drive me."

"Good grief, Mary, it's four blocks. What's wrong with you kids?"

Mary spoke for both of them. "This is just a stupid summer. My friends all went to camp and I don't have anyone to do anything with."

Josh added, "And mine are all working. When we do get together, they've got tons of money for movies and games and stuff. All I've got is the lame allowance you and Dad give me."

Wilma rolled her eyes. "Mary, we tried to get you to go to camp, but you said you needed to stay home and read. And Josh, if your friends are all working, why don't you get a job?"

"Yeah, right."

The apathy of her kids was one thing. That tone of voice was quite another. Wilma decided to get a bit more motivational.

"Josh, if you don't get up right now and go mow the lawn before lunch, you won't even get your 'lame allowance' this week. And Mary, you march yourself right down to the library. I want you to have three books read by the end of this week or I won't be taking you to the water park this weekend. But if you read five or more, I'll also take you for ice cream afterward. And Josh, when you get finished mowing, my garden needs weeding. If you want to do it for me, I'll give you some extra money."

Josh and Mary rarely saw their Mom get this aggressive, and they sat somewhat stunned.

Wilma continued, "I love you two dearly, but I'm telling you this from the bottom of my heart: Get out of my sight and go do something productive."

Five minutes later Josh was getting the mower ready when the teenage girl from the house behind theirs came out to sunbathe. They struck up a conversation and she asked if he would like to play tennis later that evening. And at the library Mary saw a couple of friends from school who hadn't gone to camp either. They all agreed to hang together during the summer. And when Joshua and Mary later told Wilma of their exciting new plans, she didn't even say, "I told you so."

Forget Your Troubles, Come On, Get Happy!

The DiCiple children are indicative of most kids—and adults, for that matter. We have a desire for the right things (a slot on the football team, awards for achievement, etc.) but soon discover that desire isn't enough. Unless desire is followed by a *drive* to accomplish those good goals, we aren't likely to accomplish them.

Nowhere is this more true than in the Christian life. Most of us quickly profess a desire to know the Bible, to pray, to discern God's will, and to live as God wants us to. And we're sincere in that desire. We really do want it. It's just that when spiritual growth starts getting more difficult, giving up is a lot easier than perseverance and drive. That's why these things are called spiritual *disciplines*. Accomplishing these goals requires persistence, determination, and hard work.

So far in this book we've been looking at things we need to do in order to find answers and meaning in the Christian life. They are external disciplines—actions we can take—that should pay off with time and faithful dedication. In this section of the book, we're making a transition to see what should be taking place *internally* as we continue our external disciplines. Unless the internal changes are taking place, the external ones aren't likely to be very meaningful.

And one of the first internal shifts that takes place as a person makes a commitment to Jesus and the Christian life should be a change of desire. We should at least *want* to please Jesus with our lives, even if we're still not doing a very good job of it. If the desire is there, the payoffs can be quite rewarding. So as we begin to consider our inner desire and what we have to look forward to, we want to examine the Beatitudes, the opening salvos of Jesus' Sermon on the Mount (Matthew 5:3-10).

By definition, "beatitudes" are declarations of blessedness. Depending on your Bible translation, the statements might be made in a number of ways. For example, here are four different translations for the opening statement of Matthew 5:3:

WELL SAID!

If enough people think of a thing and work hard enough at it, I guess it's pretty nearly bound to happen, wind and weather permitting.
—*Laura Ingalls Wilder*

ONE SMALL STEP

Pause for a moment and list the things that make you feel happy or blessed. Then, as you continue with this chapter, see how your list compares with Jesus'.

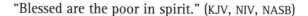

WELL SAID!

The Beatitudes set forth the balanced and variegated character of Christian people. These are not eight separate and distinct groups of disciples, some of whom are meek, while others are merciful and yet others are called upon to endure persecution. They are rather eight qualities of the same group who at one and the same time are meek and merciful, poor in spirit and pure in heart, mourning and hungry, peacemakers and persecuted. . . . The Beatitudes are Christ's own specification of what every Christian ought to be. All these qualities are to characterize all his followers. — *John R. W. Stott*

"Blessed are the poor in spirit." (KJV, NIV, NASB)

"Humble men are very fortunate!" (TLB)

"God blesses those who realize their need for him." (NLT)

"You're blessed when you're at the end of your rope." (*The Message*)

The concept of "blessed" is sometimes interpreted as being "happy," though it is much more. Happiness is fickle, coming and going with various situations we face. But a "blessed" mind-set, when properly in place, can transcend unpleasant circumstances. The Beatitudes take control away from other people or situations and establish a direct interaction between yourself and God. If the desire to get closer to God is really there, God promises to follow through with ample rewards for His faithful people.

You Poor Thing!

"God blesses those who realize their need for him, for the Kingdom of Heaven is given to them" (Matthew 5:3).

The Beatitudes begin with the importance of the proper level of desire to know God. Other translations refer to this sensation as being "poor in spirit." And to be truthful, it is sometimes difficult to admit needing anything in our affluent society. We are usually on the other side of the situation in nobly trying to "help the needy" at Thanksgiving, Christmas, and other times of year. If our thoughts or actions are the least bit condescending, it then becomes embarrassing to confess when *we* are the needy ones.

Yet that's exactly the starting point for spiritual growth. When we finally conclude that Jesus is our only option for eternal spiritual security, we need to stand before Him with our pockets turned inside out and our souls bared as well. God always responds to genuine humility. What angers Him is hypocrisy—when we realize that we can't succeed without Him, turn to Him for help, but then continue to act as if we're doing everything under our own power.

Perhaps it's easier to relate to being "poor in health." Your body simply isn't performing as it should. Your strength is drained. Your mental state is foggy. After a few days with no improvement, you decide to see a doctor, who diagnoses the problem, gives you a shot or a prescription, and soon you're better than ever. In a similar sense, being "poor in spirit" is a positive thing if it turns us from our own despair to God, who can remedy the problem once and for all.

In fact, recognizing and acting on our need for God is the first step toward the kingdom of Heaven. The world is filled with wealthy, self-sufficient people who may never acknowledge their spiritual poverty. The sooner we stop trying to substitute money or anything else for spiritual health, the sooner God can fill us with everything we need. Entrance to God's Kingdom cannot be purchased by anyone for any amount of cash or possessions. But for those who acknowledge their need for Him and respond in faith, entrance is absolutely free—and this magic kingdom never closes.

DO'S AND DON'TS

When you bow down before the Lord and admit your dependence on him, he will lift you up and give you honor. (James 4:10)

First Lessen, Then Mourn

"God blesses those who mourn, for they will be comforted" (Matthew 5:4).

Jesus suggests we not drop our guard when God deals with our spiritual poverty, because spiritual sadness is likely to follow. When we're relating to God, He will never let us down. But most of us also relate to other people—family members, coworkers, bosses, fickle friends, and others who don't always treat us with the utmost of respect. In addition, we struggle in a sin-tainted world where events don't always occur as God originally intended them. Like Job, we sometimes are at the mercy of forces that are far stronger than we are. And like Job, we sometimes sit in the ashes and wonder, "Why me?"

Spiritual suffering is never something we would wish upon ourselves, but it has its upside. As kids, skinned knees were never something we hoped for, but perhaps the trauma of falling down

WELL SAID!

Great grief is a divine and terrible radiance which transfigures the wretched. — *Victor Hugo*

ONE SMALL STEP

Diogenes was famous for carrying a lighted lantern at midday, claiming to be "looking for an honest man." Humble people are even harder to spot than honest ones, so conduct your own search this week. See how many people you can find who could honestly be described as "gentle and lowly." If you can find any, be sure to say something to encourage them.

and feeling pain revealed the extent of a parent's love. The skinned knee might have triggered Mom's mothering instincts—kisses, hugs, Bactine, a Spider-Man Band-Aid, and ice cream. In retrospect, the pain of flesh against asphalt was more than compensated by the discovery that your parents were there to see you through any crisis.

Mourning is no one's favorite activity, but it keeps our eyes turned upward, looking to God for help. And the promised result is that He indeed will provide the comfort we're looking for. We aren't promised that all our pains and struggles will disappear, but mourning at least gets results.

When things go badly, lots of people try other options: swearing, rage, retribution, despair and depression, withdrawal, lawsuits, and so forth. Some of these options only create downward emotional spirals. But when we stand before God and hold nothing back in telling Him how lousy we feel, we discover just how good He is at providing comfort.

Sweet and Lowly

"God blesses those who are gentle and lowly, for the whole earth will belong to them" (Matthew 5:5).

The more familiar translation of this verse is, "Blessed are the meek, for they will inherit the earth" (NIV). It's another of those spiritual corollaries that is just opposite of what we're accustomed to.

We are repeatedly taught that if we want to have anything to show at the end of our lives, it will require aggressiveness, hard work, insightful investing, and more. Along the way, we do whatever we can to acquire power and control. Sometimes we resort to shady (we prefer to call them "creative") techniques to get what we want because, well, we all know where nice guys finish.

But Jesus comes right out and dares us to be "gentle and lowly," even though He knows this is a dog-eat-dog world where winners have the eye of the tiger and the waters are filled with sharks in three-piece suits. How does He think a prospective boss will

respond after seeing a resumé where the applicant is seeking employment in a business environment that will allow a lot of freedom for the development of gentleness and lowliness? Do you think you'll get the job?

Yet again, Jesus also provided the promised rewards of making such a difficult choice. When God gets involved, He determines how the tables will turn. If we take the challenge of remaining gentle and lowly in a passive-aggressive world, God sees and notices.

When the herdsmen of Abraham and Lot were feuding, the uncle and nephew decided it would be best to split up. Abraham (as the elder) should have had first choice of the prime real estate, but he deferred to Lot. The younger man saw the allure and lushness of Sodom and Gomorrah and picked the easy life, leaving Abraham and his herds to forage in the desert. A bit cold, but a shrewd move on Lot's part. Right?

It might have seemed so until the sinful cities experienced a divine rainstorm of burning sulfur. Umbrellas were useless as the entire plain where the cities were located was burned to a crisp (Genesis 19:23-29). And when all was said and done, it was Abraham who "inherited the earth."

It's not a natural response to receive an insult without responding or to turn the other cheek when slapped by an aggressive and obnoxious person. But in learning to become more gentle and lowly, we become more like Jesus. And consequently, we will be rewarded more like Jesus was when He returned to His Father. It's an inheritance we can't even imagine.

FOR EXAMPLE . . .

The Rich Man and Lazarus (Luke 16:19-31)

Jesus told a stark story about how a person's fortunes can change after death, for good or for bad. A person's money, power, possessions, and so forth, have nothing to do with his or her *eternal* security. God will reward meek and lowly believers in a major way, while those who reject Him to get what they want will suffer the consequences.

Got Righteousness?

"God blesses those who are hungry and thirsty for justice, for they will receive it in full" (Matthew 5:6).

Untold millions of dollars are spent every year just to advertise food and drink. If a fraction of the money spent and hours of creativity used to sell beer were applied to science instead, we would probably be colonizing the moons of Jupiter by now. Lots of corporations

DO'S AND DON'TS

Let justice roll on like a river, righteousness like a never-failing stream. (Amos 5:24, NIV)

are out there trying to convince us we need their particular brand of fizzy sugar water or alcoholic brew, but sometimes we get to the point where the only thing that will satisfy a terrible thirst is plain cold water.

And in the Christian life, we can (and should) develop a powerful hunger for justice and thirst for righteousness. We will never be quite satisfied until God has total say and people start treating one another as they should. In a sinful world, this is an unattainable goal, of course. We can relate to the psalmist who wrote: "As the deer pants for streams of water, so I long for you, O God. I thirst for God, the living God. When can I come and stand before him? Day and night, I have only tears for food, while my enemies continually taunt me, saying, 'Where is this God of yours?'" (Psalm 42:1-3).

But God blesses those who strive for justice and righteousness against all obstacles. Jesus promises that eventually they will "receive it in full." And when it finally arrives, it's a four-star meal.

Mercy Beaucoup

"God blesses those who are merciful, for they will be shown mercy" (Matthew 5:7).

This statement actually begins in the middle of a cycle, so let's not get things backward. God doesn't wait until we show mercy to show mercy to us. Rather, He is the supreme example of both grace (giving us good things we don't deserve) and mercy (not giving us bad things we do deserve). If God weren't merciful and left us to receive what we truly deserved, we would all die for our sins and never again stand in His presence.

It is exactly because He, in His mercy, sent His Son to save us from our sin that He expects us to respond to His mercy and display it toward others. And as we perform the difficult task of offering mercy to those who (in our opinion) don't deserve it, we come to realize more completely exactly what God has done on our behalf.

So we first receive God's mercy, then learn to extend it to others, and finally discover the depth of mercy God has shown to us.

Like many of the other qualities described in the Beatitudes, mercy must be an intentional act. It won't come naturally. Showing mercy is definitely a spiritual discipline. When a kid spills milk on the floor after you told her to use both hands and she didn't, it may not be too difficult to forgive her and demonstrate mercy. But after a coworker has repeatedly stabbed you in the back to further his own career, and you are suddenly placed in the position of revealing something about him that could get him fired, it can be very difficult to hold your tongue and show mercy. Yet if we're truly hungry and thirsty for justice and righteousness, mercy should arise from that hunger.

Mercy is so rare in our day and age that it tends to get noticed. In fact, it bewilders people who don't understand how or why someone would let someone off the hook who deserved to hang on it. But if, in the Christian life, we continue our Bible study, prayer, and worship, we're reminded of the importance of mercy on a regular basis. In time, we get better at it. And if we do it often enough and well enough, people may become curious enough to ask why we're so different.

The Heart of the Matter (and Vice Versa)

"God blesses those whose hearts are pure, for they will see God" (Matthew 5:8).

When the Bible speaks of "the heart," it is usually a reference to more than an organ that pumps blood. The "heart" encapsulates a person's thoughts, feelings, and will. So in order to have a pure heart, a person should have clean thoughts, genuine emotions, and a desire to do as God instructs. (Hey! We're back to that desire thing again!)

Yet your spiritual "heart" remains a pump, in a sense. If your heart is pure, so will be your thoughts, actions, relationships, and lifestyle. But if you are harboring impurity in your heart—selfishness, greed,

FOR EXAMPLE . . .

The Parable of the Good Samaritan (Luke 10:25-37)

Jesus told the parable of the Good Samaritan to make a point. A religious/legal dialogue had arisen, and a man had asked, "Who is my neighbor?" Jesus told the parable in response, contrasting two "religious" leaders, who ignored a wounded man's needs, with a foreigner, who should have been the man's enemy but who helped him instead. Jesus followed the story by asking, "Now which of these three would you say was a neighbor to the man who was attacked by bandits?" The man who had asked the original question replied, "The one who showed him mercy."

Unexpected mercy can be powerful. And lest we think it was only a good story, Jesus concluded with a command: "Yes, now go and do the same."

FOR EXAMPLE . . .

David (1 Samuel 13:13-14; Acts 13:21-22)

Even as a young man, David was known as "a man after God's own heart," and it was a reputation that stayed with him. Yet he was by no means perfect. His adultery with Bathsheba and the "contract" he put out to murder her husband were dark deeds, to be sure (2 Samuel 11). But David's overwhelming passion for God led him to confess, repent, and return to God's favor.

lust, hatred, hypocrisy, or whatever—that's what will eventually become apparent to those around you. The person you are on the outside ultimately depends on the state of your heart.

Jesus later went into a bit more detail: "A good tree can't produce bad fruit, and a bad tree can't produce good fruit. A tree is identified by the kind of fruit it produces. Figs never grow on thornbushes or grapes on bramble bushes. A good person produces good deeds from a good heart, and an evil person produces evil deeds from an evil heart. Whatever is in your heart determines what you say" (Luke 6:43-45).

We filter our drinking water to attempt to remove all the microscopic impurities that might pollute it. Yet we may be harboring large chunks of spiritual crud that affect every other aspect of our lives. Just as we allow God to transform our minds to reflect His pure and perfect will (Romans 12:2), we also need to let Him do a little spiritual heart surgery.

People with pure hearts will see God, but that doesn't mean we have to be perfect. Moses saw God, and that was after he had killed an Egyptian and fled the scene of the crime. Elijah was close to God, but he remained quite an earthy kind of guy. Pure hearts may get a bit polluted from time to time, but the undying desire to see God will quickly motivate us to seek out God's love and help during such times. He is always willing to forgive and restore the purity level of our hearts and minds.

Peace, and Thank You

"God blesses those who work for peace, for they will be called the children of God" (Matthew 5:9).

Most of us hear a lot about peace. It's easy to point to wrongs in the world and get involved with trying to fix them. Once a year, someone is even awarded a Nobel prize in the category of peace. And until we live in a perfect world, the quest for peace will continue.

In the Christian life, however, the desire for peace need not be so wide-scale. You may never solve the conflict in the Middle East, convince the Catholics and Protestants to peacefully coexist in Ireland, or bring to a close any of the dozens of wars taking place around the world on any given day. But chances are you could resolve a personal conflict, or convince two feuding family members to peacefully coexist, or bring to an end any number of grudges you might be bearing against someone else. Don't expect to receive any Nobel prizes for your efforts, but Jesus promises a "prize" that's even better: You will be called a child of God.

Few things make a parent prouder than when someone observes of a child, "He is just like his father," or "She is just like her mother." Good parents demonstrate the traits they want their children to learn, and when the kids pick up on them, they feel rewarded. It's interesting to notice that Jesus designates the "children of God" title to peacemakers. Too many of God's children are out trying to emulate His wrath and judgment when we're exhorted to do what we can to accomplish peace.

Notice that the blessing doesn't automatically fall on anyone who wants peace but on those who work toward achieving it. The reward comes from peace*making*, not peace hoping. Lots of people in the 1960s gathered in communes and concerts and expressed a desire for peace. But when peace didn't simply happen because they wished it would, many of them pursued other options. Some committed violent acts in opposition to the Vietnam War. Some "moved on" and became the self-centered Me Generation of the 1970s. Some turned apathetic and cynical. And while the United States eventually withdrew from the war, the world is not noticeably more peaceful these days.

It's difficult to make peace with others on a personal level. It might require "taking one on the chin" and not retaliating against someone who offended you. It might mean forgiving grievances your family has been holding against someone else's family for generations. It might mean taking a bold step to narrow the distance between yourself and someone of another skin color, language, or ethnic persuasion. But when we choose to do such difficult things, we receive God's blessing.

DO'S AND DON'TS

"Never pay back evil for evil to anyone. Do things in such a way that everyone can see you are honorable. Do your part to live in peace with everyone, as much as possible." (Romans 12:17-18)

WELL SAID!

The problem is not why some pious, humble, believing people suffer, but why some do not. —*C. S. Lewis*

Hit Me with Your Best Shot

"God blesses those who are persecuted because they live for God, for the Kingdom of Heaven is theirs" (Matthew 5:10).

Jesus promises that the Christian life will be rewarding, but He never says it will be easy. Some skeptics and opponents of Christianity are rather apathetic about the whole thing, but others are outright hostile. When people resist the truth that Jesus promotes, they may also resist the carriers of the truth. Much persecution throughout the world is a result of "kill the messenger" syndrome. Their complaint is with Christ, but they take it out on Christians instead.

When it comes down to it, our Father can always whip their father, but He doesn't always choose to do so. If we consider persecution a kind of training, it can make us stronger. Just as boxers have to learn to take a punch by getting punched, Christians can only learn to withstand persecution by being persecuted. We may never discover any other explanation for it.

One's mind-set during times of persecution is crucial. In fact, Jesus followed up this final beatitude with a short pep talk: "God blesses you when you are mocked and persecuted and lied about because you are my followers. Be happy about it! Be very glad! For a great reward awaits you in heaven. And remember, the ancient prophets were persecuted, too" (Matthew 5:11-12).

Most of us in North America don't face a lot of strong persecution. We may have to endure jeers, taunts, job discrimination, comparisons to Ned Flanders, and other humiliations, but we don't see a lot of torture or death because of what we believe. The same can't be said for much of the rest of the world. In fact, it is reported that more Christian martyrs died in the twentieth century than all previous centuries combined.

It's difficult to "be very glad" when others mock, maim, or kill us simply because of our religious beliefs. But that's only the short-term view. For each of us who stand boldly (or even with knees knocking) and speak up for Jesus, the day will come when He stands boldly before His Father and speaks up for us. But if we chicken out, He won't be able to give a good report when that time comes (Mark 8:34-38).

Bless You!

So there you have it. Do you want the blessings of God? Then confess your need for Him. Be willing to mourn. Be gentle and lowly. Hunger and thirst for justice. Show mercy. Purify your heart. Work for peace. And endure persecution when it comes along.

Again, these are not easy things to do. It's quite possible to go through life reading the Bible, praying, offering a form of worship to God, and doing other things to look like a genuinely committed Christian. But until we get to this deeper, inner level of spiritual life, we won't start receiving the things Jesus has promised—the kingdom of Heaven, comfort, mercy, a better-than-ever relationship with God, and all the rest. The desire for such things is good, but it's only the beginning. We then must discipline ourselves to get beyond the legalistic practices and into the genuine growth areas.

Thank the Lord we don't have to do it alone. We have a coach, a counselor, a constant companion. In the next couple of chapters we will take a look at the part the Holy Spirit plays in the Christian life and what we can expect from Him.

ONE SMALL STEP

Read through the Beatitudes one more time (Matthew 5:3-10) and identify the challenge you find most difficult to comply with. Then come up with three specific steps you can take the next time you are faced with spiritual poverty, mourning, showing mercy, or whatever you have chosen. If you have some specific actions in mind, you will be better equipped to face the challenge and receive the blessing of God.

Questions to Ponder and/or Discuss

1. How strongly do you identify with each of the following groups (1 = lowest; 10 = highest) based on your current spiritual state?

Those who realize their need for God	1 2 3 4 5 6 7 8 9 10
Those who mourn	1 2 3 4 5 6 7 8 9 10
Those who are gentle and lowly	1 2 3 4 5 6 7 8 9 10
Those who are hungry and thirsty for justice	1 2 3 4 5 6 7 8 9 10
Those who are merciful	1 2 3 4 5 6 7 8 9 10
Those whose hearts are pure	1 2 3 4 5 6 7 8 9 10
Those who work for peace	1 2 3 4 5 6 7 8 9 10
Those who are persecuted because they live for God	1 2 3 4 5 6 7 8 9 10

2. The promises in the Beatitudes can sound like obscure theological "carrots" to convince us to behave. But what do you think it means, in practical terms:

- To belong to the Kingdom of Heaven?
- To receive comfort and mercy from God?
- To inherit the earth?
- To receive justice in full?
- To see God?
- To be a child of God?

3. Where would you place your current level of happiness on each of the following scales?

Earthly Happiness Scale

_____

Grim, Morose, Dejected   Giggling, Giddy, Euphoric

Spiritual Happiness Scale

_____

Hopeless, Defeated, Alone   Blessed, Victorious, Joyful

Which of these scales is usually more important to you? Why? (Be honest!)

CHAPTER SEVEN

Nine-Fruit Salad

THE FRUIT OF THE SPIRIT

Fred took the bratwursts off the grill. The burgers still needed a couple more minutes, but he gave Wilma the signal to have everyone gather around the outdoor table. After three weeks of waving hello as one or the other would go off to work and sharing weather observations across the backyard fence, the DiCiples had invited the Seekers over for supper.

Fred plopped the burgers down just as Wilma brought the tomatoes and lettuce from the refrigerator. The seating was a bit tight with six people, but it was still adequate. Fred said, "Do you mind if we say grace?"

George shrugged. Jane shook her head to indicate she had no objection. Fred looked at Joshua and asked, "Would you like to say it?"

"Daaaaad!" Josh pointed with his eyes to the strangers across the table. Fred may as well have asked his 14-year-old son to give the Inaugural Address, but nine-year-old Mary wasn't so reclusive. "I'll say it, Daddy."

Fred smiled at her and bowed his head. The others around the table followed his example.

SOME THINGS YOU'LL DISCOVER IN THIS CHAPTER

1. The importance of the Holy Spirit in the Christian life

2. A few of the functions and ministries of the Holy Spirit

3. Nine specific things called the "fruit" of the Holy Spirit

"God is great. God is good. Let us thank Him for our food. Amen."
Mary was capable of more elaborate prayers, but tonight she was
extra hungry so she kept it short and to the point.

The shared conversation that followed allowed the two families
to get to know each other better—comparing hobbies, previous
places they had lived or visited, job descriptions, school interests,
and so forth. Right after dessert, Josh and Mary excused themselves
to go play with some neighborhood kids.

After that followed an all-too-familiar silence where no one
knows exactly which direction to take the conversation. Fred was
gearing up to broach the subject of Christianity and was trying to
decide which topic he could bring up where he could segue into
sharing the gospel with his new neighbors. He had taken a big
breath, but just before he opened his mouth to speak, Jane broke the
silence. "You two are so nice to have us over. We still don't know
many people here, and our families are both across the country.
Good neighbors are nice, but it's even better to have good friends
next door."

Fred got a goofy "Aw, shucks" expression on his face, but Wilma
smiled and replied, "We're both looking forward to getting to know
you better."

Jane continued, "And we've been talking about what you said
about church the other day. It's true that we haven't been big on
church lately. To be honest, we've both had some experiences that
soured us on formalized religion. But we're getting ready to . . . well
. . . we're about to have our first baby and we want to raise him or
her right."

Fred had been getting ready to launch into a "Why church is
good" sermonette, but Wilma simply beamed and said, "We're so
happy for you. Let us know if there's anything we can do to help."

From there the conversation turned to baby stories about Josh
and Mary. But before the Seekers left, Wilma had made it clear,
"Whenever you're ready to check out some churches, let us know."

As Fred and Wilma were cleaning up after the Seekers had gone
home, Fred said, "I had planned to say more about our faith than I
did, but I think things turned out okay, don't you?"

Wilma grinned and replied, "Yes, dear. Even without your help, I think God might have been at work tonight."

A Change of Plans?

ONE SMALL STEP

Think back and try to identify a time or two where you had definite plans that, for one reason or another, were not carried out. What was the result of your change of plan? How did you feel at the time? How do you feel about it now? Can you detect God's involvement in the change of plans?

Anyone who devotes himself or herself to living the Christian life soon discovers the truth of Proverbs 16:9: "We can make our plans, but the Lord determines our steps." It's not by any means wrong or inappropriate to look to the future and prepare for things to come, but we need to remember that God will almost certainly interject some surprises, plot twists, challenges, opportunities, and insights that we would miss if we simply stuck to our little plans.

But how does God operate in today's world? We have His Word, and we have prayer, as we have seen. But is that it? What if there's an emergency where He wants to get our attention, or where we face a situation that doesn't seem to fit any of the verses we've read or memorized? Do we light up some shrubbery and hope He speaks again from a burning bush? Do we wait for Jesus to appear as we're on the road to Damascus . . . or to the supermarket?

Some people place a lot of stock in what they consider to be signs from God, whether they be weeping statues, the appearance of a Christ image (or something similar) on the side of a building or other unexpected place, or similar manifestations. Others place such things on a level with reported Elvis sightings or UFO abductions.

But whether or not such things are genuine miracles, God has another way to reach His people today. He is present in the lives of all who believe in Him through the presence of the Holy Spirit.

When Jesus was on earth, He could physically show and tell people what to do (or not do). It seems it should have been the best possible means of communication, yet even then His disciples were always slow to catch on to what He was trying to tell them, and He was eventually crucified by people who resisted what He was saying.

But Jesus was well aware of what was going to happen to Him, and He already had a plan that He had tried to share with His disciples. He told them He would be put to death and would leave them

WELL SAID!

What a vast distance there is between knowing God and loving Him!
—*Blaise Pascal*

alone for a while—but only a short while. And He spelled out His plan:

> If you love me, obey my commandments. And I will ask the Father, and he will give you another Counselor, who will never leave you. He is the Holy Spirit, who leads into all truth. The world at large cannot receive him, because it isn't looking for him and doesn't recognize him. But you do, because he lives with you now and later will be in you. (John 14:15-17)

And just as good teachers are wont to do, Jesus later repeated this important point for emphasis:

> But I will send you the Counselor—the Spirit of truth. He will come to you from the Father and will tell you all about me. And you must also tell others about me because you have been with me from the beginning. (John 15:26-27)

In God's master plan to redeem fallen humanity, Jesus was to come and live among us, show us what God is like, model the way God calls us to live, and then die for our sins. He would then be resurrected and return to heaven, after which time the Holy Spirit would come to earth and carry on the work Jesus had begun.

Most people have varying degrees of working knowledge about God the Father and Jesus the Son. But when it comes to the Holy Spirit, knowledge levels tend to decrease. Perhaps it's because the Bible doesn't say nearly as much about the Spirit as it does the Father or the Son. Perhaps it's because we are uncomfortable when it comes to dealing with someone so mysterious and unseen. Perhaps it's because we have seen TV preachers do strange things in the name of the Holy Spirit—speak in tongues, heal illnesses or physical ailments, or even handle snakes. Maybe it's simply because we've never given the topic much thought.

While Christian groups can vary widely in what they believe about the Holy Spirit, let's take a look at some of the clear biblical teachings.

That's the Spirit!

To begin with, the Holy Spirit is as much God as Jesus or God the Father. A few religions downplay the significance of Jesus, but most Christian denominations teach the doctrine of the Trinity, or Godhead, which consists of one God in three distinct but equally important persons: the Father, the Son, and the Holy Spirit. This can be a confusing concept that raises a lot of questions, most of which cannot be adequately covered in a self-proclaimed *No-Brainer's Guide.* But suffice it to say that we ought to be giving the Holy Spirit equal billing with God and Jesus.

One reason many of us don't is because one of the roles of the Holy Spirit is to draw attention to Jesus (John 16:13-15). While the Holy Spirit has always been around and at work, it was the incarnation (taking human form) and ministry of Jesus that triggered the coming of the Holy Spirit to indwell believers on an individual basis. And the Spirit is content to keep the spotlight on Jesus rather than Himself.

The NFL contains a number of excellent quarterbacks. The average fan in the stands or watching the game on TV might tend to compare passing and rushing statistics of different quarterbacks as if all the other variables were the same. But a good coach knows to consider other conditions. Does one guy play primarily in a dome while another endures more rain and/or snow games? How do the subtle differences between natural grass and artificial turf weigh in to the comparison? And most important of all, how well do the offensive linemen protect their quarterback? If the front line provides an average of one or two additional seconds per play for the quarterback to pass, hand off, or run, he might have better statistics than an even better quarterback who doesn't have the same kind of protection.

The Holy Spirit is no more or less important than Jesus, but the role He plays is to elevate the attention Jesus receives. Therefore, while we might usually tend to focus on Jesus, at this point we want to take a "behind the scenes" look at the work of the Holy Spirit. We won't go into great detail, but it's definitely worth your time to

WELL SAID!

It is impossible for that man to despair who remembers that his Helper is omnipotent. —*Jeremy Taylor*

FOR EXAMPLE . . .

Jesus' Baptism (Matthew 3:13-17)

Theologians frequently point to this example to demonstrate the simultaneous manifestation of all three Persons in the Godhead. Jesus was being baptized, God the Father spoke from heaven, and the Holy Spirit descended like a dove and settled on Jesus.

investigate these various aspects of the "job description" of the Holy Spirit when you have the opportunity.

1. The Holy Spirit is a person. We may tend to think of Him in terms of "the Force" in *Star Wars,* but the Bible ascribes to the Holy Spirit actions, emotions, will, and other personal qualities that an impersonal force wouldn't have.

2. The Holy Spirit has always been involved in world events. At Creation, "the Spirit of God was hovering over [the earth's] surface" (Genesis 1:2), and He has been at work ever since. While He becomes more prominent in the New Testament, the Holy Spirit was active throughout the Old Testament as well.

3. The Holy Spirit provided the insight and revelation for the Old Testament prophets and the writers of the Bible (2 Peter 1:20-21).

4. The Holy Spirit lives within all those who believe in Jesus (Romans 8:5-11).

5. The Holy Spirit enables us to understand some of the mysteries of God that are unknown to others (1 Corinthians 2:6-16).

6. The Holy Spirit is like a "down payment" of all the other wonderful things God will provide for us in eternity (Ephesians 1:13-14).

7. The Holy Spirit interprets our deepest, inexpressible feelings and "translates" them into prayer that God fully understands (Romans 8:26-27).

8. The Holy Spirit helps us in special times of need and stress (Luke 12:11-12).

These are just a few of the teachings about the importance of the Holy Spirit, but we can see clearly some of the essential functions He performs. To ignore or downplay the Spirit's place in the world is a serious mistake. In fact, Jesus taught: "I assure you that any sin can be forgiven, including blasphemy; but anyone who blasphemes against the Holy Spirit will never be forgiven. It is an eternal sin" (Mark 3:28-29). Scholars disagree as to how exactly to interpret this statement, and we don't want to open a big theological can of worms at this point. But we do want to stress the importance of treating the Holy Spirit with the same honor and respect we would show Jesus or God the Father.

More Fruit in Your Spiritual Diet

In addition to everything else, the Holy Spirit makes available to believers all sorts of things to help them live life to its fullest. We'll examine some specific and individually designated spiritual gifts in the next chapter. But He also produces "fruit" that should become evident in every believer's life.

Nine characteristics are listed that comprise the spiritual fruit that the Holy Spirit produces in our lives. Note that the nine qualities are considered the *fruit* of the Spirit rather than the *fruits* of the Spirit. The list isn't like a Chinese food menu where you pick and choose what you want. We who are pursuing the Christian life should integrate each and every item on the list into our lives.

However, the imagery of bearing fruit is telling. Much time can pass between the time a seed is planted and when the tree bears its first fruit. Similarly, just because a person becomes a Christian or rededicates himself or herself to Christ, that doesn't mean he or she will immediately bear ripe and luscious fruit of the Spirit. So for many of us, the following list will become a set of goals to work toward, knowing that these are the things the Spirit is working within us to accomplish. We may need to start working with the Holy Spirit instead of against Him.

The list of the fruit of the Spirit is found in Galatians 5:22-23. Many of these qualities will tend to overlap because these characteristics build on one another. For example, it would be very hard to have genuine joy and peace without a deep and abiding sense of love.

Love

Love is first on the list, as it should be. When describing God to his readers, John didn't just say that God is loving; he wrote that God is love itself (1 John 4:16). Most human perceptions and definitions of love are far short of the biblical definition. Love both motivates

DO'S AND DON'TS

Here are two do's and two don'ts in connection with the Holy Spirit:
- Let us follow the Holy Spirit's leading in every part of our lives. (Galatians 5:25)
- Let the Holy Spirit fill and control you. (Ephesians 5:18)
- Do not bring sorrow to God's Holy Spirit by the way you live. (Ephesians 4:30)
- Do not stifle the Holy Spirit. (1 Thessalonians 5:19)

WELL SAID!

Love is a fruit in season at all times, and within reach of every hand. Anyone may gather it, and no limit is set.
—*Mother Teresa*

everything good in life (1 Corinthians 13) and counteracts a multitude of sins (1 Peter 4:8). According to the often-quoted "love chapter" of the Bible (1 Corinthians 13), if you are jealous, you aren't showing love. If you are impatient, you aren't showing love. If you're boastful, proud, rude, or have lost hope, you need more love.

And if you need more love, where do you get it? Don't forget that this is the list of fruit of the Spirit. The Holy Spirit, who is God, is the one who provides the qualities on this list, beginning with love.

Like any other fruit, love needs time to ripen. If you talk to a couple celebrating their golden wedding anniversary, they will give you quite a different definition of love than they did at their wedding, or even at their silver anniversary. The same people. The same relationship. But as love grows and ripens, we see how "green" it used to be in contrast to what it becomes. It's not that God's love is inferior at first but that we need time and experience to detect how wonderful it really is.

Joy

A rookie mistake in the Christian life is to equate joy with happiness. Most of us have a desire to laugh, to be free of burdens, and to have an inner jubilance. But happiness comes and goes as our circumstances change. A student might be happy about acing a test until he is turned down for a date and suddenly is happy no more. Parents might be happy their teenager is learning to help out by driving the younger kids around, but they are shattered when the old car breaks down, and there's no money in the budget for another one.

Joy, on the other hand, is ongoing. Happiness cannot coexist with sadness, yet somehow joy can be felt most graphically during times of sorrow. Perhaps you or someone you know has scolded a child and, when his eyes began to well with tears, said, "I'll give you something to cry about!" Joy goes the other direction. When we're desperately trying to eke out a little happiness in life, the Holy Spirit says, "I'll give you something to rejoice about!"

Paul wrote the book of Philippians, a very upbeat letter with much to say about joy, while in the slammer. Jesus was identified as "a man of sorrows," yet He sacrificed His life "because of the joy he knew would be his afterward" (Hebrews 12:2). The inner glow of joy can keep us going through the worst of times. And if our external situations improve in the meantime, so much the better!

Peace

Similarly, peace is a frequently misunderstood fruit, as we saw in the previous chapter when thinking about what it meant to be a peacemaker. Spiritual peace isn't the absence of outer turbulence, but rather an abiding confidence in God throughout turbulent situations. Isaiah reminds us that Jesus is the Prince of Peace (Isaiah 9:6), and Jesus proved it in an impressive way during a literal storm. When the disciples, several of whom were experienced fishermen, woke Jesus and told Him they feared drowning, Jesus spoke to the storm and knocked the wind out of it, creating a dead calm (Mark 4:35-41).

The peace provided by the Holy Spirit can achieve the same emotional effect when we face "storms" of stress, despair, fear, anxiety, or any of those other nasty feelings. An unanticipated and unexplainable peace of mind can take root and help us keep a perspective of faith and hope during unpleasant circumstances.

Patience

Patience is a dying discipline in our society. Speed and efficiency are highly promoted services. If a waiter takes a bit too long, if the line at the bank is more than three people, or if a lane of traffic is a bit lethargic, some people go berserk. And when a real problem comes along such as a lingering disease or troublesome child, the lack of patience becomes even more noticeable.

Again, our mind-set probably depends on how we perceive our situations. If we think that patience is "doing nothing" or "wasting time," we're likely never to become patient people. But if we see it as consciously yielding our own timetable to God, patience becomes more of a spiritual issue. With such a mind-set, we're more likely to remember that the waiter and bank teller are real people with real feelings, just like us. And the driver holding up traffic might be an elderly woman, scared and in need of a break. (If only she would get out of the left lane!)

DO'S AND DON'TS

Always be full of joy in the Lord. I say it again—rejoice! Let everyone see that you are considerate in all you do. Remember, the Lord is coming soon. Don't worry about anything; instead, pray about everything. Tell God what you need and thank him for all he has done. If you do this, you will experience God's peace, which is far more wonderful than the human mind can understand. His peace will guard your hearts and minds as you live in Christ Jesus. (Philippians 4:4-7)

FOR EXAMPLE . . .

David Twice Spares King Saul's Life
(1 Samuel 24; 26)

Saul had not lived up to God's expectations as king, so God directed Samuel to
anoint David to be the next king. Even
though Saul repeatedly tried to kill
David, and even though David knew he
had already been chosen to be the next
king, David would do nothing to injure
"the Lord's anointed one." David's
patience to wait for God to act was
exemplary.

Lack of patience indicates a belief that our wants, time, will, and such are more important than other people's. During the time we're forced to wait, maybe God is trying to teach us something, but the lesson usually can't get through all the steam coming out our ears.

Patience is a godly quality–thankfully. If God weren't patient, none of us would be here to be impatient (2 Peter 3:8-9). Because God is so patient with us, we need to practice being patient with others. For many people, this particular fruit seems very slow to ripen. But since we're in the Christian life for the long haul, we need to learn patience (or "long-suffering" as the word was interpreted in the King James Version).

Kindness

Kindness, like love, requires another person in order to be effective. Joy, peace, and patience are qualities that we can attempt to develop in the context of the regular rigors of life. But in order to demonstrate kindness, we need someone to be kind to.

It's interesting that Paul mentions something as basic as kindness in this list of spiritual fruit, because many people today might not even consider it an adult trait. Oh, sure, we want our kindergarten-aged children to be kind to one another–to take turns, share toys, and be nice in general. But life soon becomes very competitive, and kindness is frequently left by the wayside in order to gain "the edge." We want our kids quarterbacking the team, not handing out towels on the bench. And at work we want to be the ones clambering to the top of the ladder, not kindly holding it for someone else.

But if the fruit of the Holy Spirit is maturing in our lives, kindness will find its place again. You may lose the edge in a situation or two, but having the edge on preparing for eternal life more than makes up for it.

Goodness

Goodness is another of those "wimpy" characteristics we might not take seriously at first. It's even gotten to the point where goodness is used as an insult; we take offense at being called a do-gooder or a goody-goody. But like kindness, goodness is more important than we usually realize.

After all, the ongoing battle throughout all of Scripture and history is the conflict between God and Satan, good and evil. Anything we do that isn't good puts points on the board for the other team. God is the highest possible standard for "good." If our goal is to become more like Him, we're going to have to practice being better do-gooders.

Faithfulness

The geyser in Yellowstone National Park got the name Old Faithful because it does something spectacular once every 65 minutes or so. Perhaps we think of ourselves as faithful if we do some noble act for God once a week or once a month. But frankly, we need to develop a better track record of spiritual consistency in our levels of faithfulness.

And consistency is the key word. Our spiritual lives tend to run hot and cold, active and lethargic. We need to apply the same principles we use in tennis, golf, and other sports. If we stay in shape, think about what we're doing, get lots of practice, and don't get too flustered, we tend to become more consistent. But when we lose concentration and let our minds wander, our success rates tend to slide.

Faithfulness is a matter of making ourselves available to God on a more regular basis. After we find out what He wants of us through Bible study, prayer, and worship, our spiritual commitments should faithfully become steadier and less sporadic. Just as God is faithful—available to us at all times—we need to become more faithful to Him.

Gentleness

The quality of gentleness has nothing to do with strength—or lack of it. Jesus had unlimited power to heal diseases and perform all kinds of miracles, yet He chose to be gentle in His ministry to others. From time to time He would get firm with stubborn Pharisees or dense disciples, but He never lost control.

The fruit of gentleness won't generally appear unless love and

ONE SMALL STEP

Think back over the previous week. Can you think of several examples of things you did for others for no other reason than to be good or kind? More importantly, can you think of opportunities you had where you *didn't* choose to exercise goodness or kindness? Finally, think of a recent example of someone doing a particularly good or kind favor for you. How did it make you feel?

FOR EXAMPLE . . .

Anna (Luke 2:36-38)

Anna was a prophetess who was 84 years old when Jesus was born. Seven years after being married, Anna's husband died, and she had faithfully devoted herself to God's work day and night, never even leaving the temple. She was rewarded for her faithfulness by being one of the first people to see Jesus—and recognizing who He was and what He would grow up to be.

93

FOR EXAMPLE . . .

Moses Hits a Rock (Numbers 20:1-13; Deuteronomy 32:48-52; 34)

Moses was one of the most steadfast leaders of the Bible, yet even he had moments of weakness. After decades of baby-sitting a million whining Israelites, one day he snapped. God had instructed him to speak to a rock in the desert, which would provide much-needed water. Instead, Moses struck the rock as he had done once before, and it appears he tried to share the credit for what God was doing. As a result, he was denied entrance to the Promised Land. God remained close to Moses and personally attended to his burial, but just a bit more self-control might have allowed Moses to complete what he had begun.

patience are already ripe. Otherwise it's usually too easy to snap back at someone who makes a snide comment or to use whatever power we have in inappropriate ways. Having strength yet choosing to be gentle instead requires self-control. So what do you suppose is next on the list?

Self-Control

Self-control is like the "anchor" in a relay race—the one that validates all the others and gets the job done. We can let the Holy Spirit infuse us with love, joy, peace, patience, kindness, goodness, faithfulness, and gentleness. But if we don't value these characteristics and exercise self-control to apply them to the people and situations we face, we never advance very far in our spiritual journeys.

The extent to which we get involved in the Christian life depends largely on us. It's something of a paradox. We can do nothing in our own power to get closer to God and must allow God to forgive our sins, save us from the eternal punishment we deserve, and supply us with the new characteristics we need to mature spiritually. Yet we are given much choice in the matter. Unless we want to mature, and *choose* to mature, we aren't likely to experience the entire "fruit salad" made possible by the Holy Spirit. We need self-control to keep making the right decisions without getting tempted to resume our old lifestyle or simply getting lazy along the way.

Progress in the Christian life is like attending an event where tickets are free yet still required to get in. All that is needed for attendance is securing a ticket ahead of time. As long as we keep deciding to seek God's will for our lives and supplying the drive to accomplish that goal, the Holy Spirit is our Companion and Counselor to take us as far as we are willing to go.

It sounds easy, but making the right decisions is harder than it sounds. As long as we're thinking about God, we tend to do okay. But our minds wander. Temptations are stronger than we anticipated. And sometimes in a moment of weakness we simply want to make the wrong choices.

When faced with such detours in our spiritual progress, we need

to remember that God is eager to forgive us and put us back on course. But it requires self-control on our part to resume the relationship and then maintain it.

It's Up to You

Love, joy, peace, patience, kindness, goodness, faithfulness, gentleness, and self-control. Aren't these all qualities well worth choosing?

They certainly are when we look at the other options. The fruit of the Holy Spirit is listed in a biblical passage that contrasts those qualities with the behavior we have before we know God:

> When you follow the desires of your sinful nature, your lives will produce these evil results: sexual immorality, impure thoughts, eagerness for lustful pleasure, idolatry, participation in demonic activities, hostility, quarreling, jealousy, outbursts of anger, selfish ambition, divisions, the feeling that everyone is wrong except those in your own little group, envy, drunkenness, wild parties, and other kinds of sin. Let me tell you again, as I have before, that anyone living that sort of life will not inherit the Kingdom of God. (Galatians 5:19-21)

It is extremely hard not to revert to these old habits. You may not be influenced by everything on the list, but you may have a couple (or a dozen) that are particularly hard for you to overcome. Yet the promise of the fruit of the Holy Spirit should be more than adequate motivation to forsake these old ways and move on to something much, much better.

The Holy Spirit allows us to glimpse what is involved in living "life in all its fullness" (John 10:10) and to experience more and more of it as we continue in the Christian life. The fruit of the Spirit is something available to all Christians—and that's not all. As we will see in the next chapter, we also get presents!

DO'S AND DON'TS

So, dear brothers and sisters, you have no obligation whatsoever to do what your sinful nature urges you to do. For if you keep on following it, you will perish. But if through the power of the Holy Spirit you turn from it and its evil deeds, you will live. (Romans 8:12-13)

Questions to Ponder and/or Discuss

1. To what extent are you regularly aware of the Holy Spirit's work in your life?

2. Which aspects of the Holy Spirit's "job description" do you need to be more aware of?

3. What would you say is the "ripeness level" for the fruit of the Spirit in your life at this point? (Place an X at the appropriate place on the following scales.)

	Beginning to Bud	Green	Ripening Nicely	Fully Ripe
Love				
Joy				
Peace				
Patience				
Kindness				
Goodness				
Faithfulness				
Gentleness				
Self-Control				

4. Circle any of the "desires of the sinful nature" (Galatians 5:19-21) you continue to struggle with. For everything you circle, determine which of the fruit of the Spirit would make the best "antidote." Then ask God to provide those positive qualities in greater abundance.

Sexual immorality	Impure thoughts	Eagerness for lustful pleasure

Idolatry	Hostility	Participation in demonic activities
Quarreling	Jealousy	Outbursts of anger
Selfish ambition	Divisions	Envy
Drunkenness	Wild parties	

The feeling that everyone is wrong except those in your own little group

Other kinds of sin: _____

CHAPTER EIGHT

"OK, HERE'S ANOTHER ONE FROM JOHN, AND THERE'S ONE IN HERE FROM GINNY, AND ONE FROM RANDY, AND DON'T FORGET KEVIN . . . "

The Gifts That Keep on Giving
Spiritual Gifts

Joshua, Mary, Wilma, and Fred DiCiple sat around the dinner table, taking turns talking about what had happened during their day. This had become both a tradition and a commitment for them. In spite of a hectic lifestyle and schedules that included youth soccer, Little League, band, occasional sales conferences, long hours, numerous church committee meetings, and more, the four of them made a point of landing around the table at the same time as frequently as possible.

When it was Josh's turn, he was more eager to talk than usual. "They sent information in the mail today for us to pick our class schedules, and this is going to be a great year for me!"

A teenager excited about school? Fred was pleased but mildly surprised. "Let's hear what you're going to be taking, son."

Josh began to read from the list he had pored over all afternoon. "First period, 'Introduction to Film History.' That's a class where you mostly watch movies. Second period, 'Computer Programming 201.' Third period, 'Band.' Fourth period, 'Lunch.' Fifth period,

SOME THINGS YOU'LL DISCOVER IN THIS CHAPTER

1. A list of the biblical gifts of the Holy Spirit

2. How spiritual gifts differ from talents and personal interests

3. The difference between spiritual gifts and spiritual fruit

99

'Music Theory.' Sixth period, 'Computer Gaming.'" That's where we mostly sit around and play different computer games before getting to design one of our own. And best of all, I got seventh period study hall! I thought high school might be tough, but it's going to be a breeze!"

Wilma asked, "Didn't you forget something there, Joshua?"

"Like what?"

"Like math . . . or science . . . or history . . . or English."

"That's the best part, Mom. Film history counts as English. This computer course counts as math. And I'll take some others later that count as science."

Fred spoke up. "Shakespeare is English. Geometry and algebra are math. Chemistry and biology are science. You need to sign up for some real classes."

Josh wasn't convinced. "I'm just doing what you said, Dad. You told me I should find something I'm good at and stick to it. Lots of other people are smarter than I am when it comes to math and history and science and English. But I think I can be better than anyone else at computer stuff and video games."

Fred said, "I'm glad you have an interest in computers. But let me tell you, I train new people at work all the time who have college educations, but no working knowledge of the real world. Most of them don't last long or go very far. There's more to life than what you can find on a computer monitor. I think it's fine that you take these classes, Josh, but let's intersperse them with some of the basics as well. I don't care if you're not the smartest person in class when it comes to English, science, and all the rest. But I do want you to sit through the classes and learn all you can. I promise it will make a difference later in life."

Josh wasn't happy, but he could tell by the lecture tone of Fred's voice that it would do no good to argue. He mumbled "Okay" and everyone continued their dinner. By the end of the meal, Josh was back to his old self, even doing his famous "milk out of the nose" trick that his sister hated so much—and timing it perfectly so that neither of his parents caught him.

The Eyes Have It (But So Do the Ears, Hands, Feet, Etc.)

When it comes to the Christian life, some people are a lot like Josh. They want to breeze through and do the things that are fun while leaving the hard stuff to others. Some even go so far as to claim that their "gifts" lie in other areas, so why bother with some of the more difficult disciplines? If God has gifted me with a sense of humor, for example, can't I just skip that part about being poor in spirit, or mourning with those who mourn? Doesn't it make more sense to simply establish "laughter" and "non-laughter" sections in our churches?

Few things create as much confusion in the church today as understanding and applying spiritual gifts. Perhaps you know someone like the woman who proudly affirmed, "I think it's my calling to be the grain of sand that gets under people's skin and allows them to become the pearls God wants them to be." But search as we may, we won't find the "gift of irritation" on any of the biblical lists of spiritual gifts. We'll look at some specific gifts a bit later in this chapter, but first let's try to get a better understanding of exactly what we mean by "spiritual gifts."

It might help to begin with what spiritual gifts aren't. There is a definite distinction between talents and spiritual gifts. Someone with wonderful musical ability may perform during church services on Sunday morning right after staying up all night doing bawdy songs at the Tiki Lounge. Someone with financial skills might make herself millions of dollars each year and contribute several hundred thousand to church and/or other ministries. A pro athlete might sponsor a church basketball camp and then hold out for more money and perks when it's time to renew his contract.

No one would dispute that such people are talented. And they may even use their talents for God from time to time. But that doesn't necessarily mean the talents are spiritual gifts. Similarly, a person might have a number of interests or hobbies that don't necessarily translate to spiritual gifts, although there might be some connections. An interest in cooking, for example, might connect with a spiritual gift of hospitality (if you have people into your

ONE SMALL STEP

Before going any farther in this chapter, think about the religious/spiritual people you know. What would you say are their "gifts," in a spiritual sense? Get some specific ideas in mind, and then, as you read on, compare your assessment with the definitions and descriptions of the various spiritual gifts. By the end of the chapter, see which things on your list have been verified and which you might want to reconsider.

WELL SAID!

Though every believer has the Holy Spirit, the Holy Spirit does not have every believer. —*A. W. Tozer*

home to eat) or giving (if you bake cookies or treats for others). An interest in early European military weaponry, on the other hand, might not have many spiritual applications.

Nor do spiritual gifts suggest any kind of official position or entitlement. Various gifts are distributed. No one gets them all, and no believer does without. And since everyone receives gifts, there's no justification for competition or attempting to use one's gifts for higher status than another.

Essentially everything we know about spiritual gifts comes from the writings of Paul, and he repeatedly emphasizes the importance of unity in regard to gifts. One of the primary passages is 1 Corinthians 12. Here's a key passage:

> Now there are different kinds of spiritual gifts, but it is the same Holy Spirit who is the source of them all. There are different kinds of service in the church, but it is the same Lord we are serving. There are different ways God works in our lives, but it is the same God who does the work through all of us. A spiritual gift is given to each of us as a means of helping the entire church. . . .
>
> The human body has many parts, but the many parts make up only one body. So it is with the body of Christ. Some of us are Jews, some are Gentiles, some are slaves, and some are free. But we have all been baptized into Christ's body by one Spirit, and we have all received the same Spirit.
>
> Yes, the body has many different parts, not just one part. If the foot says, "I am not a part of the body because I am not a hand," that does not make it any less a part of the body. And if the ear says, "I am not part of the body because I am only an ear and not an eye," would that make it any less a part of the body? Suppose the whole body were an eye—then how would you hear? Or if your whole body were just one big ear, how could you smell anything?
>
> But God made our bodies with many parts, and he has put each part just where he wants it. What a strange thing a body would be if it had only one part! Yes, there are many

parts, but only one body. The eye can never say to the hand, "I don't need you." The head can't say to the feet, "I don't need you." (1 Corinthians 12:4-7, 12-21)

One body, many parts. One Spirit, many gifts. Paul is clear that gifts are given (1) for the good of the church body as a whole and (2) to promote unity rather than competition or division. Just because you might be inspired and enamored by a great preacher doesn't mean you should necessarily quit your job and go to seminary. Perhaps you have the same gift, but it is just as likely (if not more so) that the other person's use of the gift might have had the intended result of making a difference in your life. And as you exercise your gifts—whatever they are—God will work in the lives of other people through you.

This is one of the best rebuttals to the argument that a person's worship is better alone with God than in a stuffy or confining church. There's more to worship than *what you might get out of it.* Based on the design and distribution of spiritual gifts, worship also includes the vital element of *what you can supply to others.*

We must also be careful not to confuse the gifts of the Spirit with the *fruit* of the Spirit. The fruit of the Spirit listed in Galatians 5:22-23 is available to all believers. We should attempt to incorporate those characteristics more thoroughly into our spiritual lives. But certain gifts of the Spirit may be given to some individuals and not others, or given in significant quantity to certain individuals and not so much to others.

With that in mind, let's take a look at the specific gifts of the Holy Spirit listed in Scripture. As we do, be aware that various groups and denominations within Christianity have different ways of interpreting and relating to the gifts of the Spirit. Some feel that certain gifts on the following list were given to the first-century church but are no longer applicable to church situations. Others disagree and believe that although the practice of the gifts may not be as prominent as it once was, the gifts are still valid and meaningful. And there may be some different ways to define some of these things.

We're not attempting in this *No-Brainer's Guide* to answer all the questions and settle all the disputes about spiritual gifts. Nor are we

FOR EXAMPLE . . .

Timothy

Timothy was a young minister in whom Paul took special interest. In a letter to Timothy, Paul reminds him of the importance of spiritual gifts: "Do not neglect the spiritual gift you received through the prophecies spoken to you when the elders of the church laid their hands on you. Give your complete attention to these matters. Throw yourself into your tasks so that everyone will see your progress" (1 Timothy 4:14-15). Paul's advice to Timothy is appropriate for all believers.

trying to promote a certain way of thinking. We're simply trying to cover the list and explain how these gifts worked for the early church and may apply to us as well.

You've Got Charisma!

The Greek word for spiritual gifts is *charisma* or *charismata*. Even today, someone who appears to be gifted with charm, grace, humor, etc., is said to be charismatic. The same statement is technically true of anyone with a spiritual gift, which is every believer. So let's check the list and see what our specific gift(s) might be. The following list is taken from three biblical passages: Romans 12:6-8; 1 Corinthians 12:8-11, 27-31; and Ephesians 4:11-13.

Prophecy (Romans 12:6; 1 Corinthians 12:10, 28; Ephesians 4:11)

Sometimes we use the term "prophets" to signify people who stood firm and spoke for God during difficult times. But more specifically, a prophet was a person to whom God revealed future events. The Old Testament prophets may be more familiar to us because of the long section of Bible books bearing their names. Yet with the coming of the Spirit in the New Testament, it appears that God continued to call numerous prophets to give hope and direction to the growing church.

We previously saw a reference to Philip's four virgin daughters who were prophetesses (see chapter 5). John had an extended vision of the future, which he recorded in the book of Revelation. And the Bible refers to several other New Testament prophets without always naming the people (see, for example, Acts 13:1).

Serving/Helping Others (Romans 12:7; 1 Corinthians 12:28)

This is one of those cases where all Christians are called to serve one another (Galatians 5:13), yet some people are especially gifted with the will and ability to serve. When considering what gifts we might have, this one may not be high on the list for most people. ("Dear God, *please* let me live my life as a maid/butler/valet/chauffeur/slave to everyone else.") Yet to exercise the gift of service is to

104

live as Jesus did (Matthew 20:28). And if your life has ever been touched by anyone with a God-given gift of service, you'll never again underestimate the importance of this gift.

Teaching (Romans 12:7; 1 Corinthians 12:28; Ephesians 4:11)

In contrast with serving, teaching is a gift that many people seem to desire. It puts them in front of others and frequently provides a degree of respect and authority. However, James warns us to be careful what we wish for with regard to teaching (James 3:1-2). When we go on record as speaking for God, then everything we say tends to carry more weight, and how many of us want to be "on the record" with everything we say?

Teaching as a spiritual gift is more than just working from a lesson plan to cram knowledge into the heads of the listeners. Rather, it requires a strong foundational knowledge of God's Word and the ability to help others know it better. Jesus was a creative teacher who used stories, word pictures, hyperbole, humor, and other techniques to help people comprehend more about the Kingdom of God. It usually doesn't take long to determine if a teacher is lacking the gift for it—although to be fair, God speaks to different people through different teachers. Someone who doesn't do a thing for you might be just the person God uses to help someone else reach new and deeper insights about Him. When it comes to teachers, as with all other things, we shouldn't be too quick to judge.

Encouragement (Exhortation) (Romans 12:8)

Life is tough. Sometimes the Christian life is even tougher. God realizes that as we struggle, we get stronger, yet He doesn't want His people to sink into discouragement, depression, or despair. Therefore, He specifically gives some people the gift of encouragement. They see the needs, failures, and emotional frailty of others, and reach out with God's love, help, and confidence.

Sometimes encouragement might even involve an element of warning. If someone with the gift of encouragement sees us doing something sinful (and therefore harmful to ourselves and/or others), they might "encourage" us to stop it before someone gets hurt.

Again, encouragement is something we're all supposed to be

DO'S AND DON'TS

Dear brothers and sisters, not many of you should become teachers in the church, for we who teach will be judged by God with greater strictness. We all make many mistakes, but those who control their tongues can also control themselves in every other way.
(James 3:1-2)

105

FOR EXAMPLE . . .

Barnabas (Acts 4:36-37)

In the early church there was a faithful member named Joseph, but the disciples gave him a nickname that stuck and by which he is better known: Barnabas, which means "Son of Encouragement."

Barnabas sold personal property and gave it willingly to the newly forming church. He later was chosen by the Holy Spirit to travel with Paul and establish new churches. After a rift between Paul and a younger believer named John Mark, Barnabas traveled with Mark while Paul took another partner. Almost everywhere Barnabas's name pops up in Scripture, he is encouraging others.

doing (1 Thessalonians 5:11), but quite frankly, many of us are pretty lousy at it. We should be thankful God equips certain individuals with large doses of this terrific gift.

Giving (Romans 12:8)

No one's going to buy it if you try the excuse, "I don't have the gift of giving, so I think I'll just hang onto all my money and let those with the gift take care of the church, the poor, new ministry opportunities, missionaries, etc." Giving money and sharing possessions are the obligation and privilege of all believers.

However, some people are especially gifted when it comes to giving. In his letters, Paul notes several examples of extreme generosity where people or churches gave even when it wasn't practical or convenient for them to do so. The size of one's bank account has nothing to do with the gift of giving, because it is possible that "wonderful joy and deep poverty [can overflow] in rich generosity" (2 Corinthians 8:2).

Don't miss the significance that since the Holy Spirit assigns gifts, those who are assigned the gift of giving perform the same act of service (to a lesser extent) as the Holy Spirit.

Leadership (Administration) (Romans 12:8; 1 Corinthians 12:28)

At last! A gift worthy of a person of your vast talents!

Don't be too sure. Leadership in churches and ministries is quite different than in business settings. God isn't looking for the equivalent of corporate CEOs to oversee churches to compete against one another in the sheep-eat-sheep world of Christian ministry. (That may be what takes place from time to time, but that's not what God desires.)

The ultimate model of leadership was Jesus, who owned nothing but the clothes on His back and had no regular source of financial security. He established no platform of His own—no local church, non-profit organization, T-shirt concession, or anything else—but spoke in synagogues, on mountainsides, at the beach, or wherever people wanted to listen. His "board of directors" were a dozen men, one of whom ultimately betrayed Him while the others fled in fear, leaving Him alone to face His enemies and die. To be a good leader under such conditions certainly requires a special gift from God.

God seeks leaders who are interested more in humility than power, in eternity than inventory, and in prophets over profits. It is indeed a God-given skill to fulfill the challenge of Jesus to "be as wary as snakes and harmless as doves" (Matthew 10:16). Good leaders can do both.

Kindness (Mercy) (Romans 12:8)

Jazz artist Mose Allison wrote, "Everybody's crying mercy, but no one knows the meaning of the word." We all want to be nice and we want other people to be nice in return. But when we're nice and they're not, then what?

Many of us have our favorite words, gestures, or other actions we reserve for such cases. But in the Christian life, showing kindness and cutting the other person a break should always be a good option.

It isn't fair, you say? Well, you've hit on the very definition of mercy. If everything were always fair, there would be no need for mercy. But in our sin-soured world, everyone makes mistakes and ends up offending other people—maybe unintentionally and maybe not. We need to be as eager to grant mercy to others as we are to receive it when we mess up. Some people are especially good at showing mercy no matter what other people say or do to them. Who knows how many stubborn people God has reached through the repeated efforts of people who have the gift of kindness? People who show repeated acts of mercy frequently get the job done long after the rest of us have given up on someone.

Wisdom and Knowledge (1 Corinthians 12:8)

These are separate gifts, though they are frequently lumped together. You might think knowledge would suggest an accumulation of facts and wisdom the ability to use those facts in practical ways. But some scholars suggest the reasoning is just the opposite. In the Christian life, insight into the ways of God requires Spirit-given wisdom, and then we also need the knowledge (or know-how) to interject those truths into our everyday lives.

The New Living Translation defines *wisdom* as "the ability to give wise advice" and *knowledge* as "special knowledge." But however

WELL SAID!

God's gifts put man's best dreams to shame. —*Elizabeth Barrett Browning*

Knowledge is proud that he has learned
so much;
   Wisdom is humble that he does not
know more.
—*William Cowper*

FOR EXAMPLE . . .

Peter Walks on Water
(Matthew 14:22-33)

When Jesus walked out across the water
to join the disciples in a boat in the
middle of the lake, for some reason Peter
demonstrated more faith than the other
disciples and asked to walk out to meet
Him. Jesus told him to come on and not
be afraid. As long as Peter's faith held
out, he too was able to walk on the
water. But when his eyes went from
Jesus to the wind and waves, he began
to sink. Similarly, some people today are
able to demonstrate more faith than
others. The gift of faith might get us "out
of the boat," but we need to keep our
focus on Jesus because faith is never
automatic.

108

you translate and apply this gift, it is clear that God is the source of truth. As we seek answers and attempt to understand His plan and what's going on in the world, some people receive clear insight. We can all add depth to Bible study with accumulated facts about history, archaeology, early cultures, different religions, and so forth. But no quantity of such facts can approach the knowledge and wisdom available only from God.

Faith (1 Corinthians 12:9)

Faith is another item that is essential in the lives of all believers. After all, it requires faith to become a believer in the first place. But again, certain believers are gifted to have greater-than-normal levels of faith.

When the going gets particularly difficult and one person crumbles while another stands strong, perhaps it's not entirely because one is hopelessly lacking faith. Maybe it's because the other has been given the gift of faith to be strong enough for both of them in critical situations.

But either way, we never discover what level of faith we have, or whether we might be gifted in this area, until we stop trying so hard to control our own lives and let God take over instead. We generally begin by showing faith in small ways and taking gradually bigger steps of faith as we go along. Some people plateau at some point, while others just seem to keep on going. Faith is something we all need to cultivate. And as we do, some of us may discover that it is a gift of the Holy Spirit to us.

Healing (1 Corinthians 12:9, 28)

Historically, healing has been one of the more attention-getting gifts. As Jesus walked through towns healing leprosy, hemorrhaging, blindness, deafness, paralysis, and so much more, people simply weren't able to keep silent about what He was doing. When Jesus sent His disciples out to minister in various cities, He gave them "power and authority to cast out demons and to heal all diseases" (Luke 9:1). As the early church was getting started, "the apostles were performing many miraculous signs and wonders among the people" (Acts 5:12).

Some people believe the gift of healing, along with certain other spiritual gifts, was given to validate the teaching of the apostles as the church was getting started and is no longer given. Others disagree. Faith healers continue to draw big crowds, though more people may now be skeptics than true believers.

This is not to say that God doesn't continue to heal, as numerous people will attest. But He also allows many of us to learn to cope with diseases and physical ailments, as Paul discovered (2 Corinthians 12:6-10). God continues to be the source of healing power whether or not He chooses to use a human representative.

Miracles (1 Corinthians 12:10, 28)

Immediate healing of a disease or infirmity is certainly a miracle, but not all miracles are healings. Perhaps the "miracles" category of spiritual gifts included casting out evil spirits. There were also instances when, like Old Testament prophets, New Testament leaders demonstrated the miraculous power of God to prove they represented Him.

Other than healing diseases, it's difficult to find a common-day equivalent of a miracle worker. Even self-professed rainmakers have essentially disappeared. Like healing, God can certainly perform miracles whenever and however He wishes, but miracles are by definition the exception rather than the rule.

Ability to Distinguish between Spirits (1 Corinthians 12:10)

When those well-dressed people knock on your door to hand out literature and want to talk to you about your faith, sometimes they seem to make a lot of sense. When they say one thing and your Christian friends and/or pastor say another, how do you know whom to trust (other than the natural inclination to go along with the people you know)?

Churches throughout history have had to deal with smooth-talking spiritual wolves in sheep's clothing. They sound intelligent, religious, and convincing. It's just that they may be peddling heresy that can destroy their listeners' lives rather than bringing them closer to God.

All of us are supposed to be ready to give a defense for what we believe (1 Peter 3:15). Some people, however, are especially good at breaking down clever-sounding arguments that are based on lies.

FOR EXAMPLE . . .
Paul's Ministry

Paul was no stranger to the healing and miracles gifts of the Holy Spirit. At one point people would hold handkerchiefs or cloths against his skin and take them back to sick people, who would then be healed of their disease or freed from the power of demonic possession (Acts 19:11-12). In other cases of miraculous power, Paul commanded a pesky sorcerer to be struck with blindness (Acts 13:4-12) and was bitten by a deadly viper with no ill effects (Acts 28:3-6). In each case, the miracle served to sway the thinking of onlookers and prove that Paul was acting with the authority of God.

Anyone who has the gift of speaking in tongues should pray also for the gift of interpretation in order to tell people plainly what has been said. For if I pray in tongues, my spirit is praying, but I don't understand what I am saying. . . . I thank God that I speak in tongues more than all of you. But in a church meeting I would much rather speak five understandable words that will help others than ten thousand words in an unknown language. (1 Corinthians 14:13-14, 18-19)

Speaking in Tongues (1 Corinthians 12:10, 28)

When the Holy Spirit first appeared and filled the people who believed in Jesus, they found they suddenly possessed the amazing ability to speak foreign languages they had never learned. As a result, everyone who was visiting Jerusalem heard the gospel in his or her own language (Acts 2:1-13).

Clearly, this kind of thing doesn't happen a lot these days. However, some people believe the Holy Spirit bestows them with the gift of speaking in a kind of heavenly linguistics that the speaker may not even understand yet that serves as a personal prayer language that God comprehends and honors.

Interpretation of Tongues (1 Corinthians 12:10, 30)

Not everyone with the gift of speaking in tongues was able to interpret what they were saying. For some reason, the Holy Spirit chose other people to have the gift of interpretation. Paul stressed the importance of using these two gifts together in public worship services. Otherwise, speaking in tongues was not to be used in a group setting (1 Corinthians 14:27-28).

Apostleship (1 Corinthians 12:28; Ephesians 4:11)

The root of the word apostle means a person who is "sent forth" or a "messenger." The term was applied to Jesus' disciples after His resurrection and ascension when they took over the work He had begun. Paul and Barnabas were also later known as apostles as they carried the good news of Jesus to new parts of the world. These people had a special opportunity to get the ball rolling in establishing the church. And since the apostles did their job well, with most of them dying martyrs' deaths for their efforts, some scholars agree the gift of apostleship no longer exists.

Evangelism (Ephesians 4:11)

All believers are supposed to be witnesses to what Jesus has done for them and the difference He makes in their lives. But some people have a specific gift of evangelism, which is the ability to present clearly the truth about Jesus to others—perhaps even people who have never heard of Him. In the biblical context, the evangelists

were the ones who got out of the churches and "hit the road" to spread the news.

In today's church, missionaries fulfill this role. It is possible, of course, to become a missionary without the spiritual gift of evangelism. But the gift of evangelism is certainly beneficial to anyone who reaches out to others with the message of the gospel. Perhaps you know certain missionaries who become so immersed in the needs and habits of the people to whom they minister that they don't really appear to be at ease in their own culture when they return.

However, the practice of evangelism is not limited to foreign missions or stadium-filling crusades. Some evangelists do quite well in one-on-one relationships and small groups. Remember: the Holy Spirit assigns the gifts, and we need to be sensitive to how and where He wants us to apply them.

Pastoring (Ephesians 4:11)

Perhaps this is the most familiar of the spiritual gifts because the role of pastor has existed throughout the historical/biblical period and hasn't changed very much over the millennia since the role was established. All believers in Jesus comprise "the church," but for practical purposes, various local churches have been established so groups of believers can assemble together on a regular basis for worship, fellowship, and ongoing learning about God.

A pastor oversees a local church. His gift touches on the teaching and leadership gifts as well but is more specific. Many times a pastor is likened to a shepherd who provides, protects, and cares for his "flock" in a spiritual, rather than a physical, sense.

When Can We Open Our Presents?

So that's the list. Some people are convinced that these are the extent of the gifts of the Holy Spirit—that there are no more than these and that several on the list are no longer valid for 21st-century believers. Other people suggest that the list is only representative of how the Holy Spirit equips believers in specific

ONE SMALL STEP

Consider: Do you think a person's spiritual gifts are always evident to others? If not, why not? If so, does that mean other believers might help you identify *your* spiritual gift(s)?

Bezalel and Oholiab (Exodus 31:2-6)

When the Old Testament tabernacle was being constructed, Scripture is clear that two men specifically received *artistic* gifts: "Look, I have chosen Bezalel. . . . I have filled him with the Spirit of God, giving him great wisdom, intelligence, and skill in all kinds of crafts. He is able to create beautiful objects from gold, silver, and bronze. He is skilled in cutting and setting gemstones and in carving wood. Yes, he is a master at every craft! And I have appointed Oholiab . . . to be his assistant."

Let love be your highest goal, but also desire the special abilities the Spirit gives. (1 Corinthians 14:1)

ways, and that other gifts exist that aren't specifically stated in Paul's letters.

Some scholars may take issue with how the gifts are paired or defined in this chapter, but this guide isn't a scholarly treatise. It's simply a brief look at how God sees fit to prepare His people to work together and face the world. It is important that all believers learn to identify and use their gifts for the church as a whole. The church was designed so members would need to rely on each other—to let each person do what he or she does best and trust God to supply all the needs.

And Paul is very clear: Unless spiritual gifts are put to use with a spirit of genuine love, they are essentially worthless. He writes:

> If I could speak in any language in heaven or on earth but didn't love others, I would only be making meaningless noise like a loud gong or a clanging cymbal. If I had the gift of prophecy, and if I knew all the mysteries of the future and knew everything about everything, but didn't love others, what good would I be? And if I had the gift of faith so that I could speak to a mountain and make it move, without love I would be no good to anybody. If I gave everything I have to the poor and even sacrificed my body, I could boast about it; but if I didn't love others, I would be of no value whatsoever. (1 Corinthians 13:1-3)

Spiritual gifts are assigned to bring people closer together, although the church has done a pretty good job over the centuries of allowing them to divide believers. That's why the emphasis on love is so crucial. Anytime a spiritual gift is used as a "badge" to exclude or demean someone else, chances are good that it isn't being used appropriately—if it is genuine to begin with.

If you are new to the Christian life, you may go through the list and not see anything that seems to apply to you. But give it time. As the fruit of the Spirit begins to blossom and ripen in your life, you will become more aware of your particular gift(s) of the Spirit.

While some of these things may sound unfamiliar and strange

at first, we should get to the point where discovering our spiritual gifts is as exciting as when we were kids waiting to rip into the presents under the tree on Christmas morning. We know what to expect in some cases; in others, we can look forward to some surprises!

If you don't yet know what your spiritual gifts are, continue to use your talents for God until you do. You may discover a connection. In any case, the work of the Holy Spirit in your life will continue to make your Christian journey vibrant, fresh, and fulfilling. And that's a gift in itself.

Questions to Ponder and/or Discuss

1. As you consider spiritual gifts, does your mental image reflect any of the following kinds of gifts as a parallel? If so, why?

- The gifts a child just can't wait to open at Christmas
- A gift from a stranger you view with a degree of suspicion
- A gift from a spouse or other very special person
- A gift given to an already spoiled child who isn't likely to appreciate it
- A gift you've saved a long, long time to acquire for yourself
- Other: _____

2. Understanding spiritual gifts requires much prayerful wisdom and insight. But as you begin to consider which gifts you might have, what is your initial feeling? Choose from the following options:

NW—No way do I have that gift!
NL—It's not likely this is my gift.
CB—Could be. I'll have to wait to see.
SP—There's a strong possibility this might be one of my gifts.
FS—For sure! I know for a fact this is how God has gifted me.

ONE SMALL STEP

If you're at a point where you want to identify and pursue your spiritual gifts, talk to your pastor or a trusted Christian friend. Many good resources are available, including some assessment questionnaires to help you ask the right questions and consider several alternatives.

SPIRITUAL GIFT	NW	NL	CB	SP	FS
Prophecy					
Serving/ Helping others					
Teaching					
Encouragement (Exhortation)					
Giving					
Leadership (Administration)					
Kindness (Mercy)					
Wisdom and/ or Knowledge					
Faith					
Healing					
Miracles					
Ability to distinguish between spirits					
Speaking in tongues					
Interpretation of tongues					
Apostleship					
Evangelism					
Pastoring					

3. Focus on any of the gifts you rated as a "Could Be" or "Strong Possibility." For each of those gifts, what are two or three ways you might demonstrate that gift?

After you get some specific ideas, choose one or two to try during the next week or so. See how it feels to practice the gift. Does God seem to lead you to pursue further development of that gift, or does He take you in a different direction?

Working on the Knight Moves
THE ARMOR OF GOD

George Seeker saw Fred DiCiple working on his lawn mower in his driveway and went over to say hello. "Looks like you've got a problem. Anything I can do?"

"No thanks," said Fred. "I think it needs a new spark plug. I'll go to the store and get one and see if that fixes it. Or maybe Josh just sabotaged it so he wouldn't have to mow this week."

George chuckled, and Fred invited him into the garage for a drink from an old fridge he kept out there. George had a root beer. Fred, ever the optimist, was sticking to diet cola.

After a bit of small talk, George asked a question out of the blue: "You're pretty serious about your religion, aren't you?"

Taken back a bit, Fred swallowed a little too quickly and sputtered before answering. But while he was coughing up the fizz, he could hear Wilma's voice in his head telling him to think before he spoke. At last he caught his breath and said, "I'm a Christian, if that's what you mean. And I work at trying to live up to the standards that are spelled out in the Bible."

George looked appreciative that Fred had taken him seriously,

115

and he continued. "Do people ever ridicule you because of what you believe?"

Fred paused to think. "I can't say it's ever been much of a problem. I encounter people from time to time who don't agree with my perspectives on life and Christianity, and I've had some spirited discussions as a result. I suppose some people think I'm a bit loony, but that's okay by me. The Bible tells believers to expect some of that kind of stuff."

"Really?" George looked relieved and confused at the same time.

"Sure. Jesus was the only person who ever had it all figured out, and He faced far worse criticism than I ever have. Anytime I feel in the least persecuted for my faith, I kind of count it as a blessing to be in the same group as Jesus. But why are you asking all of a sudden?"

George looked at the ground as he spoke. "I told some guys at work that Jane and I were thinking about going back to church and they started looking at me as if I'd told them I believed in unicorns and fairies. All of a sudden it was as if they were expecting me to explain everything they find wrong with religion. Some of them are genius-level scientists, and I had no idea what to say. I'm still new, and I barely know those guys, but it's like I've already been labeled 'the religious nut.' They don't know how wrong they are!"

Fred was sympathetic. "Well, religion is a sensitive topic for lots of people. Personally, I think it's great you and Jane are wanting to get closer to God. I know Wilma has been impressed with the questions Jane is asking in their Bible study group, and how quickly she is learning."

George interrupted: "And, uh, I guess I need to find a group like that. Could you suggest one?"

Fred said, "Sure. Our church has a couple of good ones. One meets early Tuesday mornings and gets out in plenty of time for us to get to work—if you can get up that early."

"I'm an early riser. That sounds great . . . if you're open to new members."

Fred laughed. "We're a church, not a country club. Everyone is welcome! And if you don't mind hearing a little recycled advice, I'll

tell you the same thing I just told my kids. Josh is in his first weeks of football practice, and Mary is starting guitar lessons. They both have just discovered that what they want to do is going to be harder than they anticipated. And as you start down the road of the Christian life, I bet you'll face some hard challenges too. It sounds as if you already have. But like I told Josh and Mary, the biggest obstacles are usually during the learning experience. It never gets harder than that. Once you "get the knack"—whether it's playing football, learning to play the guitar, or living the Christian life—the rewards quickly begin to outweigh the difficulties."

George started to say, "Fred, you're smarter than you look." But he wasn't sure he knew his new neighbor well enough yet. So instead he said, "Thanks. That helps a lot. I'll be glad to loan you my lawn mower in return."

Fred declined, saying he was on his way to the store to get the spark plug. Besides, he thought, if he needed to borrow the mower later, perhaps that would provide the opportunity for another good talk.

This Means War

One thing Fred tactfully didn't say to George was something George would find out soon enough. Once he stepped onto the path that would take him through the Christian life, those guys at work would become the least of his problems. It's an epiphany all believers face at some point on their spiritual journeys. We think that *people* are our problems, which may be true to a point. But if we're putting most of our time and energy into struggling with other human beings, we're fighting a losing battle.

In chapter 7 we saw that the Holy Spirit produces fruit in the lives of believers to help them get along better with each other—and even with nonbelievers. In the last chapter we saw a number of gifts He provides to help the church body operate more effectively. And certainly all those things have a real people element to them.

But in this chapter we want to take a slightly different perspective on the Christian life. Sometimes the Christian life is a walk in

DO'S AND DON'TS

Be careful! Watch out for attacks from the Devil, your great enemy. He prowls around like a roaring lion, looking for some victim to devour. Take a firm stand against him, and be strong in your faith. (1 Peter 5:8-9)

the woods. Sometimes it's a mountaintop experience where believers physically and spiritually sense the presence of God. Sometimes it's a picnic. But all the time, it's a battle. There may be a few breaks in the action where we can let our guard down long enough to walk in the woods, climb the mountain, or grab a bite to eat. But if we let down our guard too long, we're the ones who get bitten.

Paul makes it clear: "For we are not fighting against people made of flesh and blood, but against the evil rulers and authorities of the unseen world, against those mighty powers of darkness who rule this world, and against wicked spirits in the heavenly realms" (Ephesians 6:12). If you thought David vs. Goliath was an exciting story, just wait till you see the sequel: You vs. Beelzebub. The odds are about the same. If God gets involved, victory is predetermined. If not, and you're trying to fight that battle in your own power, it's not going to be pretty.

Like David, we're expected to stand on the front lines of the battle, weapon in hand, facing our huge enemies. From all appearances we may be outsized, outnumbered, and out of our minds. But from a perspective of faith, we can stand there with confidence—not in ourselves, but in God who is supplying both the power and the weapons to take down even the toughest and ugliest of our spiritual enemies.

In some cases, perhaps we've been losing the battle for a long time. In this war we don't have the opportunity to declare Swiss neutrality or '60s pacifism. If we don't fight, we lose. If we've been sitting out this battle for a while, the enemy may have made serious inroads into our lives, robbing us of much of what God intends us to have in the Christian life. But it's never too late to join the fray and take back what is rightly yours. Again, Paul addresses this possibility:

> We are human, but we don't wage war with human plans and methods. We use God's mighty weapons, not mere worldly weapons, to knock down the Devil's strongholds. With these weapons we break down every proud argument that keeps people from knowing God. With these weapons we conquer their rebellious ideas, and we teach them to obey Christ. (2 Corinthians 10:3-5)

If the devil has established strongholds in your life, it's time for some spiritual demolition. It's time to pick up your slingshot and look your opponent in the knee, if you aren't tall enough to see eye-to-eye. Don't worry about it. In the Christian life, the only size that matters is the size of your faith.

In fact, we have it a lot better than David did when he faced Goliath. David tried on King Saul's armor but found it too confining. He was so confident of God's protection that he faced Goliath with no defensive options at all (1 Samuel 17:38-40). But compared to our spiritual enemies, the nine-foot Philistine warrior was a teddy bear. So we are provided armor and are supposed to use it. The armor of God will save us from numerous spiritual defeats if we simply put it on and learn to maneuver as God wants us to.

ONE SMALL STEP

Determine what has been your experience so far with "spiritual warfare." Do you seem to be fighting battles you just can't win, perhaps because of underlying spiritual forces? If so, identify some of those "strongholds" before continuing.

Dressing for Success

When it comes to Christian fashion, forget the skirts, blouses, and three-piece suits. Instead, let's take a look at the six-piece suit of armor Paul describes to the Ephesians (and to us). God doesn't equip us so we'll look good. As you will see, if any piece of the following equipment is missing, we make ourselves unnecessarily vulnerable to attack and/or injury.

Before Paul gets specific, he issues a challenge: "Be strong with the Lord's mighty power. Put on all of God's armor so that you will be able to stand firm against all strategies and tricks of the devil.... Use every piece of God's armor to resist the enemy in the time of evil, so that after the battle you will still be standing firm" (Ephesians 6:10-11, 13).

We need to read this passage carefully. Don't overlook the fact that this is *God's* armor, and *God's* mighty power. Too many Christians are running around the battlefield wearing self-made armor of spiritual cardboard and aluminum foil, endangering themselves as well as their fellow soldiers. Few if any of us will escape some serious blows, and when they come we'd better be wearing authentic God-tempered armor that will protect us.

WELL SAID!

"Christ in you, the hope of glory." I'm not afraid of the devil. The devil can handle me—he's got judo I never heard of. But he can't handle the One to whom I'm joined; he can't handle the One to whom I'm united; he can't handle the One whose nature dwells in my nature.
—*A. W. Tozer*

DO'S AND DON'TS

Don't live in darkness. Get rid of your evil deeds. Shed them like dirty clothes. Clothe yourselves with the armor of right living, as those who live in the light. (Romans 13:12)

We also need to note that we are to put on all of God's armor and use *every piece* to resist spiritual attacks. God protects us totally. You may recall the myth of Achilles, who was dipped by his mother into the River Styx to give him invulnerability—except for the heel by which he was held. And his heel was exactly the point where an arrow later found its mark and brought him down.

As you will soon see, we have protective "shoes," but they won't do us much good if we go into battle barefoot. A helmet left behind in a closet won't protect our noggins out on the front lines. Perhaps you've been breezing through the last couple of chapters thinking, *Spiritual fruit? Cool. Spiritual gifts? That's nice.* But if you continue in this chapter with an attitude of, *Spiritual armor? How absolutely cute!*, you're likely to be in for a shock. The Holy Spirit equips us for a purpose, not because He has nothing better to do. And because He equips us, we need to stand with our fellow Christian "soldiers" on the spiritual battlefield.

Buckle Up!

A belt is one of the last accessories we select in getting dressed, but for the Roman soldiers who lived when Paul wrote about the armor of God, it was one of the first. Before any protective gear went on, the soldier would fasten a belt around his waist both to cinch loose-fitting clothing and to provide a place to attach armor.

In the Christian life, "the sturdy belt of truth" (Ephesians 6:14) should be a foundation for everything else to follow. Just as a belt encircles your body, your life should be surrounded with the desire and the commitment to be absolutely truthful.

Culturally, we've been trained to accept and deal in "little white lies," the end result of which has been the ongoing entrenchment of gradually larger and increasingly darker lies. It is becoming harder and harder to determine what is the truth, the whole truth, and nothing but the truth.

We've learned to tell other people what they want to hear—if not to spare their feelings, to ensure that we stay in their good graces.

We lie to get out of trouble. We lie to make our accomplishments sound bigger and better than reality dictates. We lie in order to feel better about ourselves. We lie for dozens of reasons and rarely think twice about it. Of course, we even lie to ourselves by not calling it lying. Instead we use softer synonyms such as *flattery, boasting, cunning, tact, spin, horse trading, stretching the truth*, and so forth. It is frequently noted that the Eskimo have dozens of words for "snow." In a similar way, we have dozens of creative ways to say, "I'm a big, fat liar." We've found so many ways to lie to one another and ourselves that we've created a wide and diverse vocabulary to cover it.

WELL SAID!

Truth is tough. It will not break, like a bubble, at a touch, nay, you may kick it about all day like a football, and it will be round and full at evening.
—Oliver Wendell Holmes

Have you ever lied to your kids, attempting to make a situation seem less threatening to them but only making it worse because they could tell you were lying? Have you ever lied to aging parents about their declining health, with similar results? Have you ever lied to a boss? a teacher? a coworker? a police officer? an insurance agent? a spouse? a close friend?

And here's the big one: Do you ever lie to yourself? Have you fooled yourself into believing you're either a better or worse person than you really are? Do you keep telling yourself that you're better than certain other people . . . that you deserve that raise . . . that it won't hurt just this once to commit that little sin . . . that the speed limit is for other people but not for good drivers like yourself?

Perhaps you don't see yourself in any of these situations, which could mean that you are an exceptionally moral and spiritual individual. Then again, you might just be lying to yourself.

DO'S AND DON'TS

Don't lie to each other, for you have stripped off your old evil nature and all its wicked deeds. In its place you have clothed yourselves with a brand-new nature that is continually being renewed as you learn more and more about Christ, who created this new nature within you. (Colossians 3:9-10)

In the Christian life, the lies have got to go. This is a clear and repeated theme of Scripture. See for yourself:

- It is impossible for God to lie (Titus 1:2; Hebrews 6:18).
- Jesus identified Himself as "the way, the truth, and the life" (John 14:6).
- The Holy Spirit is a Spirit of truth (John 14:17; 16:13).
- God's Word—the Bible—is truth (John 17:17).

ONE SMALL STEP

It is easy to overlook or downplay the things we don't like about ourselves. But since complete truth is so important and so foundational for everything that is to follow, take a few moments and try to be completely truthful with yourself. If you're not being honest with yourself, chances are you're not being completely open and honest with God either. So before going any farther, take a few moments to do a little "spiritual house-cleaning." Air out the hidden recesses, drawers, basements, crawl spaces, and other places that may be unpleasant and even painful. Let God clear them all out with the fresh air of truth and begin to heal the hurts so you can start anew. Acknowledging all the secrets, shame, and hidden "dirt" will allow you to feel a whole lot better and move forward with confidence and genuine honesty in your spiritual journey.

In fact, go get an exhaustive concordance sometime and see how many times the Bible refers to "truth." You'll find hundreds, if not thousands, of mentions.

And don't try suggesting that you have a genetic predisposition to lie, because that reveals which "family" you belong to. Jesus reminds us that the devil is "a liar and the father of lies" and that "there is no truth in him" (John 8:44). If that's the "father" who controls your thoughts and words, then yes, you are more likely to lie. But we all need to sever that "genetic" connection the moment God becomes our Father and we commit to the Christian life. As we turn our devotion from sin and Satan to salvation and God, we need to leave all the lies behind.

Truth is the belt beneath the rest of our armor. If it's sliding around rather than firmly anchored beneath your other equipment, you're apt to give yourself an enormous spiritual wedgie. But then, you probably deserve it.

Knights in Right Status

After the belt comes the breastplate, the primary piece of armor that protects the chest. And to provide this protection, in a spiritual sense, is *righteousness*. It's a big word that essentially means rightness, or having a proper status before God. Thanks to the sacrifice of Jesus on our behalf, we can place our faith in Him. God cleanses and forgives our sin, and we are deemed righteous by Him. The more confident we are of this truth, the thicker our protection against our enemy's weapons.

But in addition, righteousness becomes a lifestyle. As we continue to do the right things in various situations, based on our devotion to God, we set ourselves apart from the people who don't make those same choices. The breastplate primarily protects the heart, and the righteousness God provides can help us keep our hearts pure. If we neglect to live righteously, the purity of our heart becomes vulnerable. And conversely, if the desires of the heart stray from a commitment to righteousness, our spiritual armor develops potentially fatal chinks.

Doing the right thing at all times is a powerful defensive strategy. When falsely accused of wrongdoing, we need not huff and puff and take offense. We can simply point out where we were, what we were doing, and who saw us. Righteousness has nothing to hide. And in time, as we gain a reputation for righteousness, we may even begin to make a difference in the world around us.

God is described in the Old Testament as preparing for a quest for justice, since no one else was helping the oppressed. In doing so, He dressed Himself in a breastplate (body armor) of justice and a helmet of salvation (Isaiah 59:15-17). So He equips us with the very same spiritual armor He wears.

Righteousness is next to impossible unless it is built on truth. Attempting to do the right things is noble, but we need to ensure that those "right things" are true and not merely convenient, conventional, or otherwise askew of absolute truth. If we're not wearing some reliable body armor, the blows of the enemy are really going to sting.

No Business Like Shoe Business

With the body protected by a breastplate of righteousness, we move down to the feet. Sometimes a stubbed toe or ingrown toenail can keep us off our feet, so just think what would happen if a more serious injury impaired your ability to get around. To prevent being damaged by a low blow, the spiritual armor for our feet consists of "the peace that comes from the Good News, so that you will be fully prepared" (Ephesians 6:15).

Several years ago a shoe company ran some ads with a celebrity interviewing athletic superstars about what made them so talented. The series of questions would ultimately come down to "Is it the shoes?"

In this case, footwear can definitely make or break the success of the soldier. As you go through the Christian life and saturate yourself with the good news about Jesus, allowing the gospel to become real in your life, you are left with a sense of peace. The point comes when you realize that, ultimately, nothing terrible can happen to

DO'S AND DON'TS

Be careful how you live among your unbelieving neighbors. Even if they accuse you of doing wrong, they will see your honorable behavior, and they will believe and give honor to God when he comes to judge the world. (1 Peter 2:12)

FOR EXAMPLE . . .

Shadrach, Meshach, and Abednego (Daniel 3)

It would have been a simple matter to bow—even mockingly—in front of King Nebuchadnezzar's statue and avoid his wrath, but it wasn't the *right* thing to do. So Shadrach, Meshach, and Abednego stood tall as everyone else hit their knees. Consequently, they were tossed into the fiery furnace. And while the intense heat killed the people who threw them in, the fire didn't singe a hair or a thread of the three men's clothing. Any other armor would have let them down, yet righteousness not only saved them but made quite an impression on King Nebuchadnezzar as well.

123

Paul's life or death debate
(Philippians 1:21-24)

Paul was so consumed by the peace provided by the gospel of Jesus Christ that he had little concern over whether he lived or died. This is the way he phrased it: "For to me, living is for Christ, and dying is even better. Yet if I live, that means fruitful service for Christ. I really don't know which is better. I'm torn between two desires: Sometimes I want to live, and sometimes I long to go and be with Christ. That would be far better for me, but it is better for you that I live." (Philippians 1:21-24)

WELL SAID!

Soldiers of Christ, arise, and put your armor on,
  Strong in the strength which God supplies through His eternal Son;
  Strong in the Lord of hosts, and in His mighty power,
  Who in the strength of Jesus trusts is more than conqueror. —*Charles Wesley*

you. No matter what takes place in your life, even if you face a terrible death, just beyond is an eternity with the Person in the universe who loves you the most.

Surprisingly, feet are used several times throughout the Bible to symbolize surefootedness and/or a connection with the gospel. For example:

- God arms me with strength; he has made my way safe. He makes me as surefooted as a deer, leading me safely along the mountain heights. He prepares me for battle; he strengthens me to draw a bow of bronze (Psalm 18:32-34).
- [The Lord] lifted me out of the pit of despair, out of the mud and the mire. He set my feet on solid ground and steadied me as I walked along (Psalm 40:2).
- How beautiful on the mountains are the feet of those who bring good news of peace and salvation, the news that the God of Israel reigns! (Isaiah 52:7).

Without the peace of God in your life, you're likely to shift anxiously from foot to foot, which isn't very effective if you're trying to fight a battle. Peace allows you to stand firm and dig in. When your footing is sure, you have much better balance in life—fighting or not.

Raise Shields!

So far the descriptions have been symbolic of close-to-the-body armor. But in a first-century battle, it was always preferable if the blows and missiles of an enemy never even reached the body. So it was hard to overestimate the importance of a shield.

It was a bit tricky to design a good shield. It needed to be large enough to protect vital areas of the body but still light enough to maneuver without wearing down the soldier. The Romans had settled on wooden shields that were about four feet long and two and a half feet wide. But since their enemies would sometimes use flaming arrows, the Romans coated their shields with layers of linen and leather and then doused them in water to provide fireproofing.

According to Paul, the shield in a believer's spiritual armor is the person's *faith*. He writes: "In every battle you will need faith as your shield to stop the fiery arrows aimed at you by Satan" (Ephesians 6:16).

That's right. As soon as you step onto the path to pursue a Christian life, to God you become His child. To your enemy you become a target. God pours out His love, mercy, and grace, and Satan starts heaving fiery arrows of doubt, confusion, temptation, and worse in your direction. But the same faith you place in Jesus to become a Christian in the first place will continue to grow and shield you from much of Satan's destructive ammo. Jesus is more than a Savior; He is also a protector, and one day he will be the ultimate victor in the war that's taking place.

Until then, we are to carry our faith like a shield. Notice that faith serves a definite purpose. Sometimes we wonder what good it does to believe in things we can't see and to have confident assurance that what we hope for is going to happen (Hebrews 11:1). But that mysterious, intangible thing called faith forms an irreplaceable defensive weapon. The stronger your faith, the more sturdy and trustworthy your shield. You are likely to have numerous encounters in the Christian life where a strong faith keeps you from getting poked—or even flambéed—by one of the devil's sharp arrows.

And Now Some Protection for Your Soft Spot

Perhaps you've seen the sports video blooper where two football players are celebrating a special moment with the traditional head-butting ceremony. Something great had happened, both guys wanted to get pumped up about it, and they instinctively cracked their helmets together with great force. The problem was that in the heat of the moment, one guy had apparently forgotten he had removed his helmet. As the other guy's helmet met his skull, his expression immediately changed from one of fierce fervor to pain, anger, and confusion (if not concussion).

Suffice it to say that we can put on belts, breastplates, feet

protection, and hold a shield out in front of us. But if someone runs out to the war without a helmet, you don't have to guess his chances for success. A classic Monty Python sketch shows how a tenacious knight might continue to fight without arms and/or legs, but everyone's likelihood of success diminishes if his or her head isn't in the battle.

The spiritual equivalent of a helmet is *salvation* (Ephesians 6:17). If we haven't experienced the salvation of Jesus, we're fighting a losing battle before we even get started. But to be a bit more picky in regard to the imagery provided, the helmet is one of the final items a soldier would put on. So in this case, perhaps "salvation" refers not to the one-time decision to become a Christian, but rather the ongoing benefits of God's salvation in a believer's life. When Paul used a similar image in a letter to the Thessalonian church, he wrote of "wearing as our helmet the confidence of our salvation" (1 Thessalonians 5:8).

In other words, if we're uncertain about what God's salvation means in our lives, it will be rather easy for our spiritual enemies to "mess with our heads." But a firm assurance of salvation is like a helmet that clarifies our thinking and crystallizes our faith.

Another aspect of a helmet—whether in football or medieval battle—is to broadcast whose team you're on. A helmet of salvation identifies us clearly as belonging to Christ . . . living the Christ-ian life . . . fighting with the Christ-ian soldiers. To be honest, there may be times in our life when we're a bit embarrassed to be seen by others in His colors. But as we learn more about the Christian life and what it means, the helmet of salvation becomes a symbol of victory as well as a protective covering.

The (S)Word of God

So far it would seem that a Christian soldier is always playing defense, so to speak. The armor and shield are protective. We're not issued cannons, maces, M16s, nuclear weapons, or too much in the way of fighting back. But we do get a sword apiece, which is identified as "the sword of the Spirit, which is the word of God" (Ephesians 6:17).

The order seems to be important. We aren't to get half-dressed and then start flailing around with the sword that the Holy Spirit provides for us. Armor may feel strange enough in itself. How much more if we're trying to put it on while swinging a sword? So first we completely prepare ourselves defensively. We properly adjust the belt of truth, the breastplate of righteousness, the shoes of peace, the shield of faith, and the helmet of salvation. Only then do we pick up our offensive weapon—the Word of God, which acts as a sword.

The author of Hebrews makes a similar comparison: "The word of God is full of living power. It is sharper than the sharpest knife [or sword], cutting deep into our innermost thoughts and desires. It exposes us for what we really are" (Hebrews 4:12). So back in chapter 2 when you were considering how Bible study might be a nice thing to do, you were actually preparing to sharpen your spiritual sword in preparation for war. So many times the things we consider mere pleasantries are in fact essential for survival.

Jesus faced far greater temptations than we ever will, yet as each temptation zeroed in on Him, He fended it off with a masterful stroke of His spiritual sword—He quoted an appropriate passage from the Word of God (Matthew 4:1-11). The devil's fiery arrows never touched Him. With a bit of practice, we can get much better at spiritual swordplay as well.

ONE SMALL STEP

Review each of the items listed as "the armor of God" (Ephesians 6:10-18). Evaluate how well equipped you are at this point to go into spiritual battle. Identify your strongest point as well as where you are most vulnerable and determine what steps you need to take to become better protected.

All Dressed Up; Now Where to Go?

So there you have it: the latest fashions for the well-equipped soldier of God. But we're still not quite ready to jump into the fray. Immediately after listing the individual pieces of spiritual armor, Paul concludes by saying, "Pray at all times and on every occasion in the power of the Holy Spirit. Stay alert and be persistent in your prayers for all Christians everywhere" (Ephesians 6:18). We must never forget that even though we're wearing armor, the power and successful strategy come from God. Dressing in armor doesn't make

DO'S AND DON'TS

Endure suffering along with me, as a good soldier of Christ Jesus. And as Christ's soldier, do not let yourself become tied up in the affairs of this life, for then you cannot satisfy the one who has enlisted you in his army. Follow the Lord's rules for doing his work.
(2 Timothy 2:3-5)

someone a soldier anymore than a little girl becomes an adult by dressing in her mother's clothes and too-big shoes.

It has also been pointed out that the one vulnerable spot where armor is not specified is the back. It seems we are expected to confront our spiritual enemies head-on. As long as we're fighting, we're protected. If we turn and run, or attempt to slink away from the battlefield, we expose our vulnerable points. And if we turn on one another rather than fighting our spiritual enemies, we expose our backsides to danger. It is much better for believers to stand side by side or back-to-back, united together against our common enemy.

Another thing to notice is that our Commander tells us to "resist the enemy" and "stand your ground" (Ephesians 6:13-14). We're not told to go one-on-one against Satan or to single-handedly take on the powers of darkness. That's God's job. It's enough of a challenge for us to hold the ground we've already been given. Our enemy can put on a lot of disguises. Satan often appears as an "angel of light" (2 Corinthians 11:14). Just because someone is operating within the church doesn't necessarily mean he or she is on God's side. We must always be on guard against spies, moles, guerrilla warfare, and other sneak attacks by Satan and his devotees. Our armor and swords aren't much use if he catches us sleeping.

This is one reason why we need to take our faith seriously. If we're attempting to breeze through the Christian life, we can read the Bible casually, pray somewhat sincerely, and worship God. And we may not notice it, but as we do all those things we're actually dressing for battle. When the enemy sees us all decked out for a fight, he's happy to oblige. Yet if we haven't come to the realization that we're on a battlefield, *wearing armor*, we place ourselves at great risk. We need to keep reading, praying, and worshiping, to be sure. But we also need to consider the weight of what those things mean. They aren't simply time-passing activities for bored Christians; they are calisthenics for warriors-in-training.

And in spite of the war/armor imagery, this fight is by no means gender-specific. Women have traditionally been left out when the discussion turns to sports or military talk. But lately they have made

considerable inroads toward sports equality. And if nothing else, Xena has recently demonstrated that young ladies can also be warrior princesses. Xena is fantasy, of course (perhaps in more ways than one), but the reality of Scripture tells us that on God's battlefield, we're all equal. When it comes to Christianity, "There is no longer Jew or Gentile, slave or free, male or female" (Galatians 3:28).

The call to arms has gone out to all God's people. The battle is on. And we're faced with the same old question: "What am I going to wear?"

WELL SAID!

Let him not boast who puts his armor on
  As he who puts it off, the battle done.
—Henry Wadsworth Longfellow

Questions to Ponder and/or Discuss

1. At what level have you experienced "spiritual warfare" in your life so far? Has it been more like:

   - A squabble with a sibling in the backseat of the car?
   - An after-school fistfight with the class bully?
   - An Old West shootout?
   - Trench warfare?
   - Guerrilla warfare?
   - An all-out nuclear holocaust?
   - Other: _____

2. Take an inventory of your current spiritual armor. Check the appropriate box to indicate the condition of each piece:

PIECE OF SPIRITUAL ARMOR	MISSING	NEEDS REPAIR	BATTLE READY
The sturdy belt of truth	☐	☐	☐
The body armor of God's righteousness	☐	☐	☐

PIECE OF SPIRITUAL ARMOR	MISSING	NEEDS REPAIR	BATTLE READY
For shoes, the peace that comes from the Good News	☐	☐	☐
The shield of faith	☐	☐	☐
The helmet of salvation	☐	☐	☐
The sword of the Spirit— the Word of God	☐	☐	☐

3. What are three things you could do this week that would probably thrust you more into the line of fire in regard to the spiritual warfare that accompanies the Christian life?

CHAPTER TEN

"DO YOU, MARGARET, TAKE THIS MAN, HIS GOLF CLUBS, HIS GOLFING BUDDIES, THEIR CADDIES, WIVES, AND FRIENDS TO BE YOUR LAWFULLY WEDDED HUSBAND?"

Wedding Bell Blueprints

MARRIAGE

SOME THINGS YOU'LL DISCOVER IN THIS CHAPTER

1. God's original blueprint for marriage

2. How humans have deviated from God's original plan

3. A few biblical guidelines for Christian marriages

The Seekers and DiCiples are closer than ever. Today especially. They're all packed into a pew at the wedding of a mutual neighbor—a woman who had been attending Wilma's women's Bible study since it started. In fact, it was Betty's divorce from her husband that had motivated Wilma to start the Bible study in the first place. Now, after three years, Betty and her husband were giving marriage another chance.

Wilma and Jane were crying unashamedly. (With Jane's pregnancy several months along, her raging hormones were making many of her emotions more extreme.) Fred and George were telling "ol' ball-and-chain" jokes and making whip-cracking noises to avoid getting weepy along with their wives.

But when the couple got to their vows, there were few dry eyes in the packed church. Both bride and groom were completely open about the failures of their past—and their willingness to recommit to one another for the rest of their lives. Since none of the guests could boast of perfect marriages, the vulnerability of the couple in front impressed more than a few of those listening. Had people not been

so teary, they might have seen the loving pokes and elbow prods of couples throughout the church, signifying the recollections of good times, bad times, and the love that had seen them through *all* the times.

On the way home, the Seekers and DiCiples, who had shared a ride, also shared stories of the best and worst periods of their marriages. Regardless of having to get all dressed up on a Saturday, it turned out to be a pretty good day.

Run for Your Wife (or Husband)

Marriage is a wonderful event. When two people commit themselves to one another in selfless love, we celebrate with hearts, flowers, a fancy ceremony, and cake. Yet marriage can also be one of the biggest challenges to the Christian life.

As children grow out from under the strong influence of their parents, they learn the importance of what we sometimes call "the Christian walk." But in all honesty, as individuals we can vary the pace as we wish. It's not at all unusual for high school or college students to discover the joy of the Christian journey for themselves. They may experience a time of progress that is one of "leaps and bounds" rather than a mere "walk." At other times we might hit hard times and slow to a crawl. But progress and pace is usually an individual decision.

With marriage, however, the person's "walk" becomes essentially a three-legged race. You think you're only reciting vows at your wedding, when in reality another whole person is being strapped to you. Everything you do for a while will be clumsy and awkward. No longer can you stroll, run, or skip just because you feel like it. Your spiritual progress now depends on learning to go in the same direction at approximately the same speed as your new spouse. Otherwise, one or both of you are likely to end up on the ground.

You'll get better with practice, of course, even though it's usually difficult at first. But if you've ever seen a couple in the three-legged race work together and win the prize, it's a thing of beauty. While all the others are lying in the dirt or hobbling along with all the grace of two bobcats in a burlap bag, the winning couple stands out not only for their victory but even more for their cooperation and coordination.

Similarly, happily married couples stand out from the slew of divorce statistics and unhappily married couples. So let's turn our attention to how marriage relates to the Christian life.

Got to Get Back to the Garden

In recent years, marriage has been criticized as old-fashioned or even antiquated. And no wonder! So few couples these days even approach the potential that marriage should provide. When Olympic athletes are caught using steroids, we disqualify those contestants, but we don't do away with the Olympics. Similarly, when people cheat or hold back on their partners, it should reflect on the people and not the institution of marriage.

Let's take a look at God's model for marriage. We've tended to make changes in His original blueprint, and few if any of our changes have turned out to be improvements. Here's how the Bible describes the first union between man and woman:

> The Lord God placed the man in the Garden of Eden to tend and care for it. But the Lord God gave him this warning: "You may freely eat any fruit in the garden except fruit from the tree of the knowledge of good and evil. If you eat of its fruit, you will surely die."
>
> And the Lord God said, "It is not good for the man to be alone. I will make a companion who will help him." So the Lord God formed from the soil every kind of animal and bird. He brought them to Adam to see what he would call them, and Adam chose a name for each one. He gave names to all the livestock, birds, and wild animals. But still there was no companion suitable for him. So the Lord God caused Adam to fall into a deep sleep. He took one of Adam's ribs and closed up the place from which he had taken it. Then

ONE SMALL STEP

How many couples can you think of who are both on their first marriage and whom you would consider to be happily married? If any such couples come to mind, what qualities would you say have been crucial to the success of their marriage?

133

the Lord God made a woman from the rib and brought her
to Adam.

"At last!" Adam exclaimed. "She is part of my own flesh
and bone! She will be called 'woman,' because she was
taken out of a man." This explains why a man leaves his
father and mother and is joined to his wife, and the two are
united into one. Now, although Adam and his wife were
both naked, neither of them felt any shame. (Genesis 2:15-25)

One-to-One

The first thing we notice from God's model is that He put together
one man and one woman. Adam surely had a full set of ribs, but
God didn't see fit to take more than one just so Adam could have a
harem.

It didn't take long for human beings to deviate from this simple
one-to-one pattern. By the time we get to the fourth chapter of
Genesis, it is noted that a man named Lamech "married two
women" (Genesis 4:19). And from that point until today, people
have been trying to vary God's plan for marriage.

Polygamy was allowed in the Old Testament, but the Law provided several specific regulations to discourage the abuse of the
practice. For instance, if an Israelite male was attracted to a slave or
a foreign woman who had been taken captive, he was allowed to
marry her. But he could no longer treat her as a slave. The marriage
contract was to ensure a certain degree of status and respect (Exodus 21:7-11; Deuteronomy 21:10-14).

We must remember that this was a culture where bearing children was not just to continue the family name but was also the only
way to care for aging parents, family herds, and so forth. When
Mom and Dad got older, they didn't pack up the Caravan and move
to southern Israel to a planned retirement community for golf and
bridge. It was up to their kids to take care of them.

So if a woman was unable to bear children, the law provided the
option for the husband to take a concubine to fulfill that responsibility. The concubine was more than a one-night-stand/baby-maker.
She was legally wed to the man, had no moral stigma attached to the

relationship, and bore children who were considered legitimate. However, she didn't receive the same benefits as a full-fledged wife. A concubine had no say in running the household and could be sent away at any time with a small present as compensation for all her service. If she remained until the death of the husband, her share of the inheritance was usually considerably smaller than a wife's.

But by the beginning of the New Testament, polygamy was no longer an option for Christians. In addition to a number of spiritual considerations, church leaders were also to be faithful to a single wife (1 Timothy 3:2, 12). The mainstream churches have held to this standard throughout recent centuries. The most noted exception is probably the Mormon church, who publicly endorsed the practice of polygamy for a period. And there are other current movements that continue to promote polygamy, using the Old Testament as justification.

However, most of us have come to see that maintaining love, patience, and commitment to a single spouse is enough of a challenge. It was God's original model, and we continue to abide by it.

Male and Female

Perhaps you've heard someone make the glib observation that God created Adam and Eve, not Adam and Steve. The issues between conservative Christians and gay rights advocates are much more complex than this, of course. And we don't want to get into them here. But if we can sidestep the issue of whether contemporary gay couples should have the same rights as married heterosexual couples, let's just say that God's original blueprint was one man with one woman. And it certainly made sense at the time. His instruction to the world's first couple was to "Multiply and fill the earth and subdue it" (Genesis 1:28). Aside from any other arguments for heterosexuality, without both male and female doing their part in the multiplication process, this would have been a most difficult task.

During the process of Creation, God also originated a number of sciences—biology among them. He made a point of creating "seed-bearing plants" so they could carry on their species. And he did the same with animals and human beings.

FOR EXAMPLE . . .
Polygamy in the Old Testament

Here are a few of the better known biblical characters who had concubines. If you read the stories, you'll see that frequently the relationship with the concubine(s) created more problems than it solved.

- Abraham (Genesis 16; 21:8-21; 25:5-6)
- Jacob (Genesis 29:31–30:24)
- Gideon, also known as Jerubbaal (Judges 8:28-31)
- David (2 Samuel 5:13; 15:16; 16:21-22)
- Solomon (1 Kings 11:1-3)

DO'S AND DON'TS

Do not practice homosexuality; it is a detestable sin. (Leviticus 18:22)

WELL SAID!

Monogamous, heterosexual love is probably one of the most difficult, complex, and demanding of human relationships. —*Margaret Mead*

DO'S AND DON'TS

You will submit to one another out of reverence for Christ. You wives will submit to your husbands as you do to the Lord. For a husband is the head of his wife as Christ is the head of his body, the church; he gave his life to be her Savior. As the church submits to Christ, so you wives must submit to your husbands in everything.

And you husbands must love your wives with the same love Christ showed the church. He gave up his life for her to make her holy and clean, washed by baptism and God's word. . . . In the same way, husbands ought to love their wives as they love their own bodies. For a man is actually loving himself when he loves his wife. (Ephesians 5:21-28)

The Image of God

Yet while the differences between male and female are essential in the name of biology, there was no distinction made between them in regard to importance. The human race as a whole stands apart from the rest of the animal kingdom because people were created in God's own image. Scripture makes a clear statement: "So God created people in his own image; God patterned them after himself; male and female he created them" (Genesis 1:27).

One-to-one. Male and female. Both in His image. One could argue that it takes both male and female working in tandem to properly reflect the image of God. They were created with a mutual dependence on one another. In marriage they are to become not two very close individuals but a single union of what was previously two people.

We tend to complicate a lot of issues, but this is essentially why the biblical teachings on mutual submission are so important. Submission is not so much to establish a complicated flowchart akin to the presidential line-of-succession. Rather, submission of one spouse to the other, and vice versa, is to ensure the ongoing oneness properly reflecting the Godlikeness that is possible through marriage. Just as it is ludicrous to imagine God the Father, Jesus, and the Holy Spirit bickering about who is most important, it is equally foolish for husband and wife to spend a lot of time negotiating for power and responsibility within a marriage. If two have genuinely become one, those problems don't come up.

We're back to the three-legged race. It's important to learn to move in conjunction with, and not in opposition to, one's spouse. Under Old Testament law, newly-married men were excused from military service and other "special responsibilities" for a year. The new groom was expected to spend that year "bringing happiness to the wife he has married" (Deuteronomy 24:5). We don't always get a yearlong honeymoon these days—most of us couldn't stand that much "happiness." Yet we all could probably devote more time to learning to interact with our husbands and wives more gracefully.

The Spiritual Aspect

God didn't swoop out of the darkness, create the world, plant a couple of people and a garden full of animals, and then flit off to create even bigger galaxies and universes. Or if He did, at least He didn't desert His people in our world. We read that He would seek out Adam and Eve in the cool of the evening (Genesis 3:8). Sadly, we discover this fact after reading of how Adam and Eve disobeyed God and were hiding from Him. The tragedy of the fall of humanity is that we severed the close interpersonal connection God had established.

Yet to the extent that we are able, our marriages should include God as much as possible. An often-asked question is why God even had a forbidden tree in the paradise of Eden. Surely He could have removed it and avoided any problems for Adam and Eve—or us, for that matter.

But if God had eliminated the forbidden tree in the Garden of Eden, Adam and Eve would have been denied the option of loving Him because they *chose* to do so. Those of us who are married should be able to see the problem with this. When we truly love someone, we want the person to love us in return. But we want his or her love to be motivated by desire and not because the person has no other choice.

We think it strange to read of a husband who locks his beautiful wife away in a remote tower. Ancient kings would simply castrate all the other males who came into contact with their queens. But God never resorts to tactics of force or manipulation to convince us to love Him. He did all He could do for Adam and Eve. He gave them an ideal setting, a perfect human relationship, and a relationship with Him on top of everything else. Yet He didn't demand that they love Him—not even in a subtle way by taking away all their other options. All they had to do to prove their love for Him was to stay away from the forbidden fruit.

In contemporary marriage, we still face similar situations. You probably know couples who seemed to have a storybook life together, but one of the partners decided to have an affair. So few things are forbidden in marriage, yet droves of people continue to go out of their way to seek out "forbidden fruit."

Hosea and Gomer (Hosea 1-3)

The Old Testament prophet Hosea had a repeatedly unfaithful wife. Yet he was willing to forgive and redeem her, providing a graphic depiction of God's merciful love for His people, who have often rejected Him to pursue others.

DO'S AND DON'TS

Give honor to marriage, and remain faithful to one another in marriage. God will surely judge people who are immoral and those who commit adultery. (Hebrews 13:4)

Like Adam and Eve, our problems frequently begin when we leave God out of our marriages. Someone has compared Christian marriage to a triangle with God at the apex and each spouse on the two lower corners. If husband and wife simply try to grow closer to one another, they don't necessarily get any closer to God. But if both spouses make a commitment to continue to get closer to God, they can't help but draw closer and closer to each other.

Marriage was designed with a spiritual element in mind. The fact that so few contemporary marriages include this vital element may partially explain the divorce statistics. Some couples put more time, effort, and energy into their weddings than they do their marriages.

It is the ongoing, consoling presence of God in a marriage that prevents a lot of "issues" that trouble other couples. Until they fell out of God's favor, Adam and Eve were buck naked and un-ashamed. But as soon as they sinned, they saw things in a different (though not a better) light.

Think of how many couples you know where sin continues to create feelings of shame, guilt, depression, and other problems that would have been avoided easily if the people had only gone God's way instead of their own. We would be naïve to think we could avoid all such problems. But the more couples determine to include God in their marriage relationship, and the sooner they return to Him after making mistakes, the healthier the marriage will be—both relationally and spiritually.

Just Marred

Although God's model of marriage seems clear and rather self-explanatory, one look at our society reveals how we've distorted and twisted it to meet our own wants and wishes. As the church was being formed in the first century, Paul provided some specific guidelines to avoid marring our marriages. One of his most focused passages on marriage is 1 Corinthians 7. Let's look at some of the principles he spells out for us.

- Marriage is not the only, or even the preferable, Christian lifestyle. Paul was sold on the benefits of independence and celibacy and recommended the single life highly to anyone willing to pursue it (vv. 1, 7-8). Marriage will certainly bring problems you wouldn't otherwise have (vv. 25-28).
- Yet due to the powerful influence of sexual urges, marriage is a far better alternative than lust and/or sexual immorality (vv. 2, 9).
- Marriage partners shouldn't deprive one another of sex unless it is a mutual arrangement for a specific period of time (vv. 3-6).
- Marriage is intended to be a lifetime commitment. The two exceptions Scripture provides to justify divorce are when the other partner commits adultery (Matthew 19:3-9) or when a nonbeliever deserts a Christian spouse (1 Corinthians 7:15).
- Although a Christian married to a nonbeliever is not an ideal situation (2 Corinthians 6:14), a persevering Christian in such a relationship can exert a positive, godly influence on the other spouse and their children (1 Corinthians 7:12-16).
- As important as marriage is, it isn't the most important thing in life. Married people have shared interests and more responsibilities than most single people, yet they need to remain devoted to God's work to the extent that they are able (vv. 29-40).

WELL SAID!

Seldom, or perhaps never, does a marriage develop into an individual relationship smoothly and without crises; there is no coming to consciousness without pain. —C. G. Jung

DO'S AND DON'TS

"For I hate divorce!" says the Lord, the God of Israel. "It is as cruel as putting on a victim's bloodstained coat," says the Lord Almighty. "So guard yourself; always remain loyal to your wife." (Malachi 2:16)

Paul may seem to have some rather standoffish attitudes about marriage, but only because his own heart was so fully "married" to the work he was doing for God. We saw in chapter 5 that some of the ascetics refused to be married and saw it as some kind of spiritual shortcoming. But even as an advocate of the single life, Paul would have nothing to do with such extreme thinking.

In a letter to Timothy, Paul addressed that very attitude: "[Certain] teachers are hypocrites and liars. They pretend to be religious, but their consciences are dead. They will say it is wrong to be married and wrong to eat certain foods. But . . . since everything God created is good, we should not reject any of it. We may receive it gladly, with thankful hearts" (1 Timothy 4:2-4).

Timothy (2 Timothy 1:3-7)

Timothy is a good example of how just one Christian parent can exert a positive influence in the home. His mother and grandmother were Jewish believers in Jesus; his father was a Gentile and not mentioned as being a believer. Yet Paul was impressed with Timothy's faith and helped train the young man for the ministry.

Priscilla and Aquila (Acts 18:1-3; Romans 16:3-4)

The marriage team of Priscilla and Aquila is a shining example of how to combine marriage and ministry. They worked together both to provide income for themselves and Paul, and they also assisted Paul in his work for God. They show us life doesn't have to come down to either marriage *or* ministry. When husband and wife are working toward the same goal, life can be a rewarding interweaving of the two.

Being married and living for God is good. Being single and living for God is good. But being married and not living for God is a serious spiritual shortcoming. Marriage is supposed to be the most intimate of human relationships. It's the metaphor God uses to describe His own relationship with those who believe in Him. He is the bridegroom; the church is the bride (Revelation 19:7-8).

When our marital relationship doesn't reflect the unity and love God desires for us, it doesn't reflect well on our spiritual commitment to God either. No matter what kind of example we set at church, work, or elsewhere, if our marriages are weak, so will be our testimonies for God.

And even when we do everything right and marriage is as good as it can be here and now, we're told to expect even better things in the afterlife.

Did You Hear the One about the Woman with Seven Husbands?

The topic of marriage came up in one of Jesus' public debates with the Jewish religious leaders. A group of Sadducees, who didn't believe in resurrection, had a marriage trivia question for Jesus. In the Mosaic law, when a woman's husband died before providing her with children, it was customary for the man's brother to marry the wife and attempt to have a child with her. The Sadducees suggested that, in theory, a family with seven brothers could all marry the same woman as they died one by one and passed the responsibility for the woman on to the next of kin (Matthew 22:23-33). If that happened, the Sadducees wanted to know, and if they all were resurrected, then whose wife would the woman be in the afterlife?

This group of religious leaders were obviously trying to ridicule the likelihood of resurrection, but Jesus ridiculed their shortsightedness in reply. And in doing so, He provided us with additional insight into marriage.

Jesus clearly hinted that eternity with God is not simply a continuation of earthly life. Marriage is an earthly relationship, not an eternal one. After being resurrected, believers will live eternally, like the angels. There will be no further need either to procreate to sustain life or to limit one's devotion to a single person. The intimacy we learn to feel for spouses will be applied to everyone in attendance in the afterlife. We will at last be able to experience the fullness and perfection of God's love. As much as marriage might mean to someone now, the love and joy of heaven will quickly eclipse it.

Do You Take This Marriage for Better? Or for Worse?

You may be reading this while seated next to your fourth husband or wife. Or perhaps you're miserable in a relationship that is a marriage in name only. Is it too late to get serious about correcting previous problems and starting fresh and new?

As long as we have breath, it's never too late to commit to finding and doing God's will. It's probably not the best thing in the world that there are three ex-spouses out there somewhere. But when we come to God for forgiveness, grace, and mercy, He won't hold the mistakes of our past over our head like the sword of Damocles.

Of course, if you're sitting there with your three current wives or the other members of your Tuesday/Thursday Alternative Lifestyle Club, you're likely to need to make some permanent changes in your lifestyle and begin to take marriage (and God) seriously. Only then is it possible to discover fullness in marriage along with the intimacy, vulnerability, and other benefits that are possible.

FOR EXAMPLE . . .

The Woman at the Well (John 4:1-42)

Jesus had a most interesting conversation with a woman who had been through five husbands and was living with yet another man who wasn't her husband. Jesus took her seriously, and she took Him seriously in return. As a result, salvation came to the woman and many others in her village. Anytime we're willing to turn to God, He is willing to forgive the sins of our past and allow us to begin a healing process.

ONE SMALL STEP

Spend a few minutes considering possibilities for your life you might not have thought about before. For example, if you're single, have you assumed you would get married some day? If so, give some thought to the opportunities available if you were to remain single. If you're married, is your marriage everything you want it to be? If not, consider what changes you would like to see. And in either case, married or single, take some time to think about how you might bring about the changes you desire for your life.

Questions to Ponder and/or Discuss

1. How does your concept of marriage now vary from when you were a child? A teenager? A newlywed? Which of your perceptions seems most in line with God's original blueprint for marriage?

2. If you are currently married, look at the triangle below. If the corners are where you started on your wedding day, how far would you say you have progressed in drawing closer to one another and/or God? Place an M (for "Me") to indicate where you feel you are right now, and use an S ("Spouse") to mark his or her progress, if any.

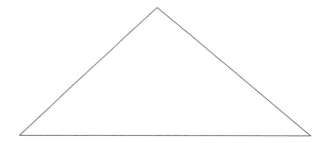

3. Based on the biblical ideals in this chapter, what are some things you could do to strengthen your marriage? Consider both short-term and long-term commitments for improvement.

Short-Term Goals   Long-Term Goals

CHAPTER ELEVEN

"A NOSE RING IS OK, BUT NO SON OF MINE IS GOING TO WEAR AN EARRING."

Kid Stuff

PARENTS AND CHILDREN

As Jane Seeker's pregnancy progressed, she and George found themselves frequently sitting on their back deck watching Fred and Wilma DiCiple interact with their kids. Today they could hear as well as see what was going on. Fred and Joshua were talking at a level just below shouting, and it was clear from their body language that today's lesson would be one in conflict management.

"Dad, I've asked you a million times to stop calling me Joshua. I want to be called 'Z-Roy,' or just 'Z' for short."

Fred looked exasperated. "For heaven's sake, Joshua, why do you want to be called 'Z-Roy'?"

"Where have you been, Dad? 'The Clone Warriors of Roy' is the coolest comic book and video game ever. This fall they're making a movie based on it."

"Well, I used to read Spider-Man comics, but I never asked my parents to start calling me Spidey."

Josh scowled. "Besides, Dad, 'Josh' is such a dorky name. I want something more . . . respectable."

Fred took a deep breath. "Son, do you know why your mom and I gave you that 'dorky' name?"

SOME THINGS YOU'LL DISCOVER IN THIS CHAPTER

1. A look at parenting problems almost as old as time itself

2. God's parenting style as a model for us

3. Qualities parents need to model for their children

"No."

"We spent six months discussing it, off and on, and went through half a dozen name books and thousands of names. We were getting pressure from family members to name you 'Manfred Junior' after me, 'Roscoe' after your mom's father, 'Brady' after my dad, and all sorts of other names. But you don't know why we chose Joshua?"

"Was it after the biblical guy?"

"Not really, although few people would have considered Joshua 'dorky' after Jericho and all his other military victories. It's because 'Joshua' meant savior, and it was the Hebrew version of the Greek name 'Jesus.' You were our first child, and we wanted you to have the most special name we could think of. Yet we didn't think you'd want to go through life with the name Jesus DiCiple."

Joshua laughed for the first time. Fred continued, "And we didn't think the Hispanic pronunciation of "Hey, Zeus" would work for you. So we gave you a name that meant the same but wouldn't cause the other kids to make fun of you. Now do you understand my bewilderment when you want to be publicly addressed as 'Z-Roy'?"

Josh was getting reasonably excited for a 14-year-old. "So 'Joshua' is actually kind of a code name?"

"In comic book terms, it's kind of like calling you 'Clark Kent,' when you, your Mom, and I secretly know you're actually pretty super."

"I guess I can live with that. I just never knew you put any thought into naming me. Hey, did you go through the same process with Mary?"

Fred made a face and asked, "What do you think?"

As Josh ran back inside, George and Jane Seeker wondered how many of the hundreds of their own parent/child confrontations that would arise in the years to come would be handled as well.

Home Is Where the Heat Is

It is sometimes pointed out that before you can take a new car out on the highway, you have to get a license that proves you know what you're doing. Not only do you have to pass a written exam to show that you've read the manual and know the rules of the road, but you also have to take a driver's test to indicate that you know how to handle the automobile. Yet any fool can take a child home from the hospital with neither knowledge nor experience of how to care for the child or ensure his or her ongoing physical, emotional, and spiritual growth.

Some conscientious couples faithfully prepare to the extent that they are able, by reading books, going to classes, watching videos, and talking to other parents who have already been through the ecstatic trauma of giving birth. Other couples seem more resigned to "faking it" as they go along. How hard can it be?

Proper care and raising of a child must be harder than many people expect. If you take a close look at many of the stories in the Bible, you'll discover that some of the biblical "heroes" with the greatest faith and best reputations were lousy parents.

Of course, in some situations, perhaps the parents had done all they could, yet the child(ren) rebelled anyway. Certainly that's the case in Jesus' parable of the Prodigal Son, where the father represents God Himself. Yet all too often, parents mentioned in Scripture seem to be too busy doing God's work while their children are being overlooked.

So by the time the first-century church was being formed, a prerequisite for leadership included not only spiritual qualities, not only monogamy (as we noted in the previous chapter), but also an emphasis on proper child rearing:

> An elder must be a man whose life cannot be spoken against. . . . He must manage his own family well, with children who respect and obey him. For if a man cannot manage his own household, how can he take care of God's church? (1 Timothy 3:2, 4-5)

> An elder must be well thought of for his good life. He must be faithful to his wife, and his children must be believers who are not wild or rebellious. (Titus 1:6)

ONE SMALL STEP

Take a little quiz to see how much you know about the child-rearing skills of some of the better known Old Testament fathers. Match the following biblical dads with their appropriate home/family situations.

ABRAHAM
(Genesis 21:8-21)

One of his sons (the first son ever that we know of) killed his younger brother.

ADAM
(Genesis 4:1-8)

He allowed jealousy between his twin boys to get out of hand to the point of death threats between them.

DAVID
(2 Samuel 13—16)

His negligence with regard to circumcising his son almost led to his untimely death.

ELI
(1 Samuel 2:12-36)

His sons should have followed him as judges, but their dishonesty prompted the Israelites to demand a king instead.

ISAAC
(Genesis 27:41-45)

While raising someone else's son, his own two crooked sons were so rotten that God took it as a personal insult.

JACOB
(Genesis 37)

One of his sons raped one of his daughters. Another son divided and almost brought down an entire nation.

JUDAH
(Genesis 38)

He played favorites among his 13 kids, provoking jealousy, bickering, and worse.

MOSES
(Exodus 4:21-26)

One son discovered him drunk and naked and was quick to broadcast the news, resulting in a curse.

NOAH
(Genesis 9:20-25)

His son's refusal to take good advice split an empire for good.

SAMUEL
(1 Samuel 8:1-9)

This dad had two sons so bad that God killed them. Later his daughter-in-law seduced him and became pregnant by him.

SOLOMON
(1 Kings 12:1-19)

This father allowed a jealous wife to deal with family turmoil, nearly causing a son to die in the wilderness.

DO'S AND DON'TS

Teach your children to choose the right path, and when they are older, they will remain upon it. (Proverbs 22:6)

Yet in spite of these biblical injunctions, the children of preachers and church leaders are still stereotyped as leaning toward out-of-control lifestyles. Perhaps there is some truth to the stereotype. Or maybe it's because we tend to hear whenever a famous pastor's kid goes off the deep end, while we never hear about all the good examples.

We won't attempt in this chapter to go into the intricacies of child rearing. To spank, or not to spank? Do you pick up a crying baby or let him cry it out? Sleep together in a family bed, or let every family member fend for himself/herself? These are all hotly-debated issues, and you can find numerous resources either endorsing or decrying these techniques.

The approach we want to take is to remember that God is a parent. In fact, Scripture refers to Him in both paternal (Isaiah 9:6; Matthew 6:9) and maternal (Isaiah 66:12-13) terms. So as a perfect being, He is also a perfect parent. If we take a look at how God provides for His children, we're likely to discover how to become better parents ourselves.

The Love Package

John couldn't be any clearer in his first letter: "God is love" (1 John 4:16). And if we pair this verse with Paul's comments in 1 Corinthians 13, we should see the qualities associated with love: patience, kindness, forgiveness, steadfastness, faithfulness, hope, endurance, and more. When God "so loved" the world, all these characteristics were wrapped in that definition of love.

When a parent tells a child, "I love you," it should mean something. According to Scripture, it should mean:

- "No matter what you do wrong, I'm here for you."
- "I will never say, 'I told you so.'"
- "Just because you made a mistake doesn't mean I like your sister more."
- "If you want to tell me something, even if it's hard, it's okay."

We tend to toss the word *love* around in regard to cars, weather, and today's choice of soda pop. And sometimes when we toss it toward our children, that's about as serious as they take it. Like God, we need to back up our verbal affirmations of love with solid examples of patience, forgiveness, mercy, grace, and oh so much more.

In Psalm 103, David connected God's love with several other traits:

> The Lord gives righteousness and justice to all who are treated unfairly. He revealed his character to Moses and his deeds to the people of Israel. The Lord is merciful and gracious; he is slow to get angry and full of unfailing love. He will not constantly accuse us, nor remain angry forever. He has not punished us for all our sins, nor does he deal with us as we deserve. For his unfailing love toward those who fear him is as great as the height of the heavens above the earth. He has removed our rebellious acts as far away from us as the east is from the west. The Lord is like a father to his children, tender and compassionate to those who fear him. (Psalm 103:6-13)

Discipline

In God's model of parenting, love is even the motivation for discipline. God doesn't discipline as a result of frustration, anger, proof of His authority, or any other imperfect motive. He wants only what is best for us and is willing to discipline us in order to spare us from straying away from Him and into something much worse.

Perhaps you've heard parents boldly proclaim a "biblical" parenting philosophy of "Spare the rod and spoil the child" based on traditional translations of verses such as Proverbs 22:15, 23:13, 29:15, and other passages. (Contemporary translations may substitute "discipline" or "spanking" for the use of a rod.) Many parents jump to the conclusion that the rod of correction is a big paddle to inflict the threat of (if not literal) pain and fear among their children. Yet in the familiar 23rd Psalm, David writes of God's rod and

WELL SAID!

Children need models rather than critics.
—*Joseph Joubert*

ONE SMALL STEP

The next time you hear yourself telling a child "I love you," pause for just a moment to consider what that really means. Try to think of at least three new ways to back up your verbal affirmation of love.

147

DO'S AND DON'TS

Be very careful never to forget what you have seen the Lord do for you. Do not let these things escape from your mind as long as you live! And be sure to pass them on to your children and grandchildren. (Deuteronomy 4:9)

staff being a source of comfort and protection. Does that sound like a big whacking stick?

If a sheep started off down the wrong fork in the path or began to stray toward a cliff, the shepherd didn't immediately grab his rod and beat the lanolin out of it. No! Usually all it took was a tap on the side to steer it in the right direction. Parents who do more whacking than steering are likely to create more problems than they solve. And yes, some animals and children are more stubborn than others and may need additional methods of discipline. But the involvement of a parent in steering the child along God's narrow path is much more effective than simply waiting for the child to do something wrong and immediately administering punishment.

The author of Hebrews makes a direct connection between God's love for His children and His discipline of them. He begins with a quote from Proverbs 3:11-12 and then continues with further explanation:

> My child, don't ignore it when the Lord disciplines you, and don't be discouraged when he corrects you. For the Lord disciplines those he loves, and he punishes those he accepts as his children.
>
> As you endure this divine discipline, remember that God is treating you as his own children. Whoever heard of a child who was never disciplined? If God doesn't discipline you as he does all of his children, it means that you are illegitimate and are not really his children after all. Since we respect our earthly fathers who disciplined us, should we not all the more cheerfully submit to the discipline of our heavenly Father and live forever?
>
> For our earthly fathers disciplined us for a few years, doing the best they knew how. But God's discipline is always right and good for us because it means we will share in his holiness. No discipline is enjoyable while it is happening—it is painful! But afterward there will be a quiet harvest of right living for those who are trained in this way. (Hebrews 12:5-11)

God loves us enough to discipline us in appropriate ways and ensure we don't lose track of what is right and good. Loving parents will do the same for their children.

Power = Protection

When we think of how God is omnipotent—all-powerful—we may tend to become a bit fearful. And to a point, fear of God is a perfectly reasonable and expected response. Yet we need to connect His omnipotence with His love for us. When we realize that God is going to use His incredible strength *for* us instead of against us, it's quite a comforting thought.

Good parents make their children feel safe and protected. However, depending on the age and maturity of the child, this can be done in a number of ways. If a loudly barking dog approaches, a small child might need to be picked up. A slightly older child might stand firm if the parent remains between the dog and the child. And if the parents have provided the child with enough courage and trust, the child might even reach out to pet the dog if the parents say it's okay.

Just because God is bigger and stronger than we are doesn't mean He will fight all our fights for us. He'll be there for us certainly, but sometimes we have to do the fighting to show that we really do trust Him to come through.

The plot for a classic episode of *The Andy Griffith Show* had a neighborhood bully stealing Opie's milk money every day. Fed up at last, Opie sought his pa's advice. Andy told him we sometimes have to take a stand and fight for what's rightfully ours. Andy was the sheriff and could have dealt with the problem from a base of power and authority. But instead we see the great concern in his eyes as he allows his beloved son to go fight his own battle. Opie emerged joyful and triumphant and never again had to yield his milk money. He received a black eye as a result, yet it was only a badge of victory to remind him of the progress he had made toward freedom.

All this is to say that sometimes God lets us know He's there for us but leaves us to deal with a particular problem. An *overly*

FOR EXAMPLE . . .

Moses' Parents (Exodus 1-2)

Moses was born under a death sentence. But rather than complying with Pharaoh's edict to put male children to death, Moses' parents trusted God and defied it. They placed their baby in a basket and floated it down the Nile River, monitored by Moses' big sister, where it was found by one of Pharaoh's daughters. Moses was officially adopted—as a "prince of Egypt," no less—and the rest is history. Moses' parents are commended for their faith in Hebrews 11:23 and are wonderful models for today's parents of the importance of protecting children.

DO'S AND DON'TS

Sing praises to God and to his name! Sing loud praises to him who rides the clouds. His name is the Lord—rejoice in his presence! Father to the fatherless, defender of widows—this is God, whose dwelling is holy. God places the lonely in families; he sets the prisoners free and gives them joy. (Psalm 68:4-6)

149

FOR EXAMPLE . . .
David and Goliath (1 Samuel 17)

David had a lot to say about the protection of God, but then, he should have. Let's not forget that he was the "baby" of his family who stood before the nine-feet-plus giant Goliath with full confidence that God would see him through his battle.

FOR EXAMPLE . . .
Hannah (1 Samuel 1; 2:18-21)

Childless and mocked by her husband's other wife, Hannah never lost hope. Rather than resorting to surrogates or the desperate means used by other Old Testament women, Hannah prayed to God. When God gave her a child, she gave him back to God to serve in the tabernacle. Her child was Samuel, who became a spiritual leader for all Israel. And God also gave Hannah three sons and two daughters. When we throw in a little faith, hope can work wonders.

protective parent is not doing his or her child any favors. Wise parents know when to step in and when to lay off. The child simply needs to know that when the going gets *too* rough, he or she can always rely on parental power to come through.

Heavy-duty Hope

As we experience God's protection in our life, we can eventually build up reasonable levels of hope for the future. Our world can be bleak if we only focus on the terror, the trauma, the tensions, and the terrible things. Sitting down to view the evening news highlights may be enough to dispel any hope you've accumulated for the day. And our children don't even have the emotional filters we have developed. They see many of the same things and are not nearly as able to cope as the adults in the room. Good parents will work to instill hope in the lives of their children. But it won't be easy.

Establishing hope, whether for oneself or one's children, requires work and dedication. Hope begins like a soufflé, which a master chef creates through a just-right recipe and hours of preparation, yet which can collapse before you know it. But genuine hope eventually grows strong.

The Bible provides a recipe for hope. It is the culmination of a series of events, not all of which are likely to be on your wish list: "We also rejoice in our sufferings, because we know that suffering produces perseverance; perseverance, character; and character, hope. And hope does not disappoint us, because God has poured out his love into our hearts by the Holy Spirit, whom he has given us" (Romans 5:3-5, NIV).

God can instill us with a heavy-duty hope that is far stronger than the "wishes and dreams" that many people think of when they hear the word *hope*. But in order to secure that kind of hope for ourselves, the process begins with suffering. As we learn to cope with suffering, we develop perseverance. As we learn to whine less and trust more, we develop character. And out of that godly character arises hope—strong, genuine, firm hope.

Armed with such hope, we can watch the evening news, face the death of a loved one, hear the insults of coworkers or fellow third-graders, and keep going. This is the kind of hope good parents attempt to instill in their children. Such hope keeps our eyes upward toward God, rather than on the crummy things of life. And whether adult or child, this kind of hope "does not disappoint us."

Trust

When we pray, we know God hears us. When we read Scripture, we trust that it's God's Word provided for our benefit. God doesn't change. He never has a bad hair day or unexplainable mood swings. We learn to count on His faithfulness. We know we can trust Him, and we take great comfort in such knowledge.

The big question is, *To what extent are we providing a similar level of faithfulness to our kids?* Do they trust us to be consistent sources of companionship, advice, and most of all, forgiveness when they need it?

Or in contrast, do we attempt to maintain the upper hand by messing with their minds? Do we try to keep them guessing as to our moods and attitudes? It doesn't take long to discover that as long as our kids are still young enough, parenthood can be a tremendous power trip. Dad is king, Mom is queen, and the motto of the land is "Because I said so!"

We need to recognize how important it is to us as adults that God is always accessible and trustworthy. Then we need to emulate those same traits for our children. If our kids get a little pesky at times when they want something, perhaps we need to review our own prayer patterns. God encourages persistence and perseverance, so we shouldn't condemn it in our children. Jesus touched on this point in His Sermon on the Mount:

> Keep on asking, and you will be given what you ask for. Keep on looking, and you will find. Keep on knocking, and the door will be opened. For everyone who asks, receives. Everyone who seeks, finds. And the door is opened to

WELL SAID!

"Totally without hope one cannot live." To live without hope is to cease to live. Hell is hopelessness. It is no accident that above the entrance to Dante's hell is the inscription: "Leave behind all hope, you who enter here."
—*Fyodor Dostoyevsky*

151

WELL SAID!

An infinite God can give all of Himself to each of His children. He does not distribute Himself that each may have a part, but to each one He gives all of Himself as fully as if there were no others.
—*A. W. Tozer*

everyone who knocks. You parents—if your children ask for a loaf of bread, do you give them a stone instead? Or if they ask for a fish, do you give them a snake? Of course not! If you sinful people know how to give good gifts to your children, how much more will your heavenly Father give good gifts to those who ask him." (Matthew 7:7-11)

The Source of Perfection

And just in case we miss anything that God the Father provides for His children, James tosses in the catchall category: "Whatever is good and perfect comes to us from God above, who created all heaven's lights. Unlike them, he never changes or casts shifting shadows. In his goodness he chose to make us his own children by giving us his true word. And we, out of all creation, became his choice possession" (James 1:17-18).

God is the source of everything good and perfect for us. Can our children say the same about us? Or do they go other places attempting to meet their needs? This is why the power trip of parenthood isn't such a good idea. As soon as the child gets old enough to seek other options elsewhere, there is little reason not to do so. But if our children discover that no one in the world cares for them nearly as much as their parents, they aren't likely to stray too far away or stay away too long.

Childlike vs. Childish

As we have already said, God is the perfect parent. And while we'll never be able to make the same claim, perhaps we can move closer to perfection than where we are right now. The pressures of parenthood are constant and demanding. Maybe you never had a decent model of parenting from which to learn. The job is that much harder for you.

The irony is that we become better parents as we become more childlike. At one point the disciples questioned Jesus about who

would be greatest in the Kingdom of Heaven. Jesus summoned a small child who was standing nearby and told them:

> I assure you, unless you turn from your sins and become as little children, you will never get into the Kingdom of Heaven. Therefore, anyone who becomes as humble as this little child is the greatest in the Kingdom of Heaven. And anyone who welcomes a little child like this on my behalf is welcoming me. But if anyone causes one of these little ones who trusts in me to lose faith, it would be better for that person to be thrown into the sea with a large millstone tied around the neck. (Matthew 18:1-6)

Yet we must be careful not to confuse childlikeness with childishness. Paul warns of the latter: "When I was a child, I spoke and thought and reasoned as a child does. But when I grew up, I put away childish things" (1 Corinthians 13:11). So it's a bit tricky in the Christian life to hold on to the best childlike traits—humility, innocence, acceptance of others, etc.—without remaining childishly petty, argumentative, and self-absorbed.

The better we are at remaining childlike, the more effective we will become in relating to our children. God has entrusted you to raise and train your child to the best of your ability, yet in another sense you're on an absolutely equal status with your child in that you are both God's children. Therefore, it's imperative to try to relate to your child exactly as God would.

So you see, bringing up a child is a breeze! All we have to do is provide unlimited, unconditional love. Be forgiving. Know just when to step in for protection and when to butt out. Provide discipline when needed and show mercy when appropriate.

But those of us in the real world realize it's impossible to be all things to all our children at all times. We know what to do, yet though we try our hardest, we still say and do things to our kids we wish we hadn't said and done. We don't do for them what we wish we *could* do. During such times we need to remember our own heavenly Parent who is eager to supply us with help, with hope, and

FOR EXAMPLE . . .

Jesus and the Children
(Matthew 19:13-15)

The disciples were frequently slow to catch on to what Jesus was saying. Not long after He had tried to teach them about the value of a small child in God's eyes, they were attempting to shoo away some kids who had been brought to receive Jesus' blessing. Jesus again reminded them, "Let the children come to me. Don't stop them! For the Kingdom of Heaven belongs to such as these."

DO'S AND DON'TS

So you should not be like cowering, fearful slaves. You should behave instead like God's very own children, adopted into his family—calling him "Father, dear Father." For his Holy Spirit speaks to us deep in our hearts and tells us that we are God's children. And since we are his children, we will share his treasures—for everything God gives to his Son, Christ, is ours, too. But if we are to share his glory, we must also share his suffering. (Romans 8:15-17)

ONE SMALL STEP

Let's not forget that we are not only God's children but also children of human parents. If your parents are still living, what can you do this week to let them know you love them, heal an old hurt, or remind them of a favorite memory? The Christian life demands that we treat our parents as well as our children with respect and honor.

with anything else we need. He can provide us with more than enough to pass along to our own children.

Questions to Ponder and/or Discuss

1. Our family might be best compared to:

- Chickens in a coop—All the youngsters are primarily dependent on Mom.
- A pack of wolves—Independent individuals who get together occasionally to howl.
- Hyenas—We spend a lot of time laughing.
- Lemmings—We're cute but somewhat self-destructive.
- Geese—We travel a lot and have our own unique formation.
- Mountain goats—Come watch us butt heads sometime.
- Other: _____

2. Think back to your growing-up years. What do you recall, good or bad, about how well your parent(s) provided each of the following characteristics:

	GOOD MEMORIES	NOT-SO-GOOD MEMORIES
Love		
Discipline		
Protection		
Hope		
Trust		
Other		

3. Now think of your current family. (If you're not a parent, skip this exercise. If your children are already grown, use this activity as a review.) In each of the following categories, what do you think you are doing right and wrong? You might want to think through the process for each of your children as individuals—not collectively.

	THINGS I'M DOING RIGHT	NEEDS IMPROVEMENT
Love		
Discipline		
Protection		
Hope		
Trust		
Other		

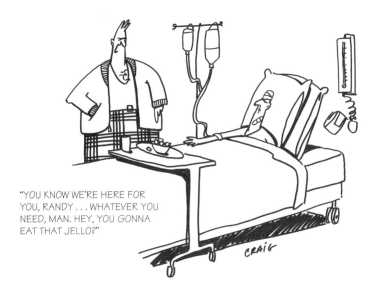

"YOU KNOW WE'RE HERE FOR YOU, RANDY . . . WHATEVER YOU NEED, MAN. HEY, YOU GONNA EAT THAT JELLO?"

CRAIG

I'll Be There for You

FRIENDS

The DiCiples and Seekers were together again, this time at the Seekers' home. The living room looked quite different now than it did the first time the DiCiples had visited. By now, Jane's skills as a decorator were evident. She had secured just the right area rugs, artwork, plants, and accessories, and she had brought them all together in a beautiful arrangement.

And while Wilma was quick to notice and comment on all the improvements that had been made, their conversations no longer depended on small talk. As their times together had become more frequent, they were also becoming more meaningful. Earlier discussions had centered around sports teams and weather, but now Jane was sharing some of her deepest fears and joys in connection with her impending motherhood. Wilma was opening up about the pain of her brother, who had recently endured a painful divorce. And Fred and George had an ongoing conversation about spirituality and Christianity.

George had recently rededicated himself to God and had begun to attend Bible studies with regularity. Fred was amazed at the depth

SOME THINGS YOU'LL DISCOVER IN THIS CHAPTER

1. The importance of perceiving God as a friend

2. Guidelines for better friendships

3. Why so few friendships mature to deep and rich levels

157

ONE SMALL STEP

This chapter focuses on friendship. Before reading it, stop long enough to rate your current friendships. How many genuine friends do you have (as opposed to casual acquaintances, coworkers, etc.) ? Rate each relationship on a scale of 1 (weakest) to 10 (strongest). Then as you go through the chapter, try to apply ideas and suggestions to bring up your average.

of insight in George's questions. He found himself surprised at how comfortable the conversation was when the other person initiated it. Maybe Wilma had been onto something when she had urged him to be patient and just be himself. To be honest, responding to George's questions was keeping Fred on his toes. It had been much easier to simply present facts from an outline, but this genuine conversation thing seemed much more effective.

In fact, Fred was already feeling closer to George than to many of the guys at church that he considered his best friends. Even with the short time they had known each other, the age difference, and the gap in their level of spiritual knowledge and maturity, the two were becoming fast friends.

Their bond was so obvious that it had become a favorite topic of discussion for Wilma and Jane, who were also getting very close. The wives were regularly amazed at the changes taking place in their husbands. They, more than anyone, realized how different Fred and George were. Yet the wonderful mystery of Christian fellowship had settled over them all, and they couldn't have been more pleased.

I'm Not a Real Friend, but I Play One on TV

Next to family, friends are perhaps the strongest influences on our lives for good or for bad. And friends may have surpassed family by now, at least if prime-time television is an indicator. Many of the greatest shows of the past seemed to focus around families: *Father Knows Best, Leave It to Beaver, I Love Lucy, The Dick Van Dyke Show, All in the Family, The Cosby Show*, etc. Friends played essential roles in these shows yet were usually secondary to the family interaction.

More recently, however, the trend has seemed to swing toward the importance of friends. Frequently family members are introduced only as celebrity walk-on ratings boosters rather than crucial elements of the story. We've seen friends in big cities *(Friends, Seinfeld)* and in stranger places *(M*A*S*H, Northern Exposure)*. We've seen friends at work *(The Mary Tyler Moore Show)* and friends at home

(The Odd Couple). We've seen single friends *(Beverly Hills 90210)* and married friends *(Mad about You, King of Queens),* old friends *(Golden Girls)* and young friends *(The Wonder Years).*

Sometimes Hollywood almost captures the deeper intricacies of friendship, but more frequently we see thin plot lines to set up jokes and gags. In reality, much more is expected of friends than a smart mouth or companionship on a wacky road trip. The latest trend in "reality" programming seems to be to thrust strangers together and see how truly bad they are at becoming friends *(The Real World, Survivor, Big Brother,* etc.).

So let's take a look at friendship and its place in the Christian life. We seem to have learned all we can from the media. But if that's all we're doing for those who consider us to be their friends, we still have a long way to go.

WELL SAID!

Associate with men of good quality, if you esteem your own reputation; for it is better to be alone than in bad company.
—*George Washington*

A Friend in High Places

There's a world of difference between being friendly and being a friend. We all tend to smile and wave at our neighbors (most of them, at least). We occasionally let other drivers into our lane. We are sometimes courteous and conversational with the checkout clerks at the grocery. But what if the clerk asked you to go home with her to attend an intervention for her alcoholic father? What if the driver in the next lane asked for a loan? What if your neighbor asked you to sign a petition to pave over Yosemite National Park in order to provide additional parking in California? Suddenly, we find ourselves not as friendly or accommodating.

We frequently tend to trivialize friendship, and we may take some of our true friends for granted. But if the friendship is genuine, we don't mind making loans, supporting one another during emotional crises, and tolerating strange quirks—even if we can't always go along with them. If he's a true friend, you can tell him he's crazy to want to pave Yosemite. If she's a more casual acquaintance, we tend to tiptoe more carefully around her oddball ideas and feelings.

It's a well-accepted biblical principle that God's love is uncondi-tional and that He does not show favoritism when it comes to

WELL SAID!

The insight of a true friend is more useful than the goodwill of others: therefore gain [friends] by choice, not by chance.
—*Baltasar Gracian*

ONE SMALL STEP

Christians are considered "friends of God." If you are a believer, spend some time thinking about exactly what that means. Determine how this bit of information should influence your spiritual growth.

people. Yet in a few instances, people are singled out as being friends of God. For example:

> Inside the Tent of Meeting, the Lord would speak to Moses face to face, as a man speaks to his friend. (Exodus 33:11)

> And so it happened just as the Scriptures say: "Abraham believed God, so God declared him to be righteous." He was even called "the friend of God." (James 2:23)

We may tend to think that friendships just happen and might not even give them any thought. Yet from these Scriptures, it appears that true friendship is an earned privilege. Therefore, making friends may be more important than we realize.

Jesus made it clear that He welcomes our friendship. It was one of the last things He promised His disciples:

> I command you to love each other in the same way that I love you. And here is how to measure it—the greatest love is shown when people lay down their lives for their friends. You are my friends if you obey me. I no longer call you servants, because a master doesn't confide in his servants. Now you are my friends, since I have told you everything that the Father told me. You didn't choose me. I chose you. (John 15:12-16)

So Jesus has initiated a friendship with each of us. Yet we can miss out on the benefits of friendship with God if we don't devote enough time and interest to the relationship. And if we've been missing out on friendship with God Himself, chances are we're also missing out on other potentially rewarding friendships with other people who aren't nearly as patient and loving toward us as God is.

Jon and Dave: Friends till the End

A classic example of friendship is the relationship between David, the young man who would become king of Israel, and Jonathan, the son of the ruling king at the time. The story is found in 1 Samuel 18. And the account leading up to this story is as gripping as any soap opera.

In the not-so-distant past, God's people, the Israelites, were living in their Promised Land and were being ruled by judges, which was by God's design. But they never drove out all their enemies, which God had told them to do. Consequently, other nations would get strong, overtake the Israelites, and cause them to cry out to God in desperation. God would then call a new judge to rally the people, face off against their enemies, win a victory, and live in peace for a period of time, during which the people would again get lazy and self-centered. This cycle repeated itself time and again.

Finally the people complained to their spiritual leader, Samuel, that they wanted a king just like all the other nations had. Samuel warned them of all the drawbacks of having a king, but they were insistent. He knew it wasn't what God wanted, yet God told him to grant the people's request.

The first king chosen was Saul, who never quite committed himself to following God as faithfully as he should have. Saul had a couple of successes but is remembered more for his spiritual shortcomings. God let Samuel know He had chosen a successor to Saul. And Samuel told Saul clearly that God had chosen "a man after his own heart" as Saul's replacement (1 Samuel 13:14). In fact, God told Samuel to go ahead and anoint David and designate him as the next king (1 Samuel 16).

However, Saul had sons of his own. Jonathan, the best-known of them, had proven himself to be faithful to God and courageous in battle (1 Samuel 14:1-23). David got more PR from his defeat of Goliath (1 Samuel 17), but Jonathan was no slouch. As soon as David was called to serve in the courts of Saul, he and Jonathan discovered they were kindred spirits: "There was an immediate bond of love between them, and they became the best of friends. . . . Jonathan made a special vow to be David's friend, and he sealed the pact by giving him his robe, tunic, sword, bow, and belt" (1 Samuel 18:1, 3).

On the other hand, David's popularity with the people created severe jealousy in King Saul. It didn't take long before Saul had

FOR EXAMPLE . . .

Ruth and Naomi (The Book of Ruth)

A good friendship during the era of the judges was between a daughter-in-law and mother-in-law. The story of Ruth and Naomi is a good one to read and see that just because someone happens to be related doesn't mean that he or she can't be a close friend as well.

DO'S AND DON'TS

As iron sharpens iron, a friend sharpens a friend. (Proverbs 27:17)

There are "friends" who destroy each other, but a real friend sticks closer than a brother. (Proverbs 18:24)

tried twice to use David for target practice with his spear (1 Samuel 18:5-12; 19:9-10). David fled for his life with the help of Jonathan and others in Saul's family. And for an extended period of time, David tried simply to keep from being killed by Saul's men. In the meantime he put together an army of his own and twice had a perfect opportunity to personally kill King Saul. But David knew that Saul too had been anointed by God, and it was up to God to establish David's reign whenever He wished.

Guidelines for Better Friendships

The purpose for this mini-history lesson is to emphasize that the rivalry between Saul and David shouldn't have done much to help the friendship between David and Jonathan. Yet it stands as one of the strongest human bonds recorded in Scripture. Let's take a closer look at this unlikely friendship and see what we might discover that we can apply to our own relationships with our friends.

We Do Well to Give Our Loyalty to Godly Friends over Ungodly Family Members.

Most of us as parents would be heartbroken to see our children choose an outsider over us. Saul was none too happy, either. When Jonathan stood up to his father on behalf of David, Saul even attempted to kill his own son (1 Samuel 20:30-34). Saul's daughter Michal, whom Saul had reluctantly allowed David to marry, also helped David escape her father's hit squad (1 Samuel 19:11-18).

Yet Scripture is clear that Saul was the one who was allowing his rage and jealousy to get out of control. If his children had blindly obeyed his wishes (or to be more accurate, his whims), they would have been directly opposing God's clearly expressed plan.

So Jonathan's loyalty to David may have been technically a rebellion against his father, but it was more correctly his expression of loyalty to David as the leader chosen by God. There may be times when we too will have to choose or lose friends based on what we believe God wants us to do.

True Friendships Have No Rivalry.

Friendship as it *should* be brings out the best qualities of everyone involved. But sometimes friends become competitive to the point of damaging the relationship. David benefited by having Jonathan inside Saul's courts, providing him with inside information (1 Samuel 20). Yet other than the love of a true friend, Jonathan had little to gain from this coalition.

Tradition and culture would dictate that Jonathan should be in line for the throne at the death of his father. Yet both he and David knew that David had been singled out by God to be the next king.

It's one thing to serve God when things are going your way. But for Jonathan to continue to be David's best friend was a true act of faith. It was an affirmation that what God wanted was more important than what Jonathan wanted. Perhaps there was also an unspoken acknowledgment that Jonathan might not even be around to attempt to claim the throne over David (which turned out to be the case).

Yet Jonathan only wished David the best, as David did for his friend.

Friends Don't Hide Their True Feelings.

As a shepherd, David had dealt with lions and bears, clubbing them to death when they tried to steal sheep (1 Samuel 17:34-35). He had stood firm as Goliath spewed verbal venom and death threats, and then David used the giant's own sword to cut off his ugly head (1 Samuel 17:41-51). But as David was forced to say good-bye to Jonathan, both young warriors were gushing tears—especially David (1 Samuel 20:41).

This unashamed expression of emotion seems embarrassing and awkward compared to what we expect of "real men" in today's society. In fact, it is a standard joke in television scriptwriting to have two male friends experience a particularly tender moment and then go out of their way to avoid any public display of their feelings.

But friends—even male friends—don't mind crying in front of one another. Or sharing sensitive information. Or confessing personal struggles. Or praying.

NO-BRAINER'S GUIDE TO HOW CHRISTIANS LIVE

FOR EXAMPLE . . .

Paul, Silas, and the Philippian Jailer (Acts 16:25-34)

Paul and Silas were not only ministry partners, but also friends. Even in prison they could unite in Christian love and sing hymns long into the night. And when they could have escaped after a divine earthquake rattled off their chains and threw open the prison doors, they chose not to. Instead they made friends with the jailer, resulting in the conversion of the man and his entire family.

You might not want to break out in heaving sobs at every fare-well party for someone at work. You might not want to hug and kiss every time a friend sinks a free throw in a league basketball game. But genuine friends mourn losses and celebrate the important victories in life.

Friends Get Good at Empathy.

The reason shared victories and losses are so essential in friendships is that friends learn to see beyond their own feelings and put themselves in someone else's shoes. David and Jonathan wept because they each could see what was in store for the other.

Jonathan realized that David was about to go on the run. The best soldiers of a very good army would join in a manhunt with him as their only target. He was a popular hero, but few people were likely to oppose King Saul in sheltering him. His would be a lifestyle of moving from place to place, never knowing when his next turn might be a wrong one—the tenth-century B.C. version of "The Fugitive."

David realized that Jonathan was going to lose out on the opportunity to rule over Israel through no fault of his own. From all we know of Jonathan, he might have made an excellent leader. Jonathan's very association with David would put him at odds with his father. Saul had tried to kill him once. If the king tried again, this time he might not miss.

No wonder two grown men were weeping openly. Neither of them could anticipate a very pleasant life in the near future. In addition to the pain of parting, surely the empathy they felt for each other added to the emotion of the moment.

Genuine Friendships Endure the Worst of Conditions.

David and Jonathan became friends as soon as David began to work for Saul—when both of them had recently made a name for themselves. They were at the top of their game, in favor with the king and the people.

As Saul began to resent David, Jonathan surely saw that the politically correct thing to do would be to bail out on the relationship. But true friendships are defined by endurance through hard times and personal challenges. Jonathan put himself on the line for David when David's situation looked bleak. And after the tragic loss of Jonathan in a subsequent battle against the Philistines, David essentially adopted Jonathan's son, who was crippled (2 Samuel 9).

Extreme circumstances can create friends who might not otherwise ever get together. People who fight together in wars frequently become lifelong friends. Cancer survivors, AA participants, students with a horrendous teacher, and others frequently bond as they resist a common enemy.

In this life we all have a common enemy—but not one of flesh and blood. The difficulties of living the Christian life should theoretically be pulling us together, but sometimes we tend to withdraw and isolate ourselves instead. The stereotype of the "fair-weather friend" is all too common in our world, but there is no place for such people in the Christian life. We're called not only to get out and fight our own battles, but also to help those who are weak and struggling. Hard times can bond us as friends if we are willing. Otherwise, we remain a collection of hurting individuals who never find the relief we seek.

Like so many other things in the Christian life, if we try to develop friendships based on what we want to get out of them, we're likely to be disappointed. It's hard to develop a deep and abiding relationship built on self-centeredness. But if we see others in need and reach out to help, many times those actions result in close friendships. If you start out dealing with tough times, the situation usually gets better and the friendship grows as you move past the crisis.

When Friendship Begins to Sink

For many people, making and keeping friends is as natural as breathing. For others, it requires more conscious effort yet is still not too difficult. But sometimes things go wrong that cause certain people to resist making friends. Let's look at a few potential drawbacks that can occur when our friendships are not quite up to par.

WELL SAID!

Prosperity provideth, but adversity proveth friends. —*Queen Elizabeth I*

DO'S AND DON'TS

Dear brothers and sisters, if another Christian is overcome by some sin, you who are godly should gently and humbly help that person back onto the right path. And be careful not to fall into the same temptation yourself. Share each other's troubles and problems, and in this way obey the law of Christ. (Galatians 6:1-2)

WELL SAID!

You can make more friends in two months by becoming interested in other people than you can in two years by trying to get other people interested in you. —*Dale Carnegie*

Too-Much-Too-Soon Friendships

Many of us have had those surreal moments when we're introduced to someone and three minutes later are hearing every detail of his emergency hernia operation. Or before she lets go of your initial handshake, she's asking your patience if she seems weird because she's going through a painful divorce and her jerk of a husband is trying to take every penny and if he doesn't have someone on the side she will be a monkey's uncle and it's definitely not too soon to let her know if you have single friends and . . . .

Genuine friendship generally takes time to grow and flourish; it doesn't spring fully formed from a first meeting. Yet some people appear unwilling to invest much time for friendship building. It's as though they are desperate to have a new friend right this second. It's like impulse shopping, but real live people are involved!

If you have a few close friends, you know how time-consuming an existing friendship can be—not to mention what it takes to make the effort to get to know a new person at that level of intimacy. Some people try to take shortcuts. To them, publicly exposing their personal lives equals friendship. It's not at all the same, but for them it will do.

The sad thing is that if you try to slow things down and let real friendship grow at a reasonable rate, such people might reject you before you reject them. Sometimes these needy people will bounce from church to church, initially basking in the attention they receive, but eventually moving on when the buzz dies down and they begin to be treated just like everyone else.

If you recognize some of these pushy traits in yourself, it's never too late to slow down and take a less threatening approach to other people. Finding the right pace to grow a friendship is never easy. But if you have some history to draw on, perhaps you can see clearly what steps to take for future friendships.

These Are the Few of My Favorite Friends

Since good, close, comfortable friendships may be few and far between, we tend to guard those relationships. Nothing wrong with that. But if we ever start excluding others in order to show preference to our friends, we've crossed a line God has drawn for us. This is especially true in church settings.

Showing favoritism is a natural thing to do, which is why it's so insidious. Most of us are naturally drawn to popular, funny, good-looking, and/or wealthy people. Meanwhile, others who don't fit those criteria are more likely to be in need of love, advice, a listening ear, or some other function of a friend. If we feel we already have "enough" friends, it can be very difficult for such people to find the help they need. It can also be difficult for someone new to the school, church, or neighborhood to break into the already tight social circles.

If we stop to think what our eternal standing might be if God showed favoritism, it's not a pretty picture. Most of us can think of others who seem more deserving, prettier, or richer when it comes to treasures in heaven. Yet God is willing to receive all of us, spiritual warts and all. So if we go out and begin to show favoritism to one group of people over another, we are guilty of blatant hypocrisy.

It's another tricky area. Genuine friendships definitely require time to grow strong. We can't have that level of commitment with many people, so we will certainly have "best friends." Yet we must beware of completely excluding others. Some people are little better than bouncers standing outside a club, turning away people who aren't "on the list." Our goal should be to never stop making new friends, while still hanging on to the ones we already have.

Friendships of Convenience

A proper friendship is like a door with an easy-access handle on both sides. Certain boundaries may be set between the people on either side, yet either person has the opportunity to initiate contact. Some friendships, however, are like exit doors at movie theaters. If you happen to be on the wrong side, you're out of luck unless someone on the other side is willing to let you in.

Some people cultivate "friends" who are there when they have problems, need a fourth for a golf game, or simply want companionship. Yet it quickly becomes clear to the other person(s) that the

DO'S AND DON'TS

My dear brothers and sisters, how can you claim that you have faith in our glorious Lord Jesus Christ if you favor some people more than others? . . . Yes indeed, it is good when you truly obey our Lord's royal command found in the Scriptures: "Love your neighbor as yourself." But if you pay special attention to the rich, you are committing a sin, for you are guilty of breaking that law. (James 2:1, 8-9)

Don't be fooled by those who say [foolish] things, for "bad company corrupts good character." (1 Corinthians 15:33)

relationship isn't at all reciprocal. If they try to initiate time with their "friend," he or she is almost always too tired, too busy, or otherwise involved and inaccessible. And unfortunately, that's good enough for a lot of people. They don't mind being taken advantage of if they can have some degree of social life. But generally they deserve better.

We need to examine our friendships to ensure that no one is repeatedly getting a door slammed in his or her face. We might need to hand out some additional sets of keys or drill some holes in the door so the other person can "get a handle" on the relationship as well.

WELL SAID!

Pure friendship is an image of the original and perfect friendship that belongs to the Trinity and is the very essence of God. —Simone Weil

Friendship: The Grown-up Version

When we're young, we don't give a lot of thought to friendship. We tend to make a few friends, desire some other friendships that never really come to pass, and lose a few along the way. But as adults, we need to consider the successes and failures of the past before we get much better at making friends.

For example, have you ever let a friendship erode because of a tiny problem that neither person was willing to deal with? Have you ever been very close to someone—perhaps even married or engaged—yet you no longer communicate with them at all? We decry couples who are married "in name only," yet how many "friendships" do you have that produce little if any evidence of their existence other than the casual acknowledgment of the relationship?

Jesus both taught and modeled that God is not only an authority figure in our lives but also our friend. So perhaps friendship is more important than we give it credit for. It's not simply a stage of growing up. If we're properly developing godly attitudes and behavior, we will reach out beyond our common interactions with acquaintances and start making new friends. We will start seeing what we can do for other people rather than vice versa. And then, when the time comes when we need a close friend, we'll discover no shortage of them.

Questions to Ponder and/or Discuss

1. If someone made a TV show about you and your friends, what would the show be called? What true story would make an interesting plot for the pilot episode?

2. What is the most sacrificial thing a friend has ever done for you? What's the biggest sacrifice you have made for a friend?

3. Who are five people you can think of with whom you are friendly but who aren't yet close friends? For each person who comes to mind, think of two specific things you might do with or for him/her that would strengthen your relationship. And as opportunities arise, put your ideas into action and see what happens.

It's Not Just a Job...

WORK RELATIONSHIPS

It was almost dark as George Seeker finished setting out a new ornamental cherry tree in his front yard. He was picking up his tools as Fred drove up. He went over to say hello but never got the chance. Fred was muttering as he got out of the car.

"If that idiot boss of mine doesn't learn what he's doing, he's going to drive our whole company down the chapter 11 expressway. He gives a whole new meaning to the word "doofus." And if he makes me stay late one more time for some lamebrained project of his, I'm going to tell him he can . . . ."

"Whoa, there," cautioned George. "Bad day at work, I take it?"

"One of many these days," conceded Fred. "But I apologize for taking it out on you. Wilma has learned just to ignore me until I let off enough steam to act normal again."

George was silent. When Fred looked up it seemed George was trying to swallow a smirk, so Fred asked, "Did I say something funny?"

George let out a soft chuckle. "Not really. It's just ironic timing. Less than two hours ago I finished another chapter in the book you gave me—the one about integrating Christian principles into

171

WELL SAID!

God gives the birds their food, but He does not throw it into their nests.
—*German proverb*

everyday life. And I had just read about how Christians should respect their bosses because the pressures of work settings provide terrific opportunities to demonstrate different behavior."

Fred winced, then grinned. "So I guess the lesson for today is, 'Do as I say, and not as I do.' That's no good. I try not to live by that motto. But I gotta tell you—some days it's hard to do as I know I'm supposed to do. Today was one of those days. Forgive me?"

"No problem."

"The challenge will be to apologize to my boss tomorrow. I didn't confront him directly, but I made sure he got the message about how I was feeling."

George was genuinely surprised. "I'm a bit amazed to see you let your feelings get the better of you. I've always assumed you had everything together in your life."

Fred stopped smiling. "I've always tried to give that impression, but I struggle just like everyone else. And lately I've been making an effort to be more genuine and honest around other people—especially those who share my beliefs. I really appreciate your being up front with me about my faults."

"Then while we're at it, let me go get my list," George deadpanned.

Fred laughed and said, "One thing at a time. But keep at it. It's good to know you're watching me and will keep me accountable."

George nodded. "And you'll do the same for me? Everything's fine for the time being, but I don't always understand or agree with the stuff your Christian writers are saying. I may need to blow off some steam one of these nights."

"You've got it," replied Fred. As he walked inside, he realized what a break it was that George was around tonight. Since George caught the full fury of his frustration instead of Wilma, Fred wouldn't have to pop for flowers tomorrow to apologize!

Is There Such a Thing As "Good Work"?

Work gets a bad reputation a lot of times—perhaps for good reason. Depending on your situation, you might be facing long hours, low

pay, irrational (or worse) bosses, backstabbing coworkers, glass ceilings, unexpected pink slips, and rock-bottom morale. When the workplace makes the news, it's frequently because some disgruntled ex-employee has returned to work with a rifle. Or maybe everyone from the CEO to the mail-room workers has been downloading porn and E-mailing it to their friends. Or in-house gossip has gotten out of hand and a melee has broken out.

WELL SAID!

There is dignity in work only when it is work freely accepted. —*Albert Camus*

Workers at bad companies get jaded and distrustful of anyone in authority. The good bosses out there search in vain for employees who will show some degree of loyalty and commitment and who will attempt to solve problems rather than whine about them. We all want raises and higher salaries but resist the harder work and greater responsibility that go along with them.

Dissatisfaction with one's work is not a new problem by any means. The Old Testament book of Ecclesiastes is a classic treatise, traditionally ascribed to King Solomon. If he was indeed the author, take a look at what the wisest man who ever lived had to say about the joys of work:

> So now I hate life because everything done here under the sun is so irrational. Everything is meaningless, like chasing the wind. I am disgusted that I must leave the fruits of my hard work to others. And who can tell whether my successors will be wise or foolish? And yet they will control everything I have gained by my skill and hard work. How meaningless!
>
> So I turned in despair from hard work. It was not the answer to my search for satisfaction in this life. For though I do my work with wisdom, knowledge, and skill, I must leave everything I gain to people who haven't worked to earn it. This is not only foolish but highly unfair. So what do people get for their hard work? Their days of labor are filled with pain and grief; even at night they cannot rest. It is all utterly meaningless. (Ecclesiastes 2:17-23)

After reading the book of Ecclesiastes, you expect archaeologists to eventually turn up one of Solomon's chariots with a bumper

ONE SMALL STEP

Not many people continue to work the earth to make a living. But all jobs have their "thorns and thistles." Mentally list the problem areas of your job. If these things were resolved or removed, how would you then feel about working? Try to determine if your complaints are about the job itself, or only about the things that go wrong on the job.

sticker bearing the first known use of the phrase "Life Stinks, Then You Die" (in the original Hebrew). If Solomon himself couldn't juxtapose work with spiritual satisfaction, how can we hope to do so at a no-brainer level?

We're not going to attempt to solve all your work-related problems. Maybe you're a poet at heart, but you work in an accounting firm. Maybe you're visually impaired with dreams of driving the big rigs. Maybe you're lazy, self-absorbed, virtually unemployable, and unwilling to change. We aren't going to try to deal with those issues. Stroll through the business section of any bookstore and you'll find ample resources to help you with your concerns. (And if you belong to the latter category, you might want to try the mental health aisle as well.)

What we do want to focus on in this chapter are your working relationships. And since you'll never have a decent relationship with anyone if your attitude is not what it should be, we need to begin by examining our attitudes toward work.

If You Don't Think Work Is a Curse, You Should Hear My Coworkers!

Some people don't try very hard to reconcile work attitudes with other elements of the Christian life. Why bother? After all, isn't work part of God's original curse on humanity? When Adam and Eve sinned, no more paradise for us. We're up at the crack of dawn and off to the salt mines. Right?

This view is only partially correct. Yes, when God was evicting Adam and Eve from the Garden of Eden, part of His sentence was as follows:

> I have placed a curse on the ground. All your life you will struggle to scratch a living from it. It will grow thorns and thistles for you, though you will eat of its grains. All your life you will sweat to produce food, until your dying day. Then you will return to the ground from which you came.

For you were made from dust, and to the dust you will return. (Genesis 3:17-19)

So Adam certainly had his work cut out for him. We envision him in Eden knocking back pineapple/guava/banana smoothies from freshly picked fruit that grew effortlessly. But after his sin, it would be okra and lima beans, and even those would require weeding, fertilizing, watering, and real manual labor for a change.

Yet if we read closely, we see that it is the earth that was afflicted. The work itself isn't the curse. If we go back even farther, we see that Adam and Eve had been given job assignments while still in Eden. It was Adam's task to name all the animals (Genesis 2:19-20). Adam and Eve were instructed to "Multiply and fill the earth and subdue it. Be masters over the fish and the birds and all the animals" (Genesis 1:28). So they weren't given jobs; they were management!

Not the same thing, you might argue. If *you* were given the job of multiplying and filling the earth, you promise we wouldn't hear any complaints? Perhaps not. And certainly it's a better job description than taking depositions all day, or filing copies, or calling strangers to sell aluminum siding, or snaking clogged drains.

But those are just the jobs we know about—the ones that were recorded. With all those animals around, perhaps Adam also had to perform a shoveling detail every once in a while. Maybe Eve had to peel the bananas and toss the salad. Maybe she did the shoveling while he cooked. But don't miss the point: Even in God's original Paradise, we see people at work. So it's not the work itself that should be repulsive. Theoretically, we should be able to have a good attitude toward work even if our specific jobs have certain problems.

Of course, God didn't stick Adam and Eve into separate cubicles and forbid them to talk to each other except during a 10-minute coffee break and at lunch. The relationship was foremost, both between Adam and Eve, and between the couple and God. And positive relationships continue to be essential for success in the workplace.

Even if your boss is a slave driver, you have no excuse. Slavery was part of the civilization when the New Testament was written,

FOR EXAMPLE . . .

Onesimus (The Book of Philemon)

The very short book of Philemon (25 verses) is the story of a runaway slave named Onesimus whom Paul met and told about Jesus, sending him back to his master with a new attitude. It's a classic story of Christian commitment versus an undesirable workplace.

and Scripture provided rules for how to cope with it. The closest most of us will come to slavery is our voluntary bondage to our jobs and/or employers. So let's see what we can adapt from the Bible's advice to slaves to help us cope with our vocational shackles. Most of the instructions are short and to the point.

Slaves, obey your earthly masters with deep respect and fear. Serve them sincerely as you would serve Christ. Work hard, but not just to please your masters when they are watching. As slaves of Christ, do the will of God with all your heart. Work with enthusiasm, as though you were working for the Lord rather than for people. Remember that the Lord will reward each one of us for the good we do, whether we are slaves or free. And in the same way, you masters must treat your slaves right. Don't threaten them; remember, you both have the same Master in heaven, and he has no favorites. (Ephesians 6:5-9; see also Colossians 3:22-4:1)

Christians who are slaves should give their masters full respect so that the name of God and his teaching will not be shamed. If your master is a Christian, that is no excuse for being disrespectful. You should work all the harder because you are helping another believer by your efforts. (1 Timothy 6:1-2)

Slaves must obey their masters and do their best to please them. They must not talk back or steal, but they must show themselves to be entirely trustworthy and good. Then they will make the teaching about God our Savior attractive in every way. (Titus 2:9-10)

These weren't obscure teachings. In several of Paul's letters, he includes instructions especially for slave/master relationships. Yet it may be difficult for us to relate to such things. We resist slavery out of principle. The thought of someone else having legal and social authority over our actions and decisions is abhorrent. We rally against such injustices. And yet in such situations, Scripture tells us we can also choose to serve God primarily and willingly, even as we serve someone else secondarily and perhaps against our wishes. And if we can foster such a mind-set in circumstances beyond our control, God will ultimately reward us—regardless of what else we get for our hard work.

We Should Choose to Serve Willingly.

In today's job market, we have options slaves didn't have. We can simply change "masters." We can complain to unions or labor boards. We have certain legal recourses when a boss oversteps his or her authority. We can do away with bosses altogether and start home businesses.

Yet as long as we are in someone's employ, that person deserves our respect. When your boss walks by, does he or she receive your "deep respect and fear"? If not, you're not living up to biblical standards.

If literal slaves were called to be willing servants rather than forced laborers, how can we sidestep the same biblical challenge? Feelings of resentment toward the person(s) in charge affect both our attitudes and actions in the workplace.

Work Should Be a Team Effort.

It's all too common to have an us-versus-them mentality at work. It even becomes a game for some. If they feel they aren't getting paid what they're worth, they'll take home the difference in legal pads, staplers, and Post-it Notes. Or they'll fudge on their time sheets. Or they'll practice a hacking cough and call in sick to get a few extra vacation days.

The goal is to learn to work with the boss, in whatever capacity you are allowed to do so. You may be much more intelligent and experienced than the person in charge. It's not really fair that he or she got the promotion rather than you. But it's still your scriptural responsibility to use your intellect and experience to help the boss rather than undermine his or her credibility.

Your boss is imperfect, no matter what he might think. And you're imperfect, no matter what you might think. So the best possible option is to pool your talents and work together to rise above your joint imperfections. Jesus was the world's only perfect leader,

FOR EXAMPLE . . .

Working for God

Many of the Bible's heroic figures worked for God under bondage, imprisonment, or other forms of slavery. Here are just a few examples:

- Joseph became the second most powerful person in Egypt after first being sold into slavery and then being sent to jail on a trumped-up rape charge (Genesis 37; 39–41).
- Moses should have drowned in the Nile as a baby yet rose to power to defy Pharaoh and lead all his people from slavery (Exodus 1–14).
- Elijah the prophet served God while being sought by Israel's king and queen who wished to put him to death (1 Kings 18:7-14; 19:2).
- Esther became queen while captive in a foreign country (Esther).
- Daniel and other prophets served during periods of captivity (Daniel).

In these and other cases, faithfulness to God's work helped these people achieve success in spite of slavery and/or other kinds of oppression.

DO'S AND DON'TS

Work for six days, and rest on the seventh. This will give your ox and donkey a chance to rest. It will also allow the people of your household, including your slaves and visitors, to be refreshed. (Exodus 23:12)

WELL SAID!

As God's fellow worker he [man] is to reflect God's creative activity on Monday in the factory no less than on Sunday when commemorating the day of rest and worship. —*Carl F. H. Henry*

and even His "workers" would regularly bicker over position, honor, rights, and so forth. So we shouldn't expect to avoid conflicts, and we should be a little quicker to acknowledge the authority of the person in charge.

Work Has a Spiritual Basis.

Scripture reminds us that God is watching, whatever we do at work. We may not get the raise, promotion, title, or recognition we deserve from the powers that be. But an even higher Power is keeping track and will reward us eventually. Of course, He is also watching if we choose to use the Xerox machine for something other than duplicating papers.

But it's not primarily God's concern that you manufacture more stereo equipment than last quarter, get the newspaper out on time, or whatever else your job requires. More important than any of these things are the relationships you're involved in.

It's something of a paradox that work is something most of us have to do, yet this workplace is where we may act less "Christian" than anywhere else. If that's the case, we need to begin to integrate all those lessons about love, mercy, forgiveness, and imitating Jesus into a work climate where they seem as out of place as Bill Gates in Amish country. If we aren't standing out at the job site, then we're probably slacking a little in a spiritual sense.

Work Is Not Church.

Having said what we have about the spiritual aspect of work, we must remember to maintain a degree of separation between church and job. At church, all believers should have equal status with no problems of status or favoritism. Yet those same believers might have certain well-defined differences as they move from Sunday services to Monday morning's business meetings.

God has certain goals for His people when they gather in church, and we should try to accomplish those goals of unity, oneness, practice of spiritual gifts, and all the rest. Your company has goals, too—among them to make money. As an employee, you've accepted your part of that goal. Seeking bigger profits may seem crass in

contrast to many spiritual goals, but it's the responsibility of all good employees. If you don't agree, you can always quit to pursue a full-time ministry somewhere. But if you've chosen a job in the secular workplace, you owe the company your best. And your boss probably feels even more pressure than you to meet the corporate expectations imposed on him.

As Paul reminded Timothy, if your boss happens to be a Christian, you need to be even more careful to respect his or her authority. Christians can pal around at church where no favoritism is shown between the mail-room employee and CEO in Bible studies and prayer groups. But the mail-room employee can embarrass the boss at work by walking into a board meeting and expecting to be treated as an equal. And the boss might embarrass the employee by coming down harder than normal to avoid any suggestion of impropriety. We should never put our fellow believers in uncomfortable positions at work by expecting or engaging in favoritism simply because we share the same faith.

Bosses Have Rules, Too.

If you happen to be a boss yourself, you might be breezing through this section shouting "Amen" at the end of every paragraph. Employees are supposed to take it on the chin when bosses are out of line. They're supposed to help the old boss look good. They're supposed to work hard—for God if not for the company. So bosses can run rampant and not have to worry about the consequences? Yippee!

Not exactly. Scripture speaks directly to Christian "masters" and doesn't let them off the hook that easily. God is Master to both boss and employee, and leaders who bear the title "Christian" have a mandate to lead as He would. That means no threats or mistreatment of those who report to them. With the privilege of leadership comes the responsibility of care and compassion as well.

Any Volunteers for Slave Duty?

So while we may not be literal slaves, we can apply some of the instructions given to slaves to make better sense of our jobs. And

ONE SMALL STEP

Evaluate your relationship with your boss, if you have one. Lately have you been making that person's job easier, or harder? Have you ever attempted to seek favor based on shared faith rather than outstanding performance? What can you do this week to fulfill the biblical mandate to give your boss "full respect"?

DO'S AND DON'TS

Work hard and cheerfully at whatever you do, as though you were working for the Lord rather than for people. Remember that the Lord will give you an inheritance as your reward, and the Master you are serving is Christ. (Colossians 3:23-24)

WELL SAID!

Do not pray for easy lives. Pray to be stronger men. Do not pray for tasks equal to your powers. Pray for powers equal to your tasks. —*Phillips Brooks*

perhaps we also need to consider that we might indeed be slaves in a sense.

Peter explains that we are slaves to whatever controls us (2 Peter 2:19). At some point in everyone's life, we are unwitting, and perhaps unwilling, slaves to sin (John 8:34). But if we wish to be free from sin, we can choose a different master. This transition is described in great detail in Romans 6–8. Look at some of the highlights:

> Our old sinful selves were crucified with Christ so that sin might lose its power in our lives. We are no longer slaves to sin. . . . Don't you realize that whatever you choose to obey becomes your master? You can choose sin, which leads to death, or you can choose to obey God and receive his approval. Thank God! Once you were slaves of sin, but now you have obeyed with all your heart the new teaching God has given you. . . . But now you are free from the power of sin and have become slaves of God. Now you do those things that lead to holiness and result in eternal life. For the wages of sin is death, but the free gift of God is eternal life through Christ Jesus our Lord. (Romans 6:6, 16-17, 22-23)

Or, as Bob Dylan put it: "You gotta serve somebody. It might be the devil, or it might be the Lord, but you're gonna have to serve somebody."

We all begin life with sin as our master. When the situation gets bad enough, we generally become willing to do almost anything to change. So we agree to follow Jesus in return for deliverance, salvation, freedom from sin, and the promise of eternal life. The problem is that we don't like being slaves—not to sin, not to work, and maybe not even to God. But until we are willing to concede that we need a loving and powerful Master to oversee our lives, we continue to struggle.

Paul proudly accepted the titles of slave and bondservant of Jesus. He frequently began his letters by using one of these terms, which put everything he had to say into context (Romans 1:1; Philippians 1:1).

The paradox is that being a "slave" of Jesus brings tremendous freedom because we need not be so burdened by other matters that weigh heavily on our peers. Other things can be cruel taskmasters; Jesus never is. And if you're a slave of Jesus, you don't feel like a slave at work—or anywhere else, for that matter. If you're working for a higher cause, then everything you do has a more intense feeling of importance.

It takes time, faith, and perseverance to develop a "slave of Jesus" mentality and see it as a positive thing. But when you eventually make that mental transition, the importance of work (and other things) becomes more evident. The opportunity to demonstrate your commitment to your heavenly Master is closely tied to the opportunities you have to please your other "masters" at work.

We opened this book by pointing out Jesus' promise to provide "life in all its fullness" (John 10:10). Perhaps nowhere is this more evident than in His ability to breathe new life into a stale old job. If we can only come to see Him as the boss, the work we do isn't nearly so dull.

A recent Army slogan promised that they provide recruits not just a job, but an adventure. But with the adventures come the mundane servant tasks. (Just ask all the privates peeling potatoes and scrubbing toilets.) The same promise applies to the Christian life. If God is King of kings and Lord of lords, He must surely be Boss of bosses as well. And when we give Him that role in our lives, our jobs can become quite adventurous.

Instead of seeing our human bosses as squinty-eyed, onion-breathed, money-grubbing worms, we might even come to see them as authority figures God has placed in our lives. And instead of resisting their position, we can learn to offer them our support, encouragement, and respect.

Having said all these things, we should also say that no one gets this part of the Christian life right all the time. Work simply consumes too much of our time—for many people, more than family, friends, and church combined. It's a powerful influence, and it's very hard not to evaluate our entire lives based on how our jobs are going.

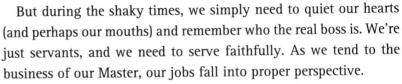

WELL SAID!

Work is not, primarily, a thing one does to live, but the thing one lives to do. It is, or it should be, the full expression of the worker's faculties. —*Dorothy L. Sayers*

DO'S AND DON'TS

You shouldn't be so concerned about perishable things like food. Spend your energy seeking the eternal life that I, the Son of Man, can give you. For God the Father has sent me for that very purpose. (John 6:27)

But during the shaky times, we simply need to quiet our hearts (and perhaps our mouths) and remember who the real boss is. We're just servants, and we need to serve faithfully. As we tend to the business of our Master, our jobs fall into proper perspective.

When we're working for God, even at a secular job, our successes mean something, and we can experience a significant degree of peace and contentment. If we're only trying to claw our way up a corporate ladder, we have no way to measure success other than money and title. And those aren't always the most valid gauges.

Unhealthy, Wealthy, and Wiser?

Psychologists have recently identified and named a new disorder in our society: sudden wealth syndrome. With all the people winning lotteries, becoming overnight millionaires with IPOs, and otherwise "succeeding" by their own definitions, many aren't prepared for the stresses that usually accompany wealth. Even though we have recently experienced the longest economic boom in history, even though the number of millionaire households are projected to quadruple between 1998 and 2008, even though so many people are realizing the once-rare dream of getting rich quick—we're seeing more psychological disorders rather than more contentment.

With wealth comes fear as people buy nicer things and then immediately begin to invest in car alarms, home security systems, and houses in gated communities. Not surprisingly, the symptoms of sudden wealth syndrome are anxiety and feelings of alienation from other people. Those with sudden wealth frequently experience guilt at having more than others, and they fear losing everything as quickly as they got it.

People with sudden wealth syndrome learn the hard way that instant millions don't always solve problems. Still, if you had to pick a disease. . . .

Contentment with God can transcend wealth or poverty, hunger or full stomachs (Philippians 4:11-12). If you get to the point where your job is simply an extension of your work for God and you feel a sense of worth and even joy in what you're doing, a wise person wouldn't trade that feeling for a million dollars.

Questions to Ponder and/or Discuss

1. Which of the following words/phrases best describes your work on an average day? (Circle all that apply.)

Adventure   Thrill   Lowest level of hell
Challenge   Confused mess   Curse
Grind   Necessary evil   Opportunity
Psycho ward   Prison sentence   Happy fun time
Routine   Downward spiral   War zone
Escape   Fulfillment   You don't want to know!
Other: _____

2. Which, if any, of the following people does your boss remind you of? Why?

- Dilbert's pointy-haired boss
- Mussolini
- Queen Elizabeth
- Mr. Rogers
- Captain Ahab
- Martha Stewart
- Other: _____

3. Suppose for a moment that Jesus had your job. What do you think He might do differently at work? (Shake the dust off His feet and go someplace else? Confront certain people about problems? Reach out to others with encouragement or help?) Think of specific people and situations, and write down everything you think of that He might do. Then spend some time thinking how you might be a bit more Christlike in those same work situations from now on.

WELL SAID!

Keep us, Lord, so awake in the duties of our callings that we may sleep in peace and awake in glory. —*John Donne*

CHAPTER FOURTEEN

"YOU GUYS ARE LEAVING JUST BECAUSE I DON'T BELIEVE IN PAYING TAXES?"

Render unto Caesar

DEALING WITH THOSE IN AUTHORITY

Fred and Josh were playing a racing video game (and Fred was *way* behind) when Mary burst through the front door chanting, "Mom got a *tic*-ket, Mom got a *tic*-ket."

Wilma followed her in, somewhat flustered and even blushing a bit. As it turned out, on her way back from picking up Mary from piano lessons she had been one of several drivers pulled over in a speed trap. Local officials had warned they were planning to crack down on "the city's chronic speeding problem," and sure enough, Wilma was one of the first to get tagged.

"Way to go, Mom!" was Josh's reaction.

She scolded, "Josh, this is nothing to joke about. I'm ashamed of this. I'm one of the first to complain about young kids whipping through our neighborhood in undependable cars with radios blaring and engines racing. We've got a lot of young children who play on the sidewalks, and it wouldn't take much for one of them to get seriously hurt. For me to be one of the offenders is not something I'm proud of."

Fred was looking at the ticket. "You were only going 42 in a 35

SOME THINGS YOU'LL DISCOVER IN THIS CHAPTER

1. Why order is important in a chaotic society

2. Resisting secular authority isn't always the best Christian response

3. How to model Jesus' attitude toward "authority," with a few precautions

185

mph. zone? Gee whiz! What's the big deal? Couldn't you have talked your way out of it? Or batted your eyelashes at the officer, or something?"

Wilma shook her head. "It's funny you should ask. I was asked to wait in the car until the police had ticketed two people in front of me. The cop—the policeman—couldn't have been older than his mid-20s. The first driver was a woman about my age, but she was flirting with him just like a girlfriend. He was trying to be professional about the whole thing and still gave her the ticket, but she did everything but take her top off to keep from getting it. And the second driver was a thirtyish businessman. He was irate and abusive. He was in the officer's face—screaming, threatening, and listing everybody he knew at city hall. A couple of times I thought the policeman's partner was going to go over to subdue the driver, but I think he was letting the younger guy get some experience handling himself. By the time the poor officer got to me, I just apologized for speeding, signed the ticket, and came home—well under the speed limit."

Fred seemed encouraged. "Then it seems we can fight it. I think if we show up in court for as slight an infraction as this, they might throw it out."

Wilma shook her head. "It's not that much. I think we should just pay it."

"It might affect our insurance rates."

"If so, then every time I pay the premium I'll be reminded to stay within the speed limit."

Fred shrugged. "It could just as easily have been me. I catch myself speeding through that stretch all the time. But I guess I'll be watching more closely now."

Josh piped up again, "Yeah, Dad. Just don't get caught."

Wilma was stern. "The point is not to speed, not simply to avoid getting caught. You'll be driving soon, Josh, and you'd better believe the police will come down a lot harder on a young driver than someone like me. The best way to avoid problems is simply to obey all the laws."

"Mom, that takes all the fun out of life."

Wilma knew he was joking, but his kidding hit close to the truth for a lot of people. Oh, well. It would be another year and a half before Josh started driving. She would have to start now to teach him the necessity of rules and the importance of following them. But first she would write a check and send it off to the city. That would be her lesson for the week.

WELL SAID!

Order is the shape upon which beauty depends" —*Pearl S. Buck*

Who Ordered This?

It should seem clear from a cursory look around that God is a God of order. We're planted on a ball in space that revolves around a larger one and is orbited by a smaller one. Yet with all the spinning, tilting, rotating, and such, we hardly notice it. Even when you multiply the activity around our sun by billions, the universe retains a sense of order.

We have enough gravity to keep us from floating off into space, but not so much that we can't move around. Some atoms are clustered into solids, allowing us to stand on firm ground and enjoy homes, cars, and all sorts of other things that don't immediately evaporate. Other atoms cluster into liquids, making it possible for us to swim and drink caffe latte. Still other atoms form gases that allow us to breathe and use helium to talk funny.

The very reason we can determine "laws of nature" is because the universe has order to it. We know what to expect, and we're glad we do. If your chair suddenly became liquid rather than solid, you would not only be sitting in a puddle, but you might be sitting there with a serious coccyx injury.

In a similar way, God has also provided a certain order for our interpersonal relationships. We have already examined family expectations, and we saw in the last chapter how we should respect our bosses ("masters"). Scripture also emphasizes the importance of government and commands a proper respect for people in positions of authority. It's sort of hard to mess up God's plan when it comes to natural laws. But lately our society has done a remarkably good job of disregarding the interpersonal standards

ONE SMALL STEP

It's time for further self-evaluation. Do you regularly berate government authority at any level? If so, what do you perceive to be the most annoying problems (big government, local police, etc.)? How do you think your attitudes toward government affect your commitment to Christ? At this point, try to identify what you feel most passionately about. As you read through the chapter, use that personal example as a mental sounding board for the comments and guidelines provided.

FOR EXAMPLE . . .

Simon of Cyrene (Matthew 27:32)

In Jesus' Sermon on the Mount, He encouraged His listeners not to resist forced labor. In fact, if forced to go one mile for someone, we should do a second mile voluntarily (Matthew 5:41). The man who helped Jesus carry His cross to Golgotha was drafted by secular soldiers, yet his act of service had a much higher purpose than simply kowtowing to the authority of government. It was true then and remains true today: When we serve others, we serve God.

WELL SAID!

The strongest poison ever known
 Came from Caesar's laurel crown. —
William Blake

God has established. Marriages continue to fail. Families are falling apart. Job satisfaction may be at an all-time low. And the hostile feelings people have toward the government may overshadow all these other problems.

Government Agents and the IRS

It's hard to be enthusiastic about supporting people who are professional bureaucrats. A few of our elected and appointed officials are hardworking and conscientious. But far too many spend their days lazing around, wasting taxpayer money, seeking bribes, and otherwise misusing their positions of power. We don't have to show respect for *those* people, do we?

Don't answer too quickly. If you think Nixon or Clinton or (You fill in the blank) have been unworthy of your respect, let's flash back to the reign of the Caesars. Imagine a time and place when your country wasn't technically yours; it was one of many possessions of the Roman Empire. Soldiers made their presence known on a regular basis. At any moment you might be drafted to help lug around a soldier's pack or otherwise serve the Empire.

And it's not like the Caesar family made much of an attempt at living upright lives. They were ruthless in their quest for power, killing off family members with little more regard than knocking down milk bottles at a carnival. They used military assassination, poison, and other creative methods to off their competing relatives and make it to the top. Some had sexual perversions that would still raise the eyebrows of *Penthouse Forum* readers. Caligula, for example, was rumored to be sleeping with his sister. It is still debated whether he was clinically insane or simply had a horrifying combination of high intelligence and nonexistent morals. Some say Nero dipped early Christians in wax and used them as human candles at parties. (Others say Nero gets blamed for a lot of stuff he didn't actually do.)

Yet during the long string of Caesars who ruled the Roman Empire, these were the instructions written to early Christians:

Obey the government, for God is the one who put it there. All governments have been placed in power by God. So those who refuse to obey the laws of the land are refusing to obey God, and punishment will follow. For the authorities do not frighten people who are doing right, but they frighten those who do wrong. So do what they say, and you will get along well. The authorities are sent by God to help you. But if you are doing something wrong, of course you should be afraid, for you will be punished. The authorities are established by God for that very purpose, to punish those who do wrong. So you must obey the government for two reasons: to keep from being punished and to keep a clear conscience.

Pay your taxes, too, for these same reasons. For government workers need to be paid so they can keep on doing the work God intended them to do. Give to everyone what you owe them: Pay your taxes and import duties, and give respect and honor to all to whom it is due. (Romans 13:1-7)

The excesses and injustices of the Roman emperors were far worse than anything that has currently made the news about our contemporary leaders. Yet these are the people God told first-century Christians to follow and obey. Their positions of authority, if not the leaders themselves, were to be respected. After all, the Old Testament contains numerous accounts of godly people who exerted powerful, positive influences on the pagan rulers of their time.

It's only natural to resist submitting to the authority of someone who is clearly not a godly or moral person. Yet we need to understand that human authority of any kind is only on loan. Only one person has ever deserved to have more authority than anyone else—Jesus. Only He led a sinless life from beginning to end. Only He overcame death and hell. And as a result, He was given "complete authority in heaven and on earth" (Matthew 28:18). He assigns "kings, kingdoms, rulers, and authorities" (Colossians 1:16). When He chooses to delegate authority to people, we sometimes question

FOR EXAMPLE . . .
People of Prominence

The following people are only a few whose faith was noticed and/or rewarded by nonbelieving national leaders.

- Joseph and Pharaoh (Genesis 41)
- Nehemiah and Artaxerxes (Nehemiah 1:1–2:10)
- Esther and Xerxes (Esther)
- Shadrach/Meshach/Abednego and King Nebuchadnezzar (Daniel 3)
- Jonah and the Assyrians (Jonah)
- Jesus and Pilate (Matthew 27:11-31)
- Paul and several Roman leaders (Acts 25–26)

WELL SAID!

Man's capacity for justice makes democracy possible, but his inclination to injustice makes democracy necessary.
—*Reinhold Niebuhr*

the right of certain people to receive power. But ultimately, we're only quibbling about who might be a little bit more sinful or less sinful than someone else.

Does that mean Jesus personally chose Hitler, Mussolini, and other tyrants who caused misery for all who came into contact with them? Of course not. But God creates systems that can work if people only put a little humility and compassion into them. The Old Testament system of judges could have worked, yet God's people were all too self-centered at the time (Judges 21:25). The Old Testament system of kings could have worked, except the kings got too absorbed in their own power rather than God's.

Monarchies can work. Democracies can work. But they can also fail. If history teaches us anything, it's that ungodly people placed in power in any system can foul everything up. Yet we also learn that ungodly people don't seem to prosper for long. Anyone can gather enough support to usurp power and control for a while, but God will ultimately balance the scales. Even as the historical atrocities are taking place, God foresees their downfall.

Shortly after God's people had been conquered and deported by the Babylonian Empire at the height of its power, Daniel interpreted a dream for King Nebuchadnezzar. The king had dreamed of a large statue with a head of fine gold (representing the Babylonian Empire), chest and arms of silver (the Medo-Persian Empire), belly and thighs of bronze (the Greek Empire), and legs of iron with feet of iron and clay (the Roman Empire).

Although this was an imposing statue, he had also dreamed of a rock carved out of a mountain, but not by human hands. It rolled like a bowling ball into the feet of the statue, causing the entire thing to fall in a heap of dust that blew away and left no trace. Meanwhile, the rock became a great mountain that covered the whole earth.

All of these empires that were foreseen by Daniel had some rulers who did whatever it took to conquer and succeed. Some of them were nasty, nasty people. Yet each empire eventually fell and was replaced by another. Today you won't find enough left of any of them to film a "Where are they now?" feature. But Jesus, the rock, remains a worldwide power to be contended with.

So while powermongers sometimes succeed in setting themselves up over other people, God never lets go of the reins of power. Evil men will not reign for long.

But the Only Caesars Today Are Salads and Casinos

You might be wondering how all this applies to us. With the exception of a few scattered places—most of them far from us—much of the world is no longer in fear of cruel leaders. Many countries that were once oppressed now enjoy free elections. The British people seem quite content with their ongoing monarchy. And here in the United States, we can vote out anyone who doesn't suit us. If things get too bad, we might go straight to impeachment without even waiting for the next election.

Yet while we might not have to worry about unlawful search and seizure or soldiers imposing tasks on us at will, our problems might lie at the other extreme. We tend to take freedom for granted, and perhaps we are even beginning to take government for granted. The percentage of people who vote is consistently low. When polled about issues, few can speak with any degree of intelligence. Some people can't even tell you the name of their mayor or governor.

And it is this distancing of the average person from his or her political representatives that can create a sense of apathy, antagonism, or worse. We have great freedom and live in a democracy. Yet while we're in perhaps the least threatening political climate ever, we find it all too easy to disparage the system that got us where we are.

Let's examine a couple more biblical passages and then see how our own attitudes stack up to the scriptural exhortations. Both of the following segments were written by Paul to people actively involved in ministry to others. His teachings apply to everyone committed to the Christian life.

DO'S AND DON'TS

Shout that people are like the grass that dies away. Their beauty fades as quickly as the beauty of flowers in a field. The grass withers, and the flowers fade beneath the breath of the Lord. And so it is with people. The grass withers, and the flowers fade, but the word of our God stands forever. (Isaiah 40:6-8)

ONE SMALL STEP

Can you name your city's mayor and chief of police? your state's governor? the Secretary of State? It's difficult to submit and pray for people when we're unaware of their existence. As you get the opportunity during the next several weeks, read the paper or watch the news with the goal of better understanding who these people are and what they stand for. (As you do, the urge to pray for them may come quite naturally!)

I urge you, first of all, to pray for all people. As you make your requests, plead for God's mercy upon them, and give thanks. Pray this way for kings and all others who are in authority, so that we can live in peace and quietness, in godliness and dignity. This is good and pleases God our Savior, for he wants everyone to be saved and to understand the truth. For there is only one God and one Mediator who can reconcile God and people. He is the man Christ Jesus. He gave his life to purchase freedom for everyone. This is the message that God gave to the world at the proper time. (1 Timothy 2:1-6)

Remind your people to submit to the government and its officers. They should be obedient, always ready to do what is good. They must not speak evil of anyone, and they must avoid quarreling. Instead, they should be gentle and show true humility to everyone. . . . These things I have told you are all true. I want you to insist on them so that everyone who trusts in God will be careful to do good deeds all the time. These things are good and beneficial for everyone. (Titus 3:1-2, 8)

It's one thing for Letterman, Leno, and countless other comedians to highlight every fault and foible of political leaders. From a purely comedic sense, many of our leaders' antics are certainly fuel for satire or laughs.

Yet how many times have you taken a cheap verbal shot at someone who wasn't your choice of leader? Christians have a mandate to avoid sinking to the lowest level of behavior—even when it comes to politics! But that doesn't stop us. Nothing gets our blood boiling faster than seeing "the other guy" giving commands, expressing opinions we don't agree with, and otherwise doing what he's entitled to do under the Declaration of Independence and the Constitution.

We are challenged to be obedient—even to the leaders we didn't vote for. We are to submit to them. We aren't to speak evil of them. We're even supposed to pray for them.

When Christians Are Losers

Christians frequently don't set good examples when it comes to obeying and supporting leaders they didn't vote for. Lately the trend has been to organize large blocs of Christian voters to attempt to sway elections. Most of the people involved are genuinely attempting to do God's will. But if their choice of candidate loses, you rarely hear those blocs of people publicly backing the newly elected official anyway. Instead, they may attempt to undermine the new leader's credibility and/or start fund-raising for the next election. Whatever would they have done in ancient Rome?

Christians aren't called to agree with all of our leaders, but we are instructed to support them. We are to comply with the laws. We are to set a good example for others.

Jesus had more knowledge, wisdom, and authority than anyone who ever lived, yet He willingly submitted to the authorities in His life. He obeyed His parents' authority even when they couldn't understand His thirst for spiritual challenge (Luke 2:48-52). And when challenged as to whether He might be a tax cheat, He paid His temple tax in a most unusual way—but it is clear that He paid it (Matthew 17:24-27).

In one instance, the religious leaders even used the issue of taxes to try to get Jesus to say something incriminating. It was a trick question: "Is it right to pay taxes to the Roman government or not?" In other words, "Should we good Jewish people support all this Roman decadence with our money?"

Jesus asked to borrow a coin, and He asked whose picture was on it. When they acknowledged Caesar's portrait, Jesus said, "Well, then, give to Caesar what belongs to him. But everything that belongs to God must be given to God" (Matthew 22:15-22).

Very rarely does the combination of religion and government become an either/or situation, unless we force certain issues. We can support God wholeheartedly, and in doing so, we also learn to respect the secular authorities in our lives.

Having said this, we should also acknowledge that Jesus broke certain rules that the Jewish religious leaders attempted to enforce.

DO'S AND DON'TS

For the Lord's sake, accept all authority—the king as head of state, and the officials he has appointed. For the king has sent them to punish all who do wrong and to honor those who do right.
(1 Peter 2:13-14)

WELL SAID!

Just be glad you're not getting all the government you're paying for.
—Will Rogers

FOR EXAMPLE . . .

Daniel (Daniel 1–6)

To justify civil disobedience under certain circumstances, we might point to Daniel. The reason he was thrown into the lions' den was because a law had been passed outlawing praying to God (Daniel 6). Yet if you read the book of Daniel from the beginning, you'll see that Daniel had been more than willing to reach tolerable compromises with his Babylonian captors (Daniel 1:8-20). He served under both Babylonian and Persian kings, demonstrating God's power rather than his own. He showed respect for those leaders, and for the most part, they showed respect for him as well. We shouldn't miss the point that his eventual disobedience to the law was a result of his total obedience to God when he had no other options.

194

He picked and ate grain on the Sabbath, which was legally considered work. He also healed people on the Sabbath, which his opponents criticized. He associated with sinners, Samaritans, women, lepers, and other people whom the religious leaders tended to shy away from. And on two occasions, He even led a cattle drive out of the temple to rid it of animals and money changers.

But we need to understand that Jesus' actions were always based on a much clearer understanding of God's intentions than the other religious leaders had. His breaking of unnecessarily binding religious laws was an object lesson about the freedom God was offering. We rarely have the same degree of certainty as to what God wants, so we need to be very careful about bending or breaking laws we don't agree with.

There may come a time and place for civil disobedience if secular laws conflict with the greater law of God. We remember the Boston Tea Party as a heroic act, not an irreligious one. We see women's suffrage and the civil rights movement as good things because of what was accomplished. But too many people lead personal, defiant crusades in the name of the Lord when perhaps the better course of action would be to submit to the authority of the person(s) in charge.

In Babylon, Persia, ancient Greece, and the Roman Empire, no one tended to mix their religion with their politics—the one exception being that those who defied the ruling parties could prepare to meet their gods before long. Political rulers did what had to be done to gain and maintain power, and religious leaders tried to guide the people as best they could under those conditions.

In contemporary society, however, many people tend to resist the separation of church and state. We want to mandate religion as law. But of course, we only want to mandate *our* religion as law. We are incensed if some other religion is pressed upon ourselves or our families.

We have fought wars to maintain the freedom of our democratic system of government. Yet we're faced with a dilemma when it comes to religion, because the same system of democracy doesn't work. God doesn't let us vote on what we will and won't accept. He is the King—a monarch and autocrat—when it comes to our religion. We exist to do His will. Besides, we can no longer assume that Christians are in the majority on many matters. If we attempt to force the issue, we are likely to be the ones voted down.

So in a sense, we're not so very different from the believers in ancient Rome. We have things a bit better, to be sure, but we need to learn the same lessons. When things don't go as we wish, we still need to respect the authorities who enforce those things. We can continue to set good examples for others and hold fast to what we believe. But it is unlikely we will always be able to determine and/or enforce the policies we desire.

We must always give to God what belongs to Him. And as we do, we must also learn to give to our governmental authorities whatever belongs to them. So the next time you're paying a speeding ticket or writing a big IRS check, think on these things. With practice, you might even learn to do it without gritting your teeth.

Questions to Ponder and/or Discuss

1. To wrap up this chapter, consider the following situations. In each case, do you tend to go along with the crowd, or do you try to stand out and set a good example?

   - At a party, the bulk of the group is president-bashing—not only speaking against his policies, but also making disparaging remarks about his personal life. It's clear none of them support him, much less pray for him. You tend to agree with them as far as the man's politics and morality go. Do you join the verbal fray? Why or why not?
   - When you sit down in April to compute your taxes, you discover you're going to have to write a big fat check to the IRS this year. But you see that if you fudge just a few deductions, you can drop to a lower bracket and save a couple thousand dollars. It was recently announced that the IRS is cutting staff members and the chances of an audit are more remote than ever. What do you do? Why?

- You're driving the kids when a police officer pulls you over and says you rolled through a stop sign. You didn't— at least, you don't believe you did. The officer looks as if he hasn't even started shaving yet, but he's clearly enjoying the authority his badge and uniform provide. How do you handle the situation? (And how would you handle it if the kids weren't in the car?)

2. When given the opportunity, do you ever defy authority? For example, if you're at a festival where people are trying to tell you where to park, do you blow past them and park where you want to? Do you ever berate teachers at your kids' schools, the people in charge of PTA meetings, or other local "authorities"? What is your attitude toward movie ushers, meter maids, park rangers, and others who have titles and responsibilities, but not much power?

CHAPTER FIFTEEN

Come Together
Church Relationships

The Seekers were attending church with the DiCiples. They had been visiting a number of different churches, including a few of the "megachurches" in the area. But once a month or so, they would come back to the DiCiples' church. It wasn't as big as some, or as ornate as others, but they liked it. The preacher's style was thought-provoking without being boring, and even though he was dealing with some pretty deep concepts, he didn't talk over their heads.

The Seekers knew a few of the people from the small-group Bible studies they had started attending. Jane and Wilma were standing in a tight cluster of women chatting away, but Fred had to go to a meeting that also included most of the guys in his Bible study. George stood in the lobby, not really knowing anyone well enough to initiate a conversation. He nodded politely to people who passed but was a bit uncomfortable and didn't know what to do with himself.

From his meeting room, Fred happened to see George shifting from one foot to another. He went to the door and shouted out to another person walking past, "Hey, Steve, introduce yourself to my

SOME THINGS YOU'LL DISCOVER IN THIS CHAPTER

1. How the biblical definition of "church" might differ from yours

2. Why church attendance may be more important than many people realize

3. What to do when church relationships go bad

ONE SMALL STEP

Think about your own church experience in the past. Do you have fond memories? Painful ones? How do you feel about church attendance on a regular basis? How important is it to your spiritual growth? Why did you start going? Why did you stop or change churches? What strengths have you detected at your local church? What weaknesses?

friend, George. He's a scientist, too. Tell him about all that quark stuff you've been working on."

As Fred returned to his meeting, Steve shook hands with George and they had a remarkable conversation. They had to be literally pulled into the sanctuary by their wives when the service started. But George missed a lot of that day's sermon because he kept thinking about how easy it had been to strike up a conversation with a total stranger. They had moved effortlessly from science to family to faith, and then back to science. George wasn't usually able to initiate meaningful discussions with such comfort. Was it simply because both he and Steve knew Fred, or was it more than that? Could it be the Christian connection that bonded them? If they had met on the street instead of in a church lobby, would their meeting have gone as smoothly?

Well, whatever the reason, George was starting to feel at home in this church.

The Church: A Body or a Building?

In chapter 4 we examined the importance of worship in the Christian life, but we focused mainly on individual worship and the attitude we need to have toward God. In this chapter we want to look more closely at church relationships. If someone is faithful in his or her individual worship to God, why bother dressing up every Sunday morning and driving to sit in a building with a bunch of other people?

Let's start by clarifying that the "church" is the people—not the building. While we may speak of going to church, the biblical perspective is that Christians *are* the church. In a common biblical metaphor, the individual believers form a collective "body" of which Jesus is the head. You can have a church without having a building—as many people have proven throughout history. If you have a building with no people, you can call it a church, but it isn't, really—even if it has a cross on the wall, a room full of pews, and a steeple on top.

Since our nation has so many church buildings sitting around, let's see how we can ensure they become genuine churches when we attend them. Below are a few reasons why it's important to get together with other believers rather than making your spiritual journey a solo effort.

Take-away Value

No one will dispute that your individual relationship with God is crucial to a successful Christian life. It is more important than any other relationship and should be developed day by day—not just once a week. An hour or two each Sunday won't do. We should frequently honor God with our prayers and praise, and He promises to supply us with all we need.

However, God frequently chooses to work through other people to meet our needs. We saw in chapter 8 that the Holy Spirit designates different gifts for different people. No Christian is created to be completely self-sufficient. We need one another. It is by brushing shoulders in the pews and shaking hands in the aisles that we begin to interact and acknowledge one another.

And that's just the start of what church attendance can do for building strong relationships. Small groups allow us to open up to express to one another our physical needs, prayer requests, hopes and dreams, and more. Bible studies help us see God's work in the past, and we can hear how He is continuing to work as other believers share their experiences.

Just as a person's social and emotional growth might be stunted if placed on a remote island to live apart from the rest of society, a believer's spiritual growth is never complete until he or she is relating to other believers. The church (the people, not the building) simply has too much to offer.

You'll Never Get So High If You're Solo

It should stand to reason that if other people have been given spiritual gifts for your growth and edification, then you have a gift or gifts for *their* benefit. If you don't associate with other believers on

WELL SAID!

There is something which only you can bring into the kingdom. —*Eric Abbott*

DO'S AND DON'TS

Let us not neglect our meeting together, as some people do, but encourage and warn each other, especially now that the day of [Jesus'] coming back again is drawing near. (Hebrews 10:25)

a regular basis, your gift is wasted to a certain extent. It's not much different from a selfish child who won't share his new Christmas presents with a sibling or friend.

Recall the spiritual gifts mentioned in chapter 8: teaching, serving, encouraging, leadership, giving, evangelism, pastoring, and such. What good are these gifts if your primary mode of worship involves isolation with God? It should be clear from the gifts themselves that they are supposed to be used in group settings. A loving parent would never give an only child a Monopoly game with the instructions to "Go to your room and have fun." It's a gift that only serves a purpose in a group.

You may not feel needed as you wander the halls of a large church or sit through a lengthy sermon. But assuming God knows what He's doing, you *are* needed. On any given day, you may make an observation that someone will remember and will take to heart. Yours may be the smile a child sees, causing her to want to return to the church where the adults are so friendly. The casual "hello" you toss out to another person may blossom into a full-fledged friendship. The eye contact you make with the preacher during the sermon may be just the affirmation he needs for all the hard work and study he invested in preparation during the week.

You need not be a preacher, teacher, speaker, or Bible scholar to be of great importance to the rest of the "body." You can be sure that you do indeed have *something* to offer, even if you haven't figured out exactly what it is yet. And whether you realize it or not, when you don't show up, you are missed.

The More the Merrier

Many churches consciously try to avoid the phrase "We've always done it that way!" It is very easy to become steeped in meaningless rituals and habits. However, a solid argument can be made for ongoing group worship by looking at how God has organized believers in the past.

No sooner had the Israelites been led from the slavery of Egypt than God sent Moses up Mount Sinai to receive a number of laws to live by. Many of these laws applied to the religious practices of the people. Much of the time Moses spent on Sinai, he was recording God's detailed plans for the construction of the tabernacle, its furnishings, the role of priests, and other details such as clothing, food, offerings, and so forth. It was clear that the practice of one's faith was not intended to be a solitary event.

Even then, the priests weren't the only people gifted for service. The Old Testament expresses great respect for stonecutters, craftspeople, musicians, and others who used their skills for the good of the people of God.

The tradition of group worship continued into the New Testament. Between the two Testaments, the Israelites were conquered by other nations and eventually came to be under Roman rule. Many of the people were carried away from their homeland into exile. It is thought that they probably gathered whenever they could to observe their Sabbaths and other special days. When they were allowed to return, they still wanted to meet on a regular basis. The temple in Jerusalem was a special place to visit for worship, but it wasn't convenient to everyone for weekly attendance. So local synagogues were established, which became more practical places for group worship. It only took a few faithful men to maintain a synagogue, so these group meetings were relatively common in the first century.

Certainly our Christian churches are even more convenient for most people. We have the luxury of "church shopping" until we find a denomination, worship style, time of worship, and so forth that fits our schedule and personal style.

Some people would say the church of today is too segmented. Young couples don't want to go to a church where there are lots of blue-hairs. Some white believers can't quite keep up with the pace of worship at many black churches. Some people's spiritual gifts make other believers uncomfortable, and ne'er the twain shall meet—at least, not on Sunday mornings.

FOR EXAMPLE . . .
Jehoshaphat (2 Chronicles 20)

If your local church were marching out to do battle against a fierce enemy, who would you put in the front lines? In this fascinating story, King Jehoshaphat had so much trust in God that he placed his *choir* in front! They sang praises to God, and the rest of the army didn't even have to fight. Instead, after God's divine intervention, they spent the next three days picking up spoils.

If two of you agree down here on earth concerning anything you ask, my Father in heaven will do it for you. For where two or three gather together because they are mine, I am there among them. (Matthew 18:19-20)

If we really wanted to open the can of worms of church problems, we would need a whole book to cover the topic adequately and fairly. So suffice it to say at this point that group worship has been the pattern from the beginning, and it continues to be important. These days you have a lot of options. If you can't find some place where you feel at home with God's people—whether you're seeking diversity or homogeny—you're probably not trying hard enough.

Huddle Up!

Another reason for gathering in a local church assembly on a regular basis is to help unify believers in reality rather than in theory. We sometimes have a mental perception of unity where we feel connected to other believers around the world, but it's a "brotherhood of man" kind of concept that may not touch the world where we live.

Unity is a noble concept that sounds as if it should be a necessity in the Christian life. But when it comes down to uniting with the same group of people week after week, the concept of unity is truly challenging. Are you really supposed to bond with the woman who has the grating voice (and multitude of problems), the guy whose case of halitosis may be coma-inducing, and the couple whose children won't stop crawling under all the seats and screaming at each other during the sermon? The answer, of course, is yes. As fellow believers, these are your brothers and sisters and will be for all of eternity (though bad breath won't be a problem after we get our spiritual, eternal bodies).

We're all out in the harsh world six days a week, fighting spiritual battles and doing our best to show God's love to the people we come into contact with. Church should be a sanctuary from such things at least once a week. Your local church body should become a shelter from the storms of life. If your family members are driving you nuts, if your boss is putting pressure on you to skirt the law to make a bigger profit, if you've been seeking God's help in making a big decision but can't seem to come to a clear conclusion, then the unity of the church is a valuable asset.

Church serves a purpose similar to a huddle for football players. The group of individuals each has a specific assignment—a tough task to perform. They know what to do. Yet the huddle is important to ensure the team is working together and running the same play. Someone might detect an especially difficult problem or a weakness in the opponent's defense that could provide an opportunity to score. By putting their heads together for a few moments on a regular basis, much good can be accomplished. Not only is it a brief respite from the action; it's also a time for essential strategy.

No matter how you feel as you walk into a church building, when you walk out you should be reenergized and ready for further action.

An Appealing Function of Church

And there's at least one more good reason for committing to regular church attendance. If worship were merely a matter of climbing a mountain by oneself to spend time with God in peace, we would run out of mountains before long. Then it would become a matter of who got there first, or who is the biggest, and soon worship would be altogether forgotten as we started bickering over who's right, who's wrong, and whose turn it is.

That's not exactly what God has in mind. He knows that disagreements between believers are bound to arise, but when they do, there should be an orderly method of achieving conflict resolution just as there is order to everything else in the Christian life. Jesus was pretty specific about what to do:

> If another believer sins against you, go privately and point
> out the fault. If the other person listens and confesses it,
> you have won that person back. But if you are unsuccessful,
> take one or two others with you and go back again, so that
> everything you say may be confirmed by two or three

WELL SAID!

The Bible knows nothing of solitary religion. —*John Wesley*

FOR EXAMPLE . . .

Euodia and Syntyche (Philippians 4:2-3)

Essentially all we know about these two ladies is that they were engaged in a public feud within the Philippian church. And settling the matter was important enough for Paul to spotlight them in his letter, encouraging them to come to terms. Wise Christians will learn from their example and resolve personal conflicts before being singled out by some other source of authority.

DO'S AND DON'TS

When you have something against another Christian, why do you file a lawsuit and ask a secular court to decide the matter, instead of taking it to other Christians to decide who is right? . . . If you have legal disputes about such matters, why do you go to outside judges who are not respected by the church? I am saying this to shame you. Isn't there anyone in all the church who is wise enough to decide these arguments? But instead, one Christian sues another—right in front of unbelievers! To have such lawsuits at all is a real defeat for you. Why not just accept the injustice and leave it at that? Why not let yourselves be cheated? But instead, you yourselves are the ones who do wrong and cheat even your own Christian brothers and sisters. (1 Corinthians 6:1, 4-8)

witnesses. If that person still refuses to listen, take your case to the church. If the church decides you are right, but the other person won't accept it, treat that person as a pagan or a corrupt tax collector. I tell you this: Whatever you prohibit on earth is prohibited in heaven, and whatever you allow on earth is allowed in heaven. (Matthew 18:15-18)

So another reason to support the organized church is because it has been given authoritative power by God. Even under the best of circumstances, believers will occasionally butt heads over certain issues. When such conflicts occur, it's good to know it's not every person for himself (or herself). If a one-to-one settlement is possible, that's the best resolution by far. If arbitration is needed, that's a second step. But in dire situations where someone simply won't listen to reason, the church can act as a ruling body.

Christians are encouraged not to air their dirty laundry in secular courts, if possible (1 Corinthians 6). It might be argued that the church sometimes leaps into political arenas, trying to resolve problems without being asked—and perhaps creating more problems than it solves. The church is even accused of misusing its power from time to time. But it is comforting to know that at a local level, we don't have to depend on the witticisms of Judge Judy or other secular courts of appeal when we have valid complaints. We can take our problems to people who have a better understanding of the Christian life, and we can count on them to rule based on knowledge and wisdom from God rather than legal technicalities and loopholes.

By nature we are all selfish and sinful people. Even years after becoming a Christian, we can revert to our old natures if we don't watch out and keep maturing spiritually. If and when we do stumble along the way, it's good to have the church body to support us, to help us see more clearly, and to guide us back to where God wants us to be. Sometimes we need God's Word applied to our lives for correction and rebuke in addition to teaching and training (2 Timothy 3:16).

When we take our complaints to the church, perhaps it will be confirmed that the other person is the problem, and the church will take action. Sometimes, however, it might be that we're the ones who are in error or who are being unreasonable. What then?

The Supreme Court

In the previous chapter we looked at several authorities in our lives to whom we should show respect and submission, among them the police, the president, the IRS, and other government officials. We have also emphasized the importance of submission within families and work settings. And you might think that submitting to church authority would be a simple matter. Unfortunately, this is not always the case.

As individual believers exercise their spiritual gifts in church settings, sometimes the church body is in for some surprises. The expectations and assumptions of the secular world don't always translate into church settings, and vice versa. A church body might include a number of corporate presidents, and you might expect them to make an effective church board. Perhaps they will, but then again, maybe not. Church leadership requires spiritual maturity and commitment, in addition to being spiritually gifted to begin with.

In the midst of the corporate officers and managerial people, perhaps the best person to oversee the administration of the church is the plumber who has studied Scripture on his own ever since childhood. The church body might include a professional singer who can induce tears with her songs (in a good way), but if she also happens to be a prima donna, she may not be the best choice to lead the choir. The youth group might benefit more from a sedate older couple who has developed patience and perseverance than from a younger, hipper person who will bail out at the first sign of difficulty or inconvenience.

This won't always be the case, of course. Many times a person's skills will meld flawlessly with his or her spiritual gifts. A CEO who has learned mercy and humility may be the best possible choice to lead a church board. A professional singer who has developed

WELL SAID!

Christians have burnt each other, quite persuaded
That all the Apostles would have done as they did.
—*Lord Byron*

teaching skills as well might become an excellent choir leader. A young person who will take on the responsibility and maturity of leadership can excel as a youth leader. It's just important to look past the "obvious" choices to see if God might have somebody else in mind for a particular area of ministry. At the local church level, people need to be careful to evaluate and choose leaders based on the gifts and talents God has designed rather than individual interests and/or abilities.

And you need to ask yourself, what if you are a CEO passed over in favor of a plumber? What if you have a heavenly voice yet are asked to sit among the choir instead of standing in front of it? What if you are a charismatic, on-the-go young leader who is asked to assist an older couple rather than take charge?

In such cases, the same rules about submitting to authority are in effect. In fact, where the unity of the church is at stake, it's even more important that we willingly submit to another person's authority. But sometimes it's harder for Christians to submit to other Christians than for them to yield the right of way to secular authorities.

The church's effectiveness will be impaired if its members aren't working together. It does us little good to individually submit to authority in all our other relationships if we don't respect one another when we gather within the church walls.

Don't You Want Some "Body" to Love?

We should grow to count on our fellow Christians within the church body, but we must be careful not to expect too much. Christians are by no means perfect, so we should expect lapses of faith, mistakes, shortcomings, and other faults.

Think about it. One day a person might be a nonbeliever, going through life grabbing for all the personal gusto he or she can get. If that person makes a decision to follow Jesus, he or she becomes a part of the church—the body of Christ. Does that mean all those old

bad habits are permanently left behind? Not likely! Each "baby" Christian has a growing, maturing process to go through.

Everyone in the church is at some stage in that process. Some are farther along than others. But everyone is likely to trip from time to time. That's the very point of coming together on a regular basis. Meeting with others in the church is a source of renewal, new commitment, additional challenge, and more.

The point of meeting together is to become more like Jesus, the head of the body. It's our ultimate goal, but we never quite get there. The "body" continues to receive new members and grow stronger. Yet on any given day the foot might fall asleep, the elbow might strike its funny bone, the little finger could get a hangnail, or the big toe could get stubbed and sore. In other words, people are going to be people, and when they aren't as "Christian" as you might like, you ought to cut them some slack. Then maybe they'll do the same for you.

It's sometimes quite a challenge to tolerate other growing Christians. Just like physical adolescence, the spiritual maturing process is likely to involve some growing pains. We can either support one another as we go through the growth process, or we can make it harder.

And if you think getting along with other Christians at church is a challenge, wait till you get a load of the next chapter.

ONE SMALL STEP

If you've tried church in the past and it hasn't been your "thing," try it again. Ask some happy-looking Christians for suggestions, and try at least three different local churches. And even if you're a regular church attender, you might want to visit some other congregations and/or denominations to see how other people worship God. You might be able to take back some fresh new ideas to your own body of believers.

WELL SAID!

The holiest moment of the church service is the moment when God's people, strengthened by preaching and sacrament, go out of the church door into the world to be the church. We don't go to church; we are the church.
—*Ernest Southcolt*

Questions to Ponder and/or Discuss

1. What would you say are the top three problems you've witnessed in local churches that, if they were satisfactorily resolved, would make a lot of people more willing to attend?

2. When you attend church, where would you say you fit on each of the following scales?

Get me out of here!	Love it!
Spectator	Participant
Old-time religion	The newer, the better
Let me sleep	Ready to learn
Sedate	Eager to use my gifts

3. What elements do you think can make or break a church service? (Pastor? Music? Fellow attenders?) List all you can think of, and rate them as to importance.

4. If you're currently attending a church, how well is your church doing in regard to each of the things you've listed? What can *you* do to make improvements?

CHAPTER SIXTEEN

"TIMEOUT!"

Mission: Unthinkable

RELATIONSHIPS WITH ENEMIES

The men's group at Fred's church had recently begun a study of the Sermon on the Mount. George Seeker had been attending regularly, as had several other men new to Christianity, so the group had chosen a topic that was down to earth and not overly theological. They had whizzed through the Beatitudes and the salt and light images and had slowed down a bit to thoroughly discuss the issues of lust and anger.

Today's meeting had come to that awkward transition from doughnuts and small talk to serious discussion. The leader finally asked: "Does anyone have any comments or questions about this week's passage?"

A moment of silence ensued as minds shifted gears. But George didn't wait long to speak. "It's probably because I'm new to Christianity and all, but I just don't get the part about loving my enemies. It seems that by definition an enemy is someone I have no respect for. I don't even *like* my enemies, much less love them. How do you guys do that? What's your secret?"

SOME THINGS YOU'LL DISCOVER IN THIS CHAPTER

1. How to reexamine our attitudes toward people we can't stand

2. Why not simply write off the people who don't like us?

3. How to be holy without being holier-than-thou

ONE SMALL STEP

President Nixon became well known for having an Enemies List, but if pressed, many of us might confess to having one. Give the matter a bit of thought. If you were asked to create a list of personal enemies, how many names immediately come to mind? What criteria do you use to determine who goes on the list and who stays off?

The silence continued, longer this time. Fred spoke up at last. "I can't say I have that little matter figured out myself. I can list a dozen people I would honestly have to classify as enemies, and I've stopped trying to be friends with them. I pray for them sometimes, but I feel like a hypocrite because I don't really mean it."

Heads started nodding. George's question and Fred's comment got a spirited discussion started that carried over into the following weeks. It was the general consensus that most men are taught—either by family or society—not to take much flak from anyone. After a reasonable time, if the other person continued to make trouble, he or she would simply be added to the Enemies List and treated with little regard from that point forward.

Yet the command to love and pray for one's enemies came from Jesus' own mouth. How could they defend such actions?

The men in the group who had grown up in the church were somewhat dumbfounded. They were well familiar with the passage, but had never really grappled with the concept. Faced with the honest question of one new Christian, they were being forced to a whole new level of understanding and commitment in their spiritual lives.

All in all, not a bad day's Bible study!

Closing All Loopholes

The previous several chapters in this book have focused on the importance of relationships in the Christian life. We've looked at marriage, family, work, church, friends, and government. Some of these have presented larger challenges than others in establishing and maintaining proper Christian attitudes and relationships.

Most of us can endorse the principle to love and respect these categories of relationships. But if you're like most people, you've been making certain exceptions for a particular harsh boss, an abusive relative, a greedy and corrupt government official, and so forth. In reality, we might have an enemy or two in each of these categories. After all, no one can be expected to get along with everyone, right?

Jesus apparently doesn't want us to be too quick to reach this conclusion. Here's what He had to say:

> You have heard that the law of Moses says, "Love your neighbor" and hate your enemy. But I say, love your enemies! Pray for those who persecute you! In that way, you will be acting as true children of your Father in heaven. For he gives his sunlight to both the evil and the good, and he sends rain on the just and on the unjust, too. If you love only those who love you, what good is that? Even corrupt tax collectors do that much. If you are kind only to your friends, how are you different from anyone else? Even pagans do that. But you are to be perfect, even as your Father in heaven is perfect. (Matthew 5:43-48)

Lest you start to think this book is about how to live "the *nice* life," we have arrived at the bottom line of "the *Christian* life." Lots of nonbelievers try very hard to respect authority, love their parents and kids, work hard, and be decent in their treatment of others. But few people (including believers) do much along the lines of loving their enemies. Yet this standard, above most other things, will convince others of the authenticity of your faith.

But Who Is My Enemy?

At one point Jesus was asked to clarify what defined a "neighbor" (Luke 10:29). In response He told the parable of the Good Samaritan, which provided a definition so broad that one's "neighbors" included even one's so-called enemies. The parable also clearly emphasized the need for showing love for those we normally tend to despise.

At this point, perhaps we need to go to the other extreme and attempt to clarify what defines an *enemy* in our thinking. Many people are quick to say, "I have no enemies," yet their thoughts, fears, and actions indicate otherwise. Below are some criteria that sometimes cause two people to become enemies.

WELL SAID!

Such ever was love's way; to rise, it stoops. —*Robert Browning*

DO'S AND DON'TS

If you call someone an idiot, you are in danger of being brought before the high council. And if you curse someone, you are in danger of the fires of hell. (Matthew 5:22)

DO'S AND DON'TS

There is no longer Jew or Gentile, slave or free, male or female. For you are all Christians—you are one in Christ Jesus. . . . So Christ has really set us free. Now make sure that you stay free, and don't get tied up again in slavery to the law. (Galatians 3:28; 5:1)

People Who Don't Look or Sound Like We Do

Some of our major prejudices arise from differences in skin color, language, accent, or gender. And it takes very little effort for those prejudices to create full-fledged enemies.

Something within us tends to want to rate and compare when presented with two options. That's no problem when you're looking for the better bargain between weed whackers or laundry detergents, but it becomes a sinister habit when dealing with people. When you stand next to someone of a different skin color, gender, weight, build, or ethnic background, it's a terrible spiritual pitfall to start comparing that person's worth to your own.

When someone looks different or has habits that are unfamiliar to us, it's easy to give them derogatory names. You can probably think of a dozen or so without even trying hard. But when we designate such names, we immediately strip away the respect those people deserve as fellow creations of God the Father.

But we don't have to go to the extremes of name-calling or other forms of degradation to put such people on our Enemies List. Our prejudices need not be nearly so overt. If we take a closer look at the parable of the Good Samaritan, we see that Jesus wasn't chiding His peers for literally harming someone—that had been done by robbers. But the cold, heartless sin of the supposedly religious people was ignoring the immediate need of a hurting person. They got within clear view, saw the blood and bruises, and just kept walking. It was the Samaritan—a person who was supposed to be an enemy—who stopped to help. In this parable, Jesus made it clear who the injured man's enemies *really* were.

Perhaps you have relatives who were shot by Iraqis in Desert Storm, the Vietcong in Vietnam, Germans or Japanese in WWII, or Prussians in WWI. Maybe your grudge goes back to the Punic Wars or before. Some families pass along resentment and even hatred toward all those countries and/or ethnic groups for generations.

We need to let go of the long-standing grudges and quit being so quick to add new ones. For some people, a simple difference in gender can trigger hostility. For others, it's a matter of tattoos,

piercings, clothing, or hairstyles. But as we take the Christian life to a deeper level, we must not allow any physical aspect of a person to immediately label him or her an "enemy." Jesus reminds us that all people are precious in His sight (red and yellow, black and white). Therefore, we need to look for ways to shorten our Enemies List, not add to it.

Geography

And we don't even have to find people who look different than we do to create enemies. All it might take is a difference in location. In high school we are urged to have "school spirit," which some students interpret as intense hatred toward all rivals. Who knows how much harm has been done between individuals just because one kid goes to one school and another kid just like him attends a neighboring school? "School spirit" frequently evolves into verbal abuse, fistfights, and worse. And as those kids grow up, sometimes all it takes is a geographic line to trigger that old "be true to your school" instinct.

Jokes abound between Texans and "Okies," between residents of other states, cities, and even suburbs. Yet as people have noted, "Many a truth is spoken in jest." Sometimes verbal jabs turn into physical ones simply because one person lives on one side of an invisible line, and someone else lives on the other. Jokes become feuds, and feuds become wars. Country turns on country and people within countries turn on each other. When we think of the American Civil War, our minds may not immediately turn to issues of slavery and economy, but rather to North vs. South.

Geographic enemies are artificial ones, but that seems to be enough for a lot of people. If you catch yourself thinking that anyone south of your location is a redneck, that all New Englanders are cold and standoffish, or that L.A. residents are all phony, those little stereotypes might lead to some very real enemies with very little effort.

Enemies by Association

Sometimes we get our dander up simply by hearing that someone belongs to a particular organization. Political affiliations are one of

FOR EXAMPLE . . .

Jesus and His Disciples (Acts 1:8)

Few groups were as tight as the Jewish people, who were bonded in social, religious, and other ways. Yet Jesus' final words to His disciples were a command to transcend geography in order to reach others. They were to start right where they were but weren't to stop until they had reached "the ends of the earth."

WELL SAID!

May I be no man's enemy, and may I be the friend of that which is eternal and abides. —*Eusebius of Caesarea*

213

DO'S AND DON'TS

If you are asked about your Christian hope, always be ready to explain it. But you must do this in a gentle and respectful way. Keep your conscience clear. Then if people speak evil against you, they will be ashamed when they see what a good life you live because you belong to Christ. (1 Peter 3:15-16)

the major examples in this category. To hear some people talk, anyone who supports a different political party is essentially voting to foster the reign of the Antichrist.

But this problem extends far beyond politics. What do you think when you hear someone is associated with the Teamsters? the NAACP? Greenpeace? the Jewish Defense League? the Freemasons? the NEA? PETA?

You might feel an immediate bond with any of these groups and what they stand for. Someone else might automatically feel a sense of suspicion or alarm. The very nature of organizing such groups is to unite as many people as possible behind a stated cause. The leaders might be extremely outspoken to the point where those outside the group feel threatened and begin to suspect any and all members of the group. The sense of suspicion might then cause outsiders to treat anyone associated with the group as a personal enemy.

This type of shortsighted thinking occurs all the time and without much thought. And again, the key is to see the individuals involved as *people,* not simply as names on a membership list. It's certainly each person's right to support or oppose any organization and what it stands for, but Christians should beware of being too quick to label the people involved enemies. As soon as we do, we severely limit our ability to reason with them and effect any degree of useful communication.

Religion

We've saved the biggie for last. Few things will cause people to raise their banners and go marching out to war faster than defending their religion. Certainly, we are expected to know what we believe and be ready to defend it. But if, as Christians, our very first instinct is to reach for a sword or sledgehammer to drive truth into the stubborn minds of any infidels we find, perhaps we're using the wrong approach to present a message of love.

Christians are privileged to serve as messengers of God, but we're supposed to be bearing Good News. If our message comes across as consistently condemning, demeaning, threatening, or otherwise negative, maybe we're not doing it right. The Christian life is supposed to include a large dose of *joy*, and people usually respond positively to their peers who don't go around scowling all the time. Yet all too often, Christians present the gospel with a hard-sell approach to convince people to turn from their sinful ways.

It's the job of the Holy Spirit to convict people of their sin and persuade them to repent (John 16:7-11). If God Himself is willing to give them the option to reject Him and walk away, who are we to deny them the same choice? Do we come on so strong because we think God needs our help strong-arming stubborn people?

It may be difficult at first to interact with people of other religions without feeling a bit threatened. Many Hindus, Buddhists, Muslims, and others are very devout—perhaps much more so than most Christians. If it were only a matter of their devotion compared to ours, a lot of us would come off looking like the spiritual slackers. Yet if Christians really believe we have discovered truth about God that others haven't yet comprehended, we should share it with patience and love. To simply label other religions as enemies is the easy (and lazy) way out. We need to save our strength to fight *spiritual* enemies, not flesh-and-blood opponents (Ephesians 6:12).

If people are actively attempting to infiltrate the church and spread false doctrine or confuse believers about the truth of Christianity, that's a different situation. Biblical precedent and instruction dictate that we should deal firmly with such problems. But if they are simply going about the practice of their own religion, we shouldn't be too quick to consider them our enemies. Perhaps a friendship will eventually lead them to the complete truth about who God really is.

We don't want to get all starry-eyed and suggest that Christianity will eliminate all problems from your relationships. It's just the opposite, as a matter of fact. As people resist God, many of them will vehemently oppose His followers. Yet those are exactly the people we need to pray for. If we don't extend God's love to them, they aren't likely to ever want to change.

So let's go back to the original question: Who is my enemy? If we are quick to define certain groups or individuals as enemies, it will

WELL SAID!

It is hard to fight an enemy who has outposts in your head. *—Sally Kempton.*

WELL SAID!

A wise man gets more use from his enemies than a fool from his friends. *—Baltasar Gracian*

FOR EXAMPLE . . .

Elisha and the Arameans
(2 Kings 6:8-23)

Reading through the Old Testament, we might assume the motto was, "See an enemy? Kill an enemy!" But in stark contrast to this practice is this story of Elisha, who had God-given insight to correctly predict the military strategies of Israel's enemies. As a result, the enemy sent an entire army to surround and capture Elisha. The prophet prayed that his enemies would be blinded, and when they became unable to see, he led them to Israel's capital city and stood them before the king. There they had their sight returned. Israel's king was thrilled. He saw a bunch of enemies and proposed they be killed on the spot. Elisha, however, commanded that they be fed and sent home safely. And from that day on, those enemies no longer threatened Israel.

be very hard to genuinely love them and pray for them. However, if *they* define themselves as our enemies, we can still love them and pray for them, even if a schism still exists in the relationship. As long as we aren't too quick to retaliate in response to their hostility, we don't close the door on eventual reconciliation.

If we are to be genuinely Christlike and relate to others the way He would, we need to do away with our Enemies List altogether. That doesn't mean your name won't be on someone else's list—perhaps a lot of people's. Sometimes that can't be helped. But in such cases, your love for that person and your prayers on his or her behalf can have surprisingly positive results. Our enemies—now defined as those who have something against us—become prime targets of prayer and compassion. If we have the proper attitudes and draw strength from God, the people who oppose us can actually strengthen our faith!

Passive Resistance to Enemies

David was very familiar with dealing with enemies—from Goliath to King Saul to members of his own household. At times he was known to slay hundreds of Philistines in a single outing. But even amid the warfare and bloodshed of the Old Testament, he composed some remarkably calming and assuring poetry. In the familiar Twenty-third Psalm, he writes: "Even when I walk through the dark valley of death, I will not be afraid, for you are close beside me. Your rod and your staff protect and comfort me. You prepare a feast for me in the presence of my enemies" (vv. 4-5).

So not even David, the mighty warrior, always resorted to extermination of his enemies. He knew what it was like to have opponents lurking around him. But his confidence in God was enough to allow him to function anyway.

Jesus also suggested that the definition of "enemy" might be someone who takes issue with us rather than vice versa. Speaking to those who had chosen to follow Him, He said, "Your enemies will be right in your own household! If you love your father or mother more than you love me, you are not worthy of being mine; or if you love your son or daughter more than me, you are not worthy of being mine" (Matthew 10:36-37).

Jesus realized that as some people put their faith in Him and others didn't, even the closest of relationships could be severed. In such cases, the key is to remain faithful to Him. If our family members or others label us as enemies, we can't help that. But we don't have to sink to the same level. That's why commitment to Jesus is so important—it's supposed to invigorate us with the love, wisdom, and logic we need to remain loving to such "enemies" and willing to pray for them.

It takes courage to love people who consider you to be their enemy. It takes perseverance. It takes faith. It's not something everyone can do.

And that's the whole point. As we get better at sensing God's leading in our lives, we can continually work at spreading the peace we feel to others, thereby reducing (and preferably, eliminating) the names on our Enemies List. And although we can't help it if others oppose us, hate us, threaten us, and so forth, we can learn to extend love to them and regularly pray for them (and really mean it).

Being Different without Being Difficult

We can't fake real love for other people. It's possible to force yourself to say or do nice things for a while, but if the other person is slow to respond, you are likely to reveal your true feelings—intentionally or not. But as you mature in the Christian life, you will eventually discover that it is possible to see other people as God sees them. Your spiritual vision clears to the point where you can see past his insults to his pain, past her rejection to her loneliness, beyond the anger to the fear and desperation.

Nonbelievers aren't likely to do this, even if they were capable of doing so. Even with the supernatural strengths and abilities available only from God, it still takes conscious choice and deep spiritual determination to overlook others' offenses and return

DO'S AND DON'TS

Try to live in peace with everyone, and seek to live a clean and holy life, for those who are not holy will not see the Lord. Look after each other so that none of you will miss out on the special favor of God. Watch out that no bitter root of unbelief rises up among you, for whenever it springs up, many are corrupted by its poison. (Hebrews 12:14-15)

WELL SAID!

Could we read the secret history of our enemies, we should find in each man's life, sorrow and suffering enough to disarm all hostility.
—*Henry Wadsworth Longfellow*

ONE SMALL STEP

It may be premature to suggest shredding your Enemies List altogether. But can you take the small step of shortening it? Can you begin to extend love to *any* of the names on it, rather than continuing to seek retaliation? Prayerfully give the matter some thought and see how many names you can cross out.

only love. If we keep reminding ourselves this is exactly what God has done for us, perhaps we can become a little better at doing the same for others.

When God looks down from heaven on you and your biggest enemy, He doesn't see much difference. God sees two people in need of His unfathomable love and forgiveness, destined for hell without it. Perhaps you are a believer while the other person isn't, but all that means is that you're in the sheepfold, so to speak, while the other person hasn't yet located the entrance. God is every bit as eager for the other person to find Him as He is glad that you already did. Few things are as grievous as believers who intentionally make it harder for others to find the serenity and security of God's kingdom. The sheep on the inside of the fold aren't supposed to place barbed wire around the walls and barricade the entrance to keep lost sheep out. The walls are there to protect the sheep from predators—not their peers. As the Shepherd attempts to rescue the perishing, those of us who have found security in His presence need to do whatever we can to support His efforts.

But let's face it: most people who call themselves Christians go throughout life with a number of people they consider enemies, whom they neither love nor attempt to pray for. And if we're not praying for them, we may not hesitate when the opportunity comes along to undermine one of them at work, to chant "I told you so" at a family reunion, or to rejoice when the wind blows a large tree on a grumpy neighbor's home instead of our own.

In other words, we act just like those who don't know God. What a shame! As the old song says, "They'll know we are Christians by our love." But if the love isn't apparent, what will they think about us?

What Did Jesus Do?

Jesus is asking us to do an extremely hard thing by loving and praying for our enemies. But if you read Scripture closely, you'll see that God never asks us to do anything that's bad for us, or that He hasn't already done Himself.

Try to put yourself in Jesus' place for a moment. He came down from heaven to save the world and redeem sinful humanity from eternal death. After three years of ministry, He had quite a following. But He also had powerful enemies who craftily saw to it that He was tried, convicted, and put to death. With a crown of thorns cutting into His head and thick spikes holding Him to a cross, He hung in utter humiliation before crowds of people.

Suppose that had been you on the cross with your enemies jeering at you, and you remembered you still had unlimited power. What would you have done?

Jesus had come to save the world—not just those who listed Him among their friends. So He didn't retaliate in response to His enemies' cruel and unfair treatment. Instead, among His final words was a prayer: "Father, forgive these people, because they don't know what they are doing" (Luke 23:34).

If Jesus could muster the will to pray for His enemies under those circumstances, surely we can learn to do the same when someone cuts us off in traffic, makes a disparaging remark about our parentage, betrays us after promising to love us "till death we do part," or treats us even worse. It's quite hard to love our enemies and pray for them, but Jesus has shown us that it is indeed possible. We first have to be willing, and then we have to make the attempt to do it. Don't expect it to be easy at first, but go ahead and give it a shot.

In this era of road rage, air rage, and rage of all sorts, we who are Christians should attempt to start a new trend. If enough of us can humble ourselves to the point of loving and praying for our enemies, our forgiveness is going to be noticed by the nonbelievers in the world. And maybe it will catch on. Let's work toward a world where love, forgiveness, mercy, and grace become all the rage.

WELL SAID!

Remember, nobody will ever get ahead of you as long as he is kicking you in the seat of the pants. —*Walter Winchell*

Questions to Ponder and/or Discuss

1. What is it about people you don't know that tends to trigger your suspicions and/or fears more than anything else? How can you resist acting prematurely and rejecting someone who might need to find a new friend . . . and possibly a connection to the Christian life?

2. What specific actions tend to put people on your Enemies List? Rate each of the following things according to how much it bothers you. (1 = Least; 10 = most)

   > Lying to you
   > Telling one of your secrets
   > Not doing something they promised to do
   > Betrayal of a trust
   > Name calling/Put downs
   > An air of superiority
   > Physical violence
   > Emotional abuse
   > Spiritual hypocrisy
   > Attempted manipulation to get what they want
   > Competitiveness
   > Other:_____

Do you consider any of these things to be unforgivable sins as far as you're concerned? Explain?

3. Who impresses you as a very forgiving person? As people come to mind, make a point of talking to them to see what offenses they have suffered (and forgiven) in the past. Choose one or two people to help hold you accountable for learning to forgive your enemies and to pray for those who persecute you.

CHAPTER SEVENTEEN

"THESE COLOR COPIES ARE SO GOOD, I THINK WE CAN PUT BACK THE ORIGINALS."

A True-to-the-Original Reproduction

SELF-IMAGE

Jane Seeker was looking at her profile in the bathroom mirror. Well into her eighth month of pregnancy, she could envision an enormous Goodyear decal across her belly. Other parts of her body were going through strange transitions to make room for the baby, resulting in a general feeling of physical yuckiness. Yet she had never been more at peace. The women in her Bible study group and others at the church had surrounded her with love, prayer, and all sorts of support. Her life had a new meaning, and she perceived the timing of her move to this area to be a gift from God, just as her new son or daughter would be. (They hadn't peeked at the sonogram.) Her initial fears for her unborn child had been quickly eased by her growing faith in God. Whatever happened was now in His hands, and she would do everything possible to be the mother He was creating her to be.

Meanwhile George Seeker was getting ready for work. As he caught a reflection of himself in the dresser mirror, he realized he was smiling. On closer inspection, he found himself humming one of the praise songs from yesterday's church service that had lodged

SOME THINGS YOU'LL DISCOVER IN THIS CHAPTER

1. Differentiating self-image from other "self" perceptions

2. What it means to be created "in the image of God"

3. Maintaining humility in light of being a unique creation of God

in his memory. He used to think such songs were a bit childish, but now they were beginning to express and reflect his inner joy and commitment to God. It was odd, this strange interdependence he was developing with Fred and the other people at church. He had always been satisfied to be independent and self-sufficient, but this new concept of "fellowship" was something special.

Fred DiCiple also happened to be looking at himself in a mirror while halfway through a workout at the health club. The chill of winter had inspired him to sign up for membership, and his morning runs were now done on a treadmill rather than asphalt. Besides, the health club also had those dreaded sit-up machines, and he had been supplementing his running with other exercises. So far it was working. He had dropped some weight, and people were just beginning to notice. But more importantly, he was feeling much more spiritually fit than ever before. His new relationship with George was a genuine friendship rather than a shallow excuse to evangelize. He thought back to previous opportunities he had probably missed out on because he had been too aggressive. That was a different person. From now on, he was going to be more sensitive to the needs of other people and then sit back to see what God would do.

Wilma DiCiple was enjoying the frigid draft coming through her slightly open window as she prepared the Bible study for this week's meeting at her house. Out of habit, she looked out at her garden. The vegetables had been gone for months, and even the late-blooming flowers had finally succumbed to the frosts and early snowfalls. Yet even though the garden was now bleak and bare, Wilma couldn't help but think about growth cycles. The regular attention she gave to her garden certainly paid off in incredible beauty for most of the year. And the women in her group—Jane Seeker foremost among them—were no less dramatic in their blossoming from green and immature seedlings into beautiful, mature people of God. She was humbled that she could be a part of that process. She wasn't responsible for the spiritual growth of her friends any more than she was responsible for the dozens of plant species that germinated from tiny seeds each year. But in both cases she could try to provide the right climate with a bit of water and attention, and then see how God brought about growth and beauty. Wilma found a tremendous satisfaction in setting the stage and then watching God work. It made her feel really good about herself.

The Definitive View of Self-Image

We've been getting to know four people whose lives have come together in strange and wonderful ways. And all of them are beginning to see themselves more clearly from a spiritual perspective. The best things in life—marriage, friendship, pregnancy, the beauty of creation, and all the rest—are only intensified when God's active presence is acknowledged. With such recognition, even the most simple and mundane aspects of life take on new meaning. And the big events are even bigger as we identify them as part of God's plan.

In this chapter we want to take a look at self-image, which can be a confusing issue for Christians. How are we supposed to perceive ourselves? It's been clear throughout this book that we're sinful, sorry people until we place our faith in God and He steps in to redeem us. The grand old hymns remind us that Jesus "saved a wretch like me" and died "for such a worm as I." Is that the extent of how we're now supposed to view ourselves? And since we're told to love our neighbors as ourselves, is that the way we're supposed to perceive other people? ("Howdy, neighbor. Beautiful day isn't it, you old wretch? How's that worm of a wife of yours?")

We've been examining all sorts of relationships a Christian is to have with other people, yet the relationship with oneself is frequently overlooked. We may make certain assumptions but never give the matter too much thought. So let's think about it for a while.

See if you can pick the definition of self-image from the following options:

___ (A) Preoccupation with oneself
___ (B) Promotion of one's own rights, claims, or opinions
___ (C) Sole concern for one's own desires, needs, or interests

WELL SAID!

A humble knowledge of thyself is a surer way to God than a deep search after learning. —*Thomas à Kempis*

FOR EXAMPLE . . .

Gideon (Judges 6—8)

Even if we tend to see ourselves as insignificant, God doesn't necessarily agree. When Gideon was called to service, he noted that "My clan is the weakest in the whole tribe of Manasseh, and I am the least in my entire family!" (Judges 6:15). He was none too eager to step into a leadership role. Yet God's angel addressed him as "mighty hero" (6:12). When Gideon agreed to let God work through him, he was for the most part a terrific judge/leader over the people of Israel. God sees us as what we can become with His help, and that's an image we need to try to cultivate for ourselves.

223

ONE SMALL STEP

Think of some specific self-improvement philosophies you have heard or read about lately. If possible, check your bookshelves or magazine racks to see what other writers have to say. Then compare those opinions to the ones presented throughout this chapter.

___ (D) An exaggerated opinion of one's own qualities or abilities

___ (E) Restraint exercised over one's own impulses, emotions, or desires

___ (F) Free choice of one's own acts or states without external compulsion

___ (G) Commitment of oneself, especially to service or sacrifice

___ (H) Correction or regulation of oneself for the sake of improvement

___ (I) The placing or keeping of oneself in the background

___ (J) A confidence and satisfaction in oneself

___ (K) Assertion of one's own individual traits

___ (L) One's conception of oneself or of one's role

___ (M) A concern for one's own advantage and well-being

___ (N) Excessive or exclusive concern for oneself

___ (O) Having confidence in and exercising one's own powers or judgment

___ (P) Conviction of one's own rightness, especially in contrast with the actions and beliefs of others

___ (Q) Governed by one's own wishes

(We'll save the correct answer for last. The other definitions, in order, are for: self-absorption, self-assertion, self-centeredness, self-conceit [or self-importance], self-control, self-determination, self-devotion, self-discipline, self-effacement, self-esteem, self-expression, self-interest, selfishness, self-reliance, self-righteousness, and self-willed. The correct definition of "self-image" was L.)

Simply put, self-image is how we see ourselves. It's a rather harmless and innocent word. Yet the inner drives we feel and the external challenges we receive to cultivate a *positive* self-image may steer us toward some of those other "self" words that aren't nearly so neutral. Some are actually quite harmful if our goal is to develop an authentic Christian lifestyle. It's a tightrope to walk. We want a certain degree of self-confidence and a lot of self-control,

but we don't want to drift into selfishness, self-absorption, and other potential problems.

So how do you see yourself? That's your self-image. Are you a lowly, wormlike wretch of an individual? Or are you the king of the world? And what *should* a Christian's self-image be?

Whom Do You See in Your Mirror?

Everyone wants to feel good about themselves. There's nothing wrong with that. But where to look to generate the good feelings we desire is crucial. Can we validate our own self-worth? And if not, who can?

One thing's for sure: We started out okay. According to the Genesis account, after God had created the oceans, stars, planets, plants, and all the other animals, He prepared to create human beings. At that point He said, "Let us make people in our image, to be like ourselves" (Genesis 1:26). As a result, "God created people in his own image; God patterned them after himself; male and female he created them" (Genesis 1:27). And when God evaluated what He had created, He deemed human beings to be "excellent in every way" (Genesis 1:31).

People were created as a mirror image of God and still reflect His image to a great extent. We're not simply another animal species, more or less equivalent with all the others, and it's not being more highly evolved that makes us special. We *started out* special in God's sight, and we remain that way.

Yet we now grapple with the problem of sin, so we don't automatically act as God would. Sin separates us from God, so we've lost much of the desire and willingness to conform to the image in which we were created. In fact, as we look at certain people we don't see much to indicate *any* form of godliness. And it's often frustrating to consider the high ideal that has been set for us and to realize how far away we remain from attaining that goal.

If it were simply a matter of working and striving to make progress, we might better deal with the process. Yet spiritual growth

WELL SAID!

Nothing is a greater impediment to being on good terms with others than being ill at ease with yourself.
—*Honoré de Balzac*

DO'S AND DON'TS

Your attitude should be the same that Christ Jesus had. Though he was God, he did not demand and cling to his rights as God. He made himself nothing; he took the humble position of a slave and appeared in human form. And in human form he obediently humbled himself even further by dying a criminal's death on a cross. Because of this, God raised him up to the heights of heaven and gave him a name that is above every other name. (Philippians 2:5-9)

WELL SAID!

If salvation could be attained only by working hard, then surely horses and donkeys would be in heaven.
—*Martin Luther*

DO'S AND DON'TS

Follow God's example in everything you do, because you are his dear children. Live a life filled with love for others, following the example of Christ, who loved you and gave himself as a sacrifice to take away your sins. And God was pleased, because that sacrifice was like sweet perfume to him. (Ephesians 5:1-2)

demands much more than our own efforts. Therein lies the problem with so many self-help philosophies. We cannot rise above our wretched problems and attain godlike status simply by thinking positively, improving our mind-set, or adhering to a regimen of meditation or other disciplines. Even within Christianity, spiritual disciplines do little good apart from the presence of the Spirit Himself acting in our lives.

If we truly want to experience what it's like to be in God's image, we must step aside and let God take over. Here's Paul's advice: "Don't copy the behavior and customs of this world, but let God transform you into a new person by changing the way you think. Then you will know what God wants you to do, and you will know how good and pleasing and perfect his will really is" (Romans 12:2).

A caterpillar doesn't keep crawling and persevering in its own efforts until one day its feet eventually leave the ground and it begins to fly. In order for the caterpillar-to-butterfly transformation to take place, the creature must give up its caterpillar-ness and let a miracle of nature take place. It enters a cocoon as a crawly wormlike creature and emerges as a magnificent airy being—able to float on the breeze and bring beauty to the world. But unless it commits to a major change by building and entering the cocoon, it will end up frozen by the winter cold or as a hearty meal for a bird or other predator.

> Similarly, if a sinful human being doesn't commit to a life-changing transformation made possible only by a supernatural act of God, the person's self-image will never improve significantly. People can work, struggle, strive, labor, and do everything within their power, but they cannot get out from under the nasty burden of sin we all inherit at birth. But God can flick away that sin problem the moment we place our faith in Jesus. At that moment we hand off our sins to Him to take care of, and we agree to carry His "yoke" instead. (Matthew 11:28-30)

It has been said that we aren't so much human beings striving to be spiritual as we are spiritual creatures trying our best to cope with being human. Scripture makes it clear that from a spiritual perspective, we can expect to live forever. So the sooner we make a commitment to Jesus here on earth, the better we can anticipate and begin to tap into the joys and wonders of the Kingdom of Heaven.

And all of this comes to bear on Webster's definition of self-image: "One's conception of oneself or of one's role." If we see ourselves as always struggling but never making any headway to rid our lives of the stench of sin, we have approximately the same self-image as a teenager at the prom without having had benefit of deodorant, toothpaste, or a shower during the past week. But if we see ourselves as forgiven and completely accepted children of God waiting for a glorious inheritance after we "go the distance" here on earth, then our self-image is going to shoot off the scale on the positive side.

As forgiven people of God, we can stop the fruitless attempts to highlight the good things about us while downplaying the bad. Instead, we can confess to our shortcomings and begin to live our lives with more vulnerability and genuineness. We can admit that we are indeed sinful yet have been pardoned and redeemed by a gracious Savior. We continue to make mistakes, but every day we become a little more conformed to the image of God. We moan and groan as our physical bodies age and break down and as outer beauty fades. But self-image can remain strong as we realize it's the inner being that is much more vital and that God will soon enough replace our temporary physical bodies with glorious eternal ones (1 Corinthians 15:53).

A Christian's self-image should begin with a confident, positive internal feeling that works its way out through our attitudes and actions. Attempting to focus on all the externals in order to feel good on the inside never works.

WELL SAID!

The grandeur of man lies in the fact that he is created in the image and likeness of God. . . . If he fails to recognize his dignity he does not know himself; if he insists on it without referring it to a greater than himself, he founders on the rock of vainglory. —*Étienne Gilson*

Been There, Dung That

If anyone could have based self-image on status and accomplishments, it would have been the Apostle Paul. His resumé looked quite impressive. He writes:

FOR EXAMPLE . . .

Paul (1 Corinthians 15:9; Ephesians 3:8; 1 Timothy 1:15)

As Paul continued to mature in the Christian life, his references to himself changed gradually. In his letter to the Corinthians he referred to himself as "the least of all the apostles." A few years later in his letter to the Ephesians, he said he was "the least deserving Christian there is." Still later, in his first letter to Timothy, Paul acknowledged himself to be the worst sinner of all. As Paul saw his human sinfulness more clearly, he placed less and less stock in any of his own accomplishments or the things he once based his self-image on. It was only in living for Christ that Paul found any lasting fulfillment. (See Philippians 1:20-24)

I could have confidence in myself if anyone could. If others have reason for confidence in their own efforts, I have even more! For I was circumcised when I was eight days old, having been born into a pure-blooded Jewish family that is a branch of the tribe of Benjamin. So I am a real Jew if there ever was one! What's more, I was a member of the Pharisees, who demand the strictest obedience to the Jewish law. And zealous? Yes, in fact, I harshly persecuted the church. And I obeyed the Jewish law so carefully that I was never accused of any fault. (Philippians 3:4-6)

Paul had credentials that would have made most of his peers jealous. Yet he realized such things had nothing to do with what was really important in life. He continues and clarifies his priorities:

I once thought all these things were so very important, but now I consider them worthless because of what Christ has done. Yes, everything else is worthless when compared with the priceless gain of knowing Christ Jesus my Lord. I have discarded everything else, counting it all as garbage, so that I may have Christ and become one with him. (Philippians 3:7-9)

Many of the values we hold and the things we do to improve our self-image are, to use Paul's word, "garbage." And even then, the translation has been sanitized a bit. The King James Version was more blunt: "I count all things but loss for the excellency of the knowledge of Christ Jesus, my Lord; for whom I have suffered the loss of all things and do count them but dung." That's right: *dung.* Sewage. Excrement. Poopoo. Perhaps you have another word for it.

The very things people cling to in order to preserve and improve self-image are equated with the stuff you try to scrape off your shoes after coming back to the house from the barn. What kind of self-image is that?! But if Jesus is the source of one's self-image, we can discover deep joy and godly pride in being among God's highest creations: human beings.

In addition to all the self-help resources sold each year, consider the number of multimillion-dollar industries fueled by money from people desperate to achieve a positive self-image through external means. In a frantic attempt to feel better about ourselves, we try hundreds of cosmetics and toiletries, designer clothing and accessories, plastic surgery, medications, health clubs, and much more. Even cars, colas, and most other products are promoted by suggesting the users stand to improve their image. While there is nothing wrong with wanting to look, feel, and smell better (or drive nice cars, for that matter), we must beware trying to compensate for an inner spiritual void with a plethora of external substitutes.

We can hide the acne on our faces. We can eliminate the stench from our armpits. We can shave certain body parts to look better and hide others for the same reason. We can sweat off dozens of pounds and diet off dozens more. But if our self-image rises and falls with our waistlines, we're only fooling ourselves. Any kind of physical determination for self-image creates spiritual problems.

Here's why. You might not mind judging *yourself* harshly based on physical traits. It might even motivate you to drop some weight, improve your personality, or whatever. But if you then seek to "love your neighbor as yourself," you're likely to impose the same standards—consciously or not. If you don't love yourself regardless of physical appearance, job status, and all the rest, then you aren't likely to cut your "neighbors" a break either. Your spouse and kids will start feeling they're never quite good enough to meet your unspoken standards. Acquaintances with a few extra pounds will never feel completely at ease around you.

ONE SMALL STEP

Think about the items in your medicine cabinet, closet, locker, jewelry boxes, etc. To what extent do you attempt to use external items to boost self-image or to improve your image in the eyes of others? Do you ever cross the line from self-care into self-centeredness, self-conceit, or similar *self*-ish problems?

DO'S AND DON'TS

Don't judge by . . . appearance or height. . . . The Lord doesn't make decisions the way you do! People judge by outward appearance, but the Lord looks at a person's thoughts and intentions. (1 Samuel 16:7)

From Dung to Gold

So while things like big homes, fancy cars, high status in the community, a toned-up physique, and other such things can be nice to have, they are little more than a dung pile as a foundation for self-image. Perhaps that's why the "love your neighbor as yourself" exhortation is the *second* part of the great commandment. First and foremost is the command to love God with all our heart, soul, mind,

FOR EXAMPLE . . .
Paul's Building Analogy
(1 Corinthians 3:10-15)

Paul confirms that Jesus is the only sure foundation for life, and adds that whatever we choose to build on that foundation will be "put through the fire to see whether or not it keeps its value. If the work survives the fire, the builder will receive a reward." Some of our accomplishments are like gold, silver, and jewels—indestructible and of lasting value. Others are closer to wood, hay, and straw, which have only momentary influence and quickly go up in smoke when tested by fire.

and strength. That step sets the stage for everything else to come in the Christian life.

Only after we begin to love God more faithfully do we realize to what extent He loves us. And all the other pieces of life begin to fall into place. We see problems as He does—merely opportunities for growth along our spiritual journeys. We see cranky people (even our enemies) as He does—as dearly beloved souls He wants to draw into His Kingdom and closer to Himself. And in time, we see ourselves as He sees us—as unique, specially created, one-of-a-kind, magnificent creations of His. That's the self-image He wants for us. Anything else is a pale imitation.

That's why Scripture says so much about choosing strong foundations and then building on them. A life built on God's truth (about Himself, ourselves, our self-image, etc.) is like a house on a rock. Any other foundation is like sand that will eventually wash away and result in "a mighty crash" (Matthew 7:24-27).

The purpose of this book has been to help establish the importance of having Jesus Christ as the only adequate foundation for the Christian life. And once we establish Him firmly as the base of everything else we do, then we can choose to build a life of great value. When our thoughts, behaviors, and actions are motivated by such a high calling, we don't tend to get caught up in shallow imitations for determining self-image. We begin to experience "life in all its fullness" (John 10:10) and will never again be satisfied with less.

Rather than wanting to hoard what we have received, we tend to want to share it with anyone and everyone willing to join us. The old ways of thinking—what Paul equated with "dung" (or the equivalent term of your choice)—are transformed into gold, silver, and jewels. And the Golden Rule of life is summed up succinctly by Jesus Himself: "Do for others what you would like them to do for you. This is a summary of all that is taught in the law and the prophets" (Matthew 7:12).

It's another of those odd contradictions of the Christian life: The more we try to focus on "self," the more screwed up our self-image becomes. But as we keep our focus on God and show our devotion

to Him by attending to the needs of our "neighbors," self-image begins to soar.

In conjunction with our commitment to the Christian life, God provides numerous rewards and benefits to regularly encourage us and keep us on track. Many of those things will be described in the next chapter–the final chapter. It is our hope to send you away from this book on a positive note.

Questions to Ponder and/or Discuss

1. To what extent do each of the following factors tend to affect your self-image? (1 = least; 10 = most)

How I look on any given day	1 2 3 4 5 6 7 8 9 10
What other people say about me	1 2 3 4 5 6 7 8 9 10
The way I've been brought up	1 2 3 4 5 6 7 8 9 10
What I'm wearing	1 2 3 4 5 6 7 8 9 10
How I feel	1 2 3 4 5 6 7 8 9 10
Recent successes/failures	1 2 3 4 5 6 7 8 9 10
Other:_____	1 2 3 4 5 6 7 8 9 10

2. In 25 words or less, what does it mean to you that you are created "in the image of God"?

_____

_____

_____

3. If you were to cultivate a more consistent biblical outlook in regard to your self-image, what are three significant changes you might expect to see in your life?

ONE SMALL STEP

If self-image has been an ongoing concern of yours, spend some time thinking about how God sees you. If you aren't convinced He is eager to wrap His arms around you and make available to you everything in His kingdom, reread the parable of the Prodigal Son (Luke 15:11-32) and think some more.

CHAPTER EIGHTEEN

"LOOK, EITHER NOAH THROWS IN STOCK OPTIONS AS PART OF THE PACKAGE, OR MY CLIENT WALKS."

The Benefits Package

WHAT GOD PROVIDES FOR THOSE WHO SEEK THE CHRISTIAN LIFE

Fred and Wilma DiCiple sat, as patiently as possible, in the hospital waiting room. George Seeker had waited until after sunrise to call them, even though Jane had already been in labor for much of the night. But as soon as they arrived, George had been called into the delivery room.

Fred wasn't quite as nervous this time as when Joshua and Mary had been born, but almost. Wilma had a book with her, but her mind wouldn't absorb the words. She, too, was thinking about the births of her own children. How could anyone witness something so seemingly impossible and not believe in miracles?

Fred reached out and took her hand, and they sat in silence, reminiscing silently but together. It was still early, with few people around. Every time someone came to the door, they both looked up expectantly. After about a dozen false alarms, the person in the door was George Seeker. "It's a girl. The doctor says she's perfect . . . and who am I to argue?"

Not long afterward the five of them were clustered in Jane's

SOME THINGS YOU'LL DISCOVER IN THIS CHAPTER

1. A review of benefits of the Christian life

2. A few additional benefits to add to the list

3. A preview of even better things yet to come

WELL SAID!

Does being born into a Christian family make one a Christian? No! God has no grandchildren. —*Corrie ten Boom*

room. She looked exhausted, but exhilarated. George was holding the baby as the DiCiples cooed over her. Wilma spoke for both of them: "What are you going to name her?"

Jane smiled. "If it had been a boy we probably would have gone with George Junior. But for a girl, we both really like Hope."

"Hope Seeker. Wow! What better name for a darling little girl just starting out in this scary world." Fred barely got the words out before his voice choked up.

Wilma took over. "After all these months, it's really good to know that there's a new Seeker in the world. We're so happy for you."

"Thanks," replied Jane. "And if we have anything to say about the matter, it won't be long before she's a new disciple as well. We owe you two so much."

"You don't owe us a thing," countered Fred. "We're privileged to have such tremendous neighbors and friends."

And right there, right then, the first of a lifetime of prayers was said, through tears of joy, for the young Hope. And to think she was only one of the thousands of God's new children born that day!

No Happy Endings?

With this we say good-bye to the Seekers and DiCiples. But don't forget these four fictional friends because most of us will see ourselves in one or more of them. We're all seekers at different levels, even those of us who are disciples as well. As long as we're on earth, the process of seeking God and trying to follow Him will continue. The more we discover about Him, the more we realize how much we need to continue seeking.

So far we, the authors, have been blathering on about the Christian life for 17 chapters. Much of this stuff you probably already knew, so we've just been reminding you of some basics. Yet we hope a few of the things we've said have been worthwhile and thought-provoking for you. And we've tried to save much of the best stuff for last.

One final question we would like to pose is this: At what point does the Christian life end?

Don't be too quick to answer. This isn't baseball, where "It ain't over till it's over." If we're talking about the life Jesus has in store for us, it ain't ever going to be over.

When Paul was writing letters to the churches, he knew that other teachers of the time were denying the reality of the resurrection of the dead. Like many people today, they believed that you live, you die, and that's that. So for those who bought into that philosophy, it made little sense to adhere to Paul's (and Jesus') admonitions to deny oneself, live for others, sacrifice oneself, and so forth. The Christian life was a joke to such people.

And if Paul weren't so sure about resurrection, he probably would have agreed with them. In fact, he went on record that, "If we have hope in Christ only for this life, we are the most miserable people in the world" (1 Corinthians 15:19). As we have seen, the Christian life offers peace, joy, wisdom, a deeper level of love for others, and much more. It's a pretty good deal for those willing to commit to it, yet few of those who have enlisted can deny that it also requires much sacrifice and self-denial. If this life is all we get, it does indeed seem foolish to "waste" so much time on behalf of others that we could be using to pamper ourselves.

But if this life *isn't* all we get, that's a different story. This life then becomes only the appetizer for a lush and endless banquet yet to come.

FOR EXAMPLE . . .

Paul's Visit to the "Third Heaven" (2 Corinthians 12:1-10)

Why was Paul so convinced of the resurrection? In this account, he speaks of knowing a man who "was caught up into paradise and heard things so astounding that they cannot be told." Most people assume Paul is speaking of his own experience. As a result of his "wonderful revelations from God," he wrote of resurrection and eternal life with great authority.

Review

We've touched on a number of benefits to the Christian life as we've gone through this book. But we want to ensure that they are spotlighted as we wrap things up. Below are a few of the things we've noted so far.

Salvation/Redemption

We said from the beginning that the Christian life can be little more than a label unless we depend on God to take care of our sin

DO'S AND DON'TS

Don't let anyone lead you astray with empty philosophy and high-sounding nonsense that come from human thinking and from the evil powers of this world, and not from Christ.
(Colossians 2:8)

problem and make us different from all those who are spiritually dead or dying. Only He can do it. And only after He does it can we begin to experience "life in all its fullness" (John 10:10).

Salvation is so wonderfully simple that it may not seem as essential as it truly is. Perhaps you've seen prayers you can repeat, short and to the point, in which you invite God to oversee your life from here on. But it's less a matter of the words you say as it is the intention of your heart. A prayer for salvation should include a confession of one's sinful status, a desire to lead a righteous and godly life, and a genuine expression that the life, death, and resurrection of Jesus Christ is the only effective remedy for the sin problem. And that's all it takes—no matter what words you use or how clumsily you attempt to express yourself. God is smart enough to know what you're trying to say and when you're being sincere, and He responds immediately.

The moment you make this commitment, God writes your name in His Book of Life—and heaven's pencils don't have erasers! Jesus becomes your Savior and Friend, and you can relate to Him in an entirely new and deeper way. In addition, the Holy Spirit enters your life to provide guidance, support, power, and everything else you need for day-to-day living.

God doesn't require a particular SAT (Spiritual Aptitude Test) score before bestowing salvation. He doesn't demand you attend religion boot camp for rigorous training. If you want to wait until your dying breath to make this commitment, that's your loss, not His. The loving heavenly Father will gladly wrap His arms around any prodigal, any time, who wishes to find his or her way home. It's simply that the sooner in life we make the decision, the better we can make sense out of the trials and blessings of life itself.

Sometimes this process of salvation is also called redemption. In the most basic sense, you have great value to God, but you're like a coupon. Until you submit yourself to God, your value is little more than any other slip of paper. When He redeems you, however, you discover how much worth He assigns you, and you may be quite surprised.

Access to God

Along with your newfound salvation, you will discover an amazing level of improvement in your communication with God. Just as sin separated humanity from God in the Garden of Eden, salvation restores the connection to a great extent. You might remember that at the death of Jesus, the veil that hid the Most Holy Place in the temple was "torn in two, from top to bottom" (Matthew 27:51). It was as if God declared, "No more separation! Enough of that!"

WELL SAID!

God is not greater if you reverence Him, but you are greater if you serve Him.
—*Augustine of Hippo*

We are now encouraged to "come boldly to the throne of our gracious God. There we will receive his mercy, and we will find grace to help us when we need it" (Hebrews 4:16). We can certainly expect to experience times when our prayers don't seem to be working and we feel a sense of isolation. These are feelings common to all Christians from time to time. Yet they are only temporary feelings. For the most part, God seems much closer and more involved after our salvation. It's as if He adopts us to be Jesus' brothers and sisters—His children with all the same benefits Jesus has received (Romans 8:15-17).

Fellowship/Unity

The changes in one's personal life that arise from the marvel of salvation at first seem so unique and miraculous that we are surprised to discover how many other people have already been through the same transformation. But soon enough we find ourselves drawn to those who truly understand the mysterious spiritual metamorphosis that has taken place. We begin to identify our spiritual gifts and look for ways to put them to good use. And as we learn to leave behind the bickering and jealousy, church becomes a place where we find kindred spirits, renew our commitment to God on a regular basis, and recharge our spiritual batteries to go out into the secular world for another week.

As church ceases to be a place to attend infrequently out of guilt or obligation, we are freed to discover how great it feels to belong to a group whose single most important goal is to worship God. And when worship is genuine, it usually doesn't take long for the love expressed toward God to quickly filter down into expressions of

WELL SAID!

If you love, you will suffer, and if you do not love, you do not know the meaning of a Christian life. —*Agatha Christie*

love and concern for one another. This newfound unity and fellowship in a church setting is a benefit of the Christian life that comes as a total surprise to many new believers.

An Emotional Shift

We tend to think of the Christian life as being primarily a spiritual thing, yet another tremendous benefit is the change that tends to take place at a deep emotional level. You may recall that the fruit of the Holy Spirit is love, joy, peace, patience, kindness, goodness, faithfulness, gentleness, and self-control. These are spiritual qualities, in a sense, yet they are also so down-to-earth that we can immediately start applying them to bad hairdressers, grumpy great-aunts, harsh teachers, and everyone else we come into contact with. Rather than allowing the setbacks of life to automatically trigger negative reactions, we now have a choice of how we *want* to respond.

As love for God tends to integrate with our love for one another, so do the spiritual elements of life begin to blend with the emotional ones. This is primarily a good thing, although we are no longer able to claim to be a good and holy person at church on Sunday morning while remaining a holy terror at work the rest of the week. Consistency of behavior becomes not only a goal, but also a passion.

New View

Most of the previous section has been little more than a review, yet it is material that is certainly worthy of a second look. In this section we want to continue the list of benefits of the Christian life. These will be things we might have touched on throughout the book but that are so important we don't want to wrap things up without going into just a bit more detail.

Grace

For a little word, grace carries a lot of significance. Lots of people toss it around as if they fully understand it, but few truly comprehend the depth of its meaning.

Simply put, grace translates as "undeserved favor." In other words, anything good God does for us that we don't deserve is an act of grace. So the very basics of the Christian life that we've already examined—salvation, access to God, Christian fellowship, the presence of the Holy Spirit in our lives, and all the rest—are free gifts. We can do nothing in our own power to deserve such things, and must simply receive them from God.

God's primary act of grace, of course, was sending His Son to earth as a final sacrifice for sin. Thanks to Jesus' death and resurrection, we are freed from a strict, legalistic system based on sacrifices. We need not worry about working hard enough to "earn" heaven on our own merits. Instead, we can joyfully live and worship in the light of God's grace. We are still expected to follow the basic teachings of Scripture, but our motivation should no longer be the fear of God's judgment if we make a mistake or stumble along the way. Instead, we should be thrilled to follow God out of sheer gratitude for all He has done for us.

ONE SMALL STEP

Read a book about grace, which has been a popular topic lately. If you don't find one on the shelves of your home, bookstore, or church library, you might ask for *The Grace Awakening* by Charles Swindoll or *What's So Amazing about Grace?* by Philip Yancey.

Mercy

Mercy is quite similar to grace. But while grace consists of the good things God does for us that we don't deserve, mercy is a reprieve from receiving all the bad stuff we *do* deserve as a result of our sin.

Perhaps you've noticed that every time you tell a lie your nose doesn't begin to grow like Pinocchio's. You can look at pornography and not go blind (no matter what Grandma used to tell you). You can occasionally call in sick to work and go to a ball game instead, and you aren't always the one singled out for a close-up on the JumboTron. Sometimes when we get by with such things, we tend to think we're pretty clever. But God sees each of our sins, and it grieves Him whenever someone supposedly devoted to the Christian life behaves more like someone belonging to the Prince of Darkness's House of Follies.

The fact that we don't get caught by other people every time we sin isn't mercy. But the fact that God, from whom nothing is hidden, doesn't zap us into carbon dust when we consistently oppose Him and His standards is certainly due to His mercy. And if we

DO'S AND DON'TS

So since God's grace has set us free from the law, does this mean we can go on sinning? Of course not! Don't you realize that whatever you choose to obey becomes your master? You can choose sin, which leads to death, or you can choose to obey God and receive his approval. (Romans 6:15-16)

239

FOR EXAMPLE . . .

Ananias and Sapphira (Acts 5:1-11)

This rather harsh story is in the Bible for anyone who begins to think God is so full of grace and mercy that He is a "pushover" for anything we want to do or try to take credit for. God is a wonderful proponent of grace and mercy, but the day will come when He will also fulfill His role as judge, and justice will be served.

ONE SMALL STEP

If you have a neighbor who works hard to tend to flowers for the neighborhood to enjoy, make a note of thanking him or her this week. You can keep the conversation at a horticultural level if you wish, or it might take a spiritual turn if you want to express your appreciation for "God's creation" in your neighbor's garden.

refuse to respond to His repeated examples of grace and mercy, someday we will discover we should not have taken such valuable gifts for granted.

Creation

People brought up in church sometimes tend to think of the original Creation story with great sadness and trauma. God created a perfect world, the serpent entered, and Adam and Eve threw it all away. From that point there have been curses, thorns, thistles, and sweat.

And while it's true that the world is a lot less perfect now than it was created to be, we forget what a truly sweet place it is. It seems in our world of concrete and asphalt that it's harder these days for God to get our attention when it comes to natural things. But perhaps you can recall a day not so long ago when you were stopped in your tracks by a sunrise or sunset, by the first warm day of spring or what might turn out to be the final one of fall, by a butterfly working a flower, by a hummingbird, a wild coyote on the edge of your suburb, a meteor shower, a spectacular sighting on a whale-watching expedition, or any of a hundred thousand other things that usually go by unnoticed.

We tend to plead with God for the few things we don't have as we take for granted a hefty percentage of the gifts He offers us each day. If dandelions were very rare instead of so plentiful, don't you suppose many people would pay big money to watch the almost overnight miracle of bright yellow flower transforming into a spherical puff of seeds to be disbursed in the first gust of wind? But since we see them as little more than nuisance weeds, we hardly notice the miracle each spring.

God's amazing creation surrounds us whether we're aware of it or not. The more we make an effort to notice, the more we discover to thank Him for.

Variety

And while we're at it, have you ever considered why God went to such lengths to provide us with such a *variety* of creation? The weather changes with the rotation of seasons. We have a vast selection of foods and tastes to choose from—even more these days now that shipments can be overnighted from one side of the world to the other. If you want a dog as a pet, you have approximately 300 breeds to choose from, or you can go to a shelter and get your own one-of-a-kind friend. We perceive colors across a wide spectrum.

And again, we tend to take these options for granted. Think how drab the world would be if the weather never changed, or if everything were the same color. What if you never had a choice of what to eat?

And this may not seem to be much of a spiritual matter at first, but indeed it is. God, in His infinite wisdom, could have created the world with a lot less variety. He could have created people just alike as well—same look, same personality, same sense of humor. Yet He saw fit to equip different people with different gifts and talents. Variety seems to be important to Him. When things are working as they should, our differences draw us closer to one another. The gifts one person lacks are those others have in abundance. So if we learn to depend on one another, we never come up short.

You can be who you were created to be, and so can your spouse and your friends. And in doing so you may be just about as different as people can be. Good! Enjoy the gift of variety that only God the Creator can make possible.

WELL SAID!

To see a World in a Grain of Sand
And a Heaven in a wild Flower,
Hold Infinity in the palm of your hand
And Eternity in an hour.
—*William Blake*

Benefits Unlimited

We could go on enumerating gifts of God until we run out of ink, and we would still have hardly begun. But perhaps you're getting the idea. We'll let you continue with your own list from here on. But let's not forget the reminder we find in James: "Whatever is good and perfect comes to us from God above, who created all heaven's lights. Unlike them, he never changes or casts shifting shadows. In his goodness he chose to make us his own children by giving us his true word. And we, out of all creation, became his choice possession" (James 1:17-18).

Everything good and perfect is a gift of God—and therefore another benefit of the Christian life. And as far as God is concerned,

DO'S AND DON'TS

God has made everything beautiful for its own time. He has planted eternity in the human heart, but even so, people cannot see the whole scope of God's work from beginning to end. So I concluded that there is nothing better for people than to be happy and to enjoy themselves as long as they can. And people should eat and drink and enjoy the fruits of their labor, for these are gifts from God. (Ecclesiastes 3:11-13)

you are the "choice possession" at the top of His list of great creations. The benefits of the Christian life shouldn't necessarily be limited to things spiritual. If it's good, it's from God. That might include pet iguanas, lightning storms, tree houses and other special places, your favorite meal at a downtown restaurant, the cooling wind on your face after a hard day's work outdoors, trips to the zoo, or whatever good pursuits seem to enthrall you.

One of the best benefits of the here-and-now Christian life is that we start to see God in lots of places other than church. And as our spiritual eyes are opened, we see that His daily miracles are every bit as awe-inspiring as walking on the sea or turning water into wine.

And that's just here and now. He promises that the best is yet to come.

Preview

All things considered, the benefits of living the Christian life on earth seem pretty tremendous. Yet don't forget what we have learned from 1 Corinthians 15:19: "If we have hope in Christ only for this life, we are the most miserable people in the world." So let's see what's in store in our future after we have lived out this "miserable" existence.

Resurrection

Paul's point in his "miserable people" statement was to emphasize the importance of resurrection. If resurrection of the dead were only a myth, as certain people in his time (and ours) were promoting, then Christians are only fooling themselves. For one thing, if Jesus didn't rise from the dead, there is no adequate provision for sin. In that case, we would be living a sad and pathetic pipe dream—miserable without even knowing it.

This is why Jesus' resurrection is such a crucial element of Christianity. If He never rose from the dead and entered heaven, what hope is there for us? But if indeed Jesus rose from the dead, then He leads the way for the rest of us to do the same. Because He conquered death and sin, we too can glide into the afterlife on His holy coattails.

In connection with resurrection, we're even promised new, eternal bodies to replace these physically deteriorating ones we have now (1 Corinthians 15:40-44). That in itself is a tremendous benefit for many of us.

An Eternal Home

Some people might question the benefit of an eternal body if they must look forward to the same neglect and isolation they face in their earthly lives. But Jesus tells us to expect a family relationship with Him—and a permanent home. One of the last things He told His disciples before His death was: "Don't be troubled. You trust God, now trust in me. There are many rooms in my Father's home, and I am going to prepare a place for you. If this were not so, I would tell you plainly. When everything is ready, I will come and get you, so that you will always be with me where I am" (John 14:1-3).

Not only do we have assurance of eternal life. We also are promised an eternal home and family to go along with it. We've already mentioned the concept of how God adopts us and gives us an inheritance. But the real prize in eternal life will be to find ourselves in His presence.

Authority

Since Jesus is the ultimate authority, and since those in the Christian life are bonded to Him for eternity, we too are promised a degree of authority in the afterlife. Scripture doesn't go into a lot of detail about this, but here are a few relevant passages:

> Don't you know that someday we Christians are going to judge the world? And since you are going to judge the world, can't you decide these little things among yourselves? Don't you realize that we Christians will judge angels? So you should surely be able to resolve ordinary disagreements here on earth. (1 Corinthians 6:2-4)

And Jesus replied [to His disciples], "I assure you that when I, the Son of Man, sit upon my glorious throne in the

FOR EXAMPLE . . .

Old Testament Believers

Even in the Old Testament, a number of people were given a preview or a first-hand look at the afterlife:

- Jacob dreamed of a ladder (staircase) with angels ascending and descending, and was convinced the place was "none other than the house of God—the gateway to heaven" (Genesis 28:10-22).
- Enoch (Genesis 5:23-24) and Elijah (2 Kings 2:11-12) were both escorted into heaven by God, apparently without the trauma of physical death.
- Isaiah (Isaiah 6) and Ezekiel (Ezekiel 1), among other prophets, had detailed visions of God's throne and related heavenly events.

Kingdom, you who have been my followers will also sit on twelve thrones, judging the twelve tribes of Israel." (Matthew 19:28)

This is a true saying: If we die with him, we will also live with him. If we endure hardship, we will reign with him. (2 Timothy 2:11-12)

Then I saw thrones, and the people sitting on them had been given the authority to judge. And I saw the souls of those who had been beheaded for their testimony about Jesus, for proclaiming the word of God. And I saw the souls of those who had not worshiped the beast or his statue, nor accepted his mark on their forehead or their hands. They came to life again, and they reigned with Christ for a thousand years. (Revelation 20:4)

So the words of Jesus and the writings of Paul and John all attest that believers will one day have some kind of special authority. It's not to create a thirst for power within us, but these promises should more than compensate for the times we currently endure suffering or choose to submit to someone else on behalf of the kingdom of God.

Bliss

People often talk (and preach) a lot about the things we're expected to do without as we're living the Christian life. We're willingly supposed to eliminate a lot of behaviors that other people seem to enjoy. But in return, God sees to it that we'll also do without certain things in heaven. For example:

I heard a loud shout from the throne, saying, "Look, the home of God is now among his people! He will live with them, and they will be his people. God himself will be with them. He will remove all of their sorrows, and there will be no more death or sorrow or crying or pain. For the old world and its evils are gone forever." (Revelation 21:3-4)

No temple could be seen in the city [new Jerusalem], for the Lord God Almighty and the Lamb are its temple. And the city has no need of sun or moon, for the glory of God illuminates the city, and the Lamb is its light. . . . Its gates never close at the end of day because there is no night. And all the nations will bring their glory and honor into the city. Nothing evil will be allowed to enter. (Revelation 21:22-27)

WELL SAID!

Power cannot, as some demand, simply be abolished. That is an illusion. But in the light of the Christian conscience power . . . can be used for service instead of domination. —*Hans Küng*

No death. No sorrow. No pain. No evil. No sun or any other pale imitation of the real Light of the world. Nothing to stand between us and God—not even a temple or church.

Few of us can conceive of a place without fear, doubt, anxiety, guilt, shame, dread, tears, aches and pains, and other imperfections. Such things have become too real and too much a part of everyday life—even the Christian life. But once we move onward from this waiting area to the final destination God has in store for us, we discover the reality of all the promises He has ever made. It will be an unprecedented and unimaginable level of bliss that we should look forward to with great hope and expectation.

And They All Live Perfectly Ever After

From chapter 1 we have repeatedly noted that Jesus came to earth so we could have "life in all its fullness" (John 10:10). And one of His final promises before returning to heaven was that He was leaving in order to prepare a place for His followers in His Father's home (John 14:2). So, it would seem, following Jesus is a pretty good idea. Where He goes, things get a lot better.

When we devote ourselves to Him and commit to the Christian life, we soon discover numerous levels of depth and meaning to life that we never before knew existed. But even those wonderful discoveries pale in light of what is to follow.

So if you decide to pursue the Christian life, live it for all it's worth. Jesus surrounds you with His love and makes your life rich and full, in spite of any sufferings or setbacks you might encounter. But don't for a moment start to think that's all there is to it. The

Christian life here on earth will always be imperfect and frequently difficult.

Yet the Christian life is *eternal* life. It is during the next phase, at long last, we will all discover just how perfect God designed our lives to be. And of all the benefits we've discussed, being forever in God's presence will be the greatest blessing of them all.

Questions to Ponder and/or Discuss

1. Review the lists of benefits in this chapter. Which ones, if any, have you been less aware of than you should for some reason? Which benefits do you desire to receive in greater doses? What can you do to maximize each of these benefits in your life?

2. When you finally come into God's presence, what are the first three questions you would like to ask Him about your life on earth?

3. Think back to previous chapters in this book. What aspects of the Christian life still seem unclear to you and need further explanation?

4. Who are some people you can consult during the next few weeks to get better clarification on the points you have listed?

Appendix

GOD'S PART OF THE BARGAIN

Here are verses from the Bible that identify who God is and what He has done on our behalf to enable us to succeed in the Christian life.

All Scripture is inspired by God and is useful to teach us what is true and to make us realize what is wrong in our lives. It straightens us out and teaches us to do what is right. It is God's way of preparing us in every way, fully equipped for every good thing God wants us to do. (2 Timothy 3:16-17)

I assure you, those who listen to my message and believe in God who sent me have eternal life. They will never be condemned for their sins, but they have already passed from death into life. (John 5:24)

God is our refuge and strength, always ready to help in times of trouble. (Psalm 46:1)

Every word of God proves true. He defends all who come to him for protection. (Proverbs 30:5)

Trust in the LORD with all your heart; do not depend on your own understanding. Seek his will in all you do, and he will direct your paths. (Proverbs 3:5-6)

Your word is a lamp for my feet and a light for my path. (Psalm 119:105)

The LORD says, "I will guide you along the best pathway for your life. I will advise you and watch over you." (Psalm 32:8)

The wages of sin is death, but the free gift of God is eternal life through Christ Jesus our Lord. (Romans 6:23)

God saved you by his special favor when you believed. And you can't take credit for this; it is a gift from God. (Ephesians 2:8)

Sin is no longer your master, for you are no longer subject to the law, which enslaves you to sin. Instead, you are free by God's grace. (Romans 6:14)

If you confess with your mouth that Jesus is Lord and believe in your heart that God raised him from the dead, you will be saved. (Romans 10:9)

Jesus told her, "I am the resurrection and the life. Those who believe in me, even though they die like everyone else, will live again." (John 11:25)

Once you were wandering like lost sheep. But now you have turned to your Shepherd, the Guardian of your souls. (1 Peter 2:25)

I will rejoice in the LORD! I will be joyful in the God of my salvation. (Habakkuk 3:18)

The Lord is faithful; he will make you strong and guard you from the evil one. (2 Thessalonians 3:3)

So you see, the Lord knows how to rescue godly people from their trials, even while punishing the wicked right up until the day of judgment. (2 Peter 2:9)

Each time he said, "My gracious favor is all you need. My power works best in your weakness." So now I am glad to boast about my weaknesses, so that the power of Christ may work through me. (2 Corinthians 12:9)

God knew his people in advance, and he chose them to become like his Son, so that his Son would be the firstborn, with many brothers and sisters. (Romans 8:29)

All who are victorious will be clothed in white. I will never erase their names from the Book of Life, but I will announce before my Father and his angels that they are mine. (Revelation 3:5)

So be strong and take courage, all you who put your hope in the LORD! (Psalm 31:24)

So I advise you to live according to your new life in the Holy Spirit. Then you won't be doing what your sinful nature craves. (Galatians 5:16)

We can make our plans, but the LORD determines our steps. (Proverbs 16:9)

So, you see, it is impossible to please God without faith. Anyone who wants to come to him must believe that there is a God and that he rewards those who sincerely seek him. (Hebrews 11:6)

The person who loves God is the one God knows and cares for. (1 Corinthians 8:3)

I lavish my love on those who love me and obey my commands, even for a thousand generations. (Exodus 20:6)

Don't worry about anything; instead, pray about everything. Tell God what you need, and thank him for all he has done. If you do this, you will experience God's peace, which is far more wonderful than the human mind can understand. His peace will guard your hearts and minds as you live in Christ Jesus. (Philippians 4:6-7)

And let the peace that comes from Christ rule in your hearts. For as members of one body you are all called to live in peace. And always be thankful. (Colossians 3:15)

I will give you the right words and such wisdom that none of your opponents will be able to reply! (Luke 21:15)

True wisdom and power are with God; counsel and understanding are his. (Job 12:13)

We know the one who said, "I will take vengeance. I will repay those who deserve it." He also said, "The Lord will judge his own people." (Hebrews 10:30)

Get rid of all bitterness, rage, anger, harsh words, and slander, as well as all types of malicious behavior. Instead, be kind to each other, tenderhearted, forgiving one another, just as God through Christ has forgiven you. (Ephesians 4:31-32)

There was a time when some of you were just like that, but now your sins have been washed away, and you have been set apart for God. You have been made right with God because of what the Lord Jesus Christ and the Spirit of our God have done for you. (1 Corinthians 6:11)

Since he himself has gone through suffering and temptation, he is able to help us when we are being tempted. (Hebrews 2:18)

If we confess our sins to him, he is faithful and just to forgive us and to cleanse us from every wrong. (1 John 1:9)

If you need wisdom—if you want to know what God wants you to do—ask him, and he will gladly tell you. He will not resent your asking. (James 1:5)

I am sure that God, who began the good work within you, will continue his work until it is finally finished on that day when Christ Jesus comes back again. (Philippians 1:6)

I can do everything with the help of Christ who gives me the strength I need. (Philippians 4:13)

If you believe, you will receive whatever you ask for in prayer. (Matthew 21:22)

When they call on me, I will answer; I will be with them in trouble. I will rescue them and honor them. (Psalm 91:15)

Ask me and I will tell you some remarkable secrets about what is going to happen here. (Jeremiah 33:3)

In that day you will sing: "Praise the LORD! He was angry with me, but now he comforts me." (Isaiah 12:1)

We are God's masterpiece. He has created us anew in Christ Jesus, so that we can do the good things he planned for us long ago. (Ephesians 2:10)

Remember this—a farmer who plants only a few seeds will get a small crop. But the one who plants generously will get a generous crop. You must each make up your own mind as to how much you should give. Don't give reluctantly or in response to pressure. For God loves the person who gives cheerfully. And God will generously provide all you need. Then you will always have everything you need and plenty left over to share with others. (2 Corinthians 9:6-8)

Honor the LORD with your wealth and with the best part of everything your land produces. Then he will fill your barns with grain, and your vats will overflow with the finest wine. (Proverbs 3:9-10)

Therefore, obey the terms of this covenant so that you will prosper in everything you do. (Deuteronomy 29:9)

Don't forget to do good and to share what you have with those in need, for such sacrifices are very pleasing to God. (Hebrews 13:16)

Sell what you have and give to those in need. This will store up treasure for you in heaven! And the purses of heaven have no holes in them. Your treasure will be safe—no thief can steal it and no moth can destroy it. (Luke 12:33)

If you keep looking steadily into God's perfect law—the law that sets you free—and if you do what it says and don't forget what you heard, then God will bless you for doing it. (James 1:25)

When you pray, go away by yourself, shut the door behind you, and pray to your Father secretly. Then your Father, who knows all secrets, will reward you. (Matthew 6:6)

Take delight in the LORD, and he will give you your heart's desires. (Psalm 37:4)

Keep on praying. No matter what happens, always be thankful, for this is God's will for you who belong to Christ Jesus. (1 Thessalonians 5:17-18)

Restore to me again the joy of your salvation, and make me willing to obey you. Then I will teach your ways to sinners, and they will return to you. (Psalm 51:12-13)

Give all your worries and cares to God, for he cares about what happens to you. (1 Peter 5:7)

Stay away from the love of money; be satisfied with what you have. For God has said, "I will never fail you. I will never forsake you." (Hebrews 13:5)

The LORD is good. When trouble comes, he is a strong refuge. And he knows everyone who trusts in him. (Nahum 1:7)

Listen! The LORD is not too weak to save you, and he is not becoming deaf. He can hear you when you call. (Isaiah 59:1)

If you forgive those who sin against you, your heavenly Father will forgive you. (Matthew 6:14)

God has not given us a spirit of fear and timidity, but of power, love, and self-discipline. (2 Timothy 1:7)

Since God did not spare even his own Son but gave him up for us all, won't God, who gave us Christ, also give us everything else? (Romans 8:32)

Then he adds, "I will never again remember their sins and lawless deeds." (Hebrews 10:17)

The Lord does not abandon anyone forever. Though he brings grief, he also shows compassion according to the greatness of his unfailing love. For he does not enjoy hurting people or causing them sorrow. (Lamentations 3:31-33)

Don't get tired of doing what is good. Don't get discouraged and give up, for we will reap a harvest of blessing at the appropriate time. (Galatians 6:9)

The LORD is like a father to his children, tender and compassionate to those who fear him. (Psalm 103:13)

Don't be afraid, for I am with you. Do not be dismayed, for I am your God. I will strengthen you. I will help you. I will uphold you with my victorious right hand. (Isaiah 41:10)

Those who have been ransomed by the LORD will return to Jerusalem, singing songs of everlasting joy. Sorrow and mourning will disappear, and they will be overcome with joy and gladness. (Isaiah 51:11)

He will remove all of their sorrows, and there will be no more death or sorrow or crying or pain. For the old world and its evils are gone forever. (Revelation 21:4)

He satisfies the thirsty and fills the hungry with good things. (Psalm 107:9)

So humble yourselves before God. Resist the Devil, and he will flee from you. (James 4:7)

No, despite all these things, overwhelming victory is ours through Christ, who loved us. (Romans 8:37)

We can rejoice, too, when we run into problems and trials, for we know that they are good for us—they help us learn to endure. And endurance develops strength of character in us, and character strengthens our confident expectation of salvation. And this expectation will not disappoint us. For we know how dearly God loves us, because he has given us the Holy Spirit to fill our hearts with his love. (Romans 5:3-5)

He was wounded and crushed for our sins. He was beaten that we might have peace. He was whipped, and we were healed! (Isaiah 53:5)

This High Priest of ours understands our weaknesses, for he faced all of the same temptations we do, yet he did not sin. So let us come boldly to the throne of our gracious God. There we will receive his mercy, and we will find grace to help us when we need it. (Hebrews 4:15-16)

Once I was young, and now I am old. Yet I have never seen the godly forsaken, nor seen their children begging for bread. (Psalm 37:25)

All praise to the God and Father of our Lord Jesus Christ. He is the source of every mercy and the God who comforts us. He comforts us in all our troubles so that we can comfort others. When others are troubled, we will be able to give them the same comfort God has given us. You can be sure that the more we suffer for Christ, the more God will shower us with his comfort through Christ. (2 Corinthians 1:3-5)

That is what the Scriptures mean when they say, "No eye has seen, no ear has heard, and no mind has imagined what God has prepared for those who love him." (1 Corinthians 2:9)

OUR PART OF THE BARGAIN

Here are verses from the New Testament that identify what we need to do in order to succeed in the Christian life.

You have heard that the law of Moses says, "Do not murder. If you commit murder, you are subject to judgment." But I say, if you are angry with someone, you are subject to judgment! If you call someone an idiot, you are in danger of being brought before the high council. And if you curse someone, you are in danger of the fires of hell. (Matthew 5:21-22)

If you are standing before the altar in the Temple, offering a sacrifice to God, and you suddenly remember that someone has something against you, leave your sacrifice there beside the altar. Go and be reconciled to that person. Then come and offer your sacrifice to God. (Matthew 5:23-24)

Come to terms quickly with your enemy before it is too late and you are dragged into court, handed over to an officer, and thrown in jail. I assure you that you won't be free again until you have paid the last penny. (Matthew 5:25-26)

You have heard that the law of Moses says, "Do not commit adultery." But I say, anyone who even looks at a woman with lust in his eye has already committed adultery with her in his heart. So if your eye—even if it is your good eye —causes you to lust, gouge it out and throw it away. It is better for you to lose one part of your body than for your whole body to be thrown into hell. And if your hand—even if it is your stronger hand —causes you to sin, cut it off and throw it away. It is better for you to lose one part of your body than for your whole body to be thrown into hell. (Matthew 5:27-30)

You have heard that the law of Moses says, "A man can divorce his wife by merely giving her a letter of divorce." But I say that a man who divorces his wife, unless she has been unfaithful, causes her to commit adultery. And anyone who marries a divorced woman commits adultery. (Matthew 5:31-32)

Again, you have heard that the law of Moses says, "Do not break your vows; you must carry out the vows you have made to the Lord." But I say, don't make any vows! If you say, "By heaven!" it is a sacred vow because heaven is God's throne. And if you say, "By the earth!" it is a sacred vow because the earth is his footstool. And don't swear, "By Jerusalem!" for Jerusalem is the city of the great King. Don't even swear, "By my head!" for you can't turn one hair white or black. Just say a simple, "Yes, I will," or "No, I won't." Your word is enough. To strengthen your promise with a vow shows that something is wrong. (Matthew 5:33-37)

You have heard that the law of Moses says, "If an eye is injured, injure the eye of the person who did it. If a tooth gets knocked out, knock out the tooth of the person who did it." But I say, don't resist an evil person! If you are slapped on the right cheek, turn the other, too. If you are ordered to court and your shirt is taken from you, give your coat, too. If a soldier demands that you carry his gear for a mile, carry it two miles. Give to those who ask, and don't turn away from those who want to borrow. (Matthew 5:38-42)

You have heard that the law of Moses says, "Love your neighbor" and hate your enemy. But I say, love your

enemies! Pray for those who persecute you! In that way, you will be acting as true children of your Father in heaven. For he gives his sunlight to both the evil and the good, and he sends rain on the just and on the unjust, too. If you love only those who love you, what good is that? Even corrupt tax collectors do that much. If you are kind only to your friends, how are you different from anyone else? Even pagans do that. But you are to be perfect, even as your Father in heaven is perfect. (Matthew 5:43-48)

When you give to someone, don't tell your left hand what your right hand is doing. Give your gifts in secret, and your Father, who knows all secrets, will reward you. (Matthew 6:3-4)

When you pray, go away by yourself, shut the door behind you, and pray to your Father secretly. Then your Father, who knows all secrets, will reward you. When you pray, don't babble on and on as people of other religions do. They think their prayers are answered only by repeating their words again and again. Don't be like them, because your Father knows exactly what you need even before you ask him! (Matthew 6:6-8)

If you forgive those who sin against you, your heavenly Father will forgive you. But if you refuse to forgive others, your Father will not forgive your sins. (Matthew 6:14-15)

When you fast, comb your hair and wash your face. Then no one will suspect you are fasting, except your Father, who knows what you do in secret. And your Father, who knows all secrets, will reward you. (Matthew 6:17-18)

Don't store up treasures here on earth, where they can be eaten by moths and get rusty, and where thieves break in and steal. Store your treasures in heaven, where they will never become moth-eaten or rusty and where they will be safe from thieves. Wherever your treasure is, there your heart and thoughts will also be. (Matthew 6:19-21)

No one can serve two masters. For you will hate one and love the other, or be devoted to one and despise the other. You cannot serve both God and money. (Matthew 6:24)

I tell you, don't worry about everyday life—whether you have enough food, drink, and clothes. Doesn't life consist of more than food and clothing? (Matthew 6:25)

Stop judging others, and you will not be judged. For others will treat you as you treat them. Whatever measure you use in judging others, it will be used to measure how you are judged. (Matthew 7:1-2)

Don't give what is holy to unholy people. Don't give pearls to swine! They will trample the pearls, then turn and attack you. (Matthew 7:6)

Keep on asking, and you will be given what you ask for. Keep on looking, and you will find. Keep on knocking, and the door will be opened. For everyone who asks, receives. Everyone who seeks, finds. And the door is opened to everyone who knocks. (Matthew 7:7-8)

You can enter God's Kingdom only through the narrow gate. The highway to hell is broad, and its gate is wide for the many who choose the easy way. But the gateway to life is small, and the road is narrow, and only a few ever find it. (Matthew 7:13-14)

Beware of false prophets who come disguised as harmless sheep, but are really wolves that will tear you apart. You can detect them by the way they act, just as you can identify a tree by its fruit. You don't pick grapes from thornbushes, or figs from thistles. A healthy tree produces good fruit, and an unhealthy tree produces bad fruit. (Matthew 7:15-17)

Not all people who sound religious are really godly. They may refer to me as "Lord," but they still won't enter the Kingdom of Heaven. The decisive issue is whether they obey my Father in heaven. (Matthew 7:21)

Anyone who listens to my teaching and obeys me is wise, like a person who builds a house on solid rock. Though the rain comes in torrents and the floodwaters rise and the winds beat against that house, it won't collapse, because it is built on rock. But anyone who hears my teaching and ignores it is foolish, like a person who builds a house on

NO-BRAINER'S GUIDE TO HOW CHRISTIANS LIVE

sand. When the rains and floods come and the winds beat against that house, it will fall with a mighty crash. (Matthew 7:24-27)

What I tell you now in the darkness, shout abroad when daybreak comes. What I whisper in your ears, shout from the housetops for all to hear! Don't be afraid of those who want to kill you. They can only kill your body; they cannot touch your soul. Fear only God, who can destroy both soul and body in hell. (Matthew 10:27-28)

If anyone acknowledges me publicly here on earth, I will openly acknowledge that person before my Father in heaven. But if anyone denies me here on earth, I will deny that person before my Father in heaven. (Matthew 10:32-33)

If you love your father or mother more than you love me, you are not worthy of being mine; or if you love your son or daughter more than me, you are not worthy of being mine. If you refuse to take up your cross and follow me, you are not worthy of being mine. (Matthew 10:37-38)

If you cling to your life, you will lose it; but if you give it up for me, you will find it. (Matthew 10:39)

And if you give even a cup of cold water to one of the least of my followers, you will surely be rewarded. (Matthew 10:42)

Then Jesus said, "Come to me, all of you who are weary and carry heavy burdens, and I will give you rest. Take my yoke upon you. Let me teach you, because I am humble and gentle, and you will find rest for your souls. For my yoke fits perfectly, and the burden I give you is light." (Matthew 11:28-30)

Then Jesus said to the disciples, "If any of you wants to be my follower, you must put aside your selfish ambition, shoulder your cross, and follow me. If you try to keep your life for yourself, you will lose it. But if you give up your life for me, you will find true life." (Matthew 16:24-25)

"You didn't have enough faith," Jesus told them. "I assure you, even if you had faith as small as a mustard seed you could say to this mountain, 'Move from here to there,' and it

would move. Nothing would be impossible."
(Matthew 17:20)

Jesus called a small child over to him and put the child among them. Then he said, "I assure you, unless you turn from your sins and become as little children, you will never get into the Kingdom of Heaven. Therefore, anyone who becomes as humble as this little child is the greatest in the Kingdom of Heaven." (Matthew 18:2-4)

So if your hand or foot causes you to sin, cut it off and throw it away. It is better to enter heaven crippled or lame than to be thrown into the unquenchable fire with both of your hands and feet. And if your eye causes you to sin, gouge it out and throw it away. It is better to enter heaven half blind than to have two eyes and be thrown into hell. (Matthew 18:8-9)

Jesus told him, "If you want to be perfect, go and sell all you have and give the money to the poor, and you will have treasure in heaven. Then come, follow me." (Matthew 19:21)

And everyone who has given up houses or brothers or sisters or father or mother or children or property, for my sake, will receive a hundred times as much in return and will have eternal life. But many who seem to be important now will be the least important then, and those who are considered least here will be the greatest then.
(Matthew 19:29-30)

Jesus replied, "'You must love the Lord your God with all your heart, all your soul, and all your mind.' This is the first and greatest commandment. A second is equally important: 'Love your neighbor as yourself.'" (Matthew 22:37-39)

So be prepared, because you don't know what day your Lord is coming. Know this: A homeowner who knew exactly when a burglar was coming would stay alert and not permit the house to be broken into. You also must be ready all the time. For the Son of Man will come when least expected.
(Matthew 24:42-44)

He will give eternal life to those who persist in doing what is good, seeking after the glory and honor and immortality that God offers. But he will pour out his anger and wrath on those who live for themselves, who refuse to obey the truth and practice evil deeds. (Romans 2:7-8)

Do you think that God will judge and condemn others for doing them and not judge you when you do them, too? Don't you realize how kind, tolerant, and patient God is with you? Or don't you care? Can't you see how kind he has been in giving you time to turn from your sin? (Romans 2:3-4)

Because of our faith, Christ has brought us into this place of highest privilege where we now stand, and we confidently and joyfully look forward to sharing God's glory. We can rejoice, too, when we run into problems and trials, for we know that they are good for us—they help us learn to endure. And endurance develops strength of character in us, and character strengthens our confident expectation of salvation. And this expectation will not disappoint us. For we know how dearly God loves us, because he has given us the Holy Spirit to fill our hearts with his love. (Romans 5:2-5)

So you should consider yourselves dead to sin and able to live for the glory of God through Christ Jesus. Do not let sin control the way you live; do not give in to its lustful desires. Do not let any part of your body become a tool of wickedness, to be used for sinning. Instead, give yourselves completely to God since you have been given new life. And use your whole body as a tool to do what is right for the glory of God. Sin is no longer your master, for you are no longer subject to the law, which enslaves you to sin. Instead, you are free by God's grace. (Romans 6:11-14)

And since we are his children, we will share his treasures—for everything God gives to his Son, Christ, is ours, too. But if we are to share his glory, we must also share his suffering. (Romans 8:17)

And so, dear brothers and sisters, I plead with you to give your bodies to God. Let them be a living and holy sacrifice—the kind he will accept. When you think of what he has done for you, is this too much to ask? Don't copy the behav-

ior and customs of this world, but let God transform you into a new person by changing the way you think. Then you will know what God wants you to do, and you will know how good and pleasing and perfect his will really is. (Romans 12:1-2)

As God's messenger, I give each of you this warning: Be honest in your estimate of yourselves, measuring your value by how much faith God has given you. (Romans 12:3)

God has given each of us the ability to do certain things well. So if God has given you the ability to prophesy, speak out when you have faith that God is speaking through you. If your gift is that of serving others, serve them well. If you are a teacher, do a good job of teaching. If your gift is to encourage others, do it! If you have money, share it generously. If God has given you leadership ability, take the responsibility seriously. And if you have a gift for showing kindness to others, do it gladly. (Romans 12:6-8)

Don't just pretend that you love others. Really love them. Hate what is wrong. Stand on the side of the good. (Romans 12:9)

Love each other with genuine affection, and take delight in honoring each other. (Romans 12:10)

Never be lazy in your work, but serve the Lord enthusiastically. (Romans 12:11)

Be glad for all God is planning for you. Be patient in trouble, and always be prayerful. (Romans 12:12)

When God's children are in need, be the one to help them out. And get into the habit of inviting guests home for dinner or, if they need lodging, for the night. (Romans 12:13)

If people persecute you because you are a Christian, don't curse them; pray that God will bless them. When others are happy, be happy with them. If they are sad, share their sorrow. (Romans 12:14-15)

Live in harmony with each other. Don't try to act important, but enjoy the company of ordinary people. And don't think you know it all! (Romans 12:16)

Never pay back evil for evil to anyone. Do things in such a way that everyone can see you are honorable. Do your part to live in peace with everyone, as much as possible. (Romans 12:17-18)

Dear friends, never avenge yourselves. Leave that to God. For it is written, "I will take vengeance; I will repay those who deserve it," says the Lord. (Romans 12:19)

Instead, do what the Scriptures say: "If your enemies are hungry, feed them. If they are thirsty, give them something to drink, and they will be ashamed of what they have done to you." (Romans 12:20)

Don't let evil get the best of you, but conquer evil by doing good. (Romans 12:21)

Obey the government, for God is the one who put it there. All governments have been placed in power by God. So those who refuse to obey the laws of the land are refusing to obey God, and punishment will follow. (Romans 13:1-2)

Give to everyone what you owe them: Pay your taxes and import duties, and give respect and honor to all to whom it is due. (Romans 13:7)

Pay all your debts, except the debt of love for others. You can never finish paying that! If you love your neighbor, you will fulfill all the requirements of God's law. (Romans 13:8)

The night is almost gone; the day of salvation will soon be here. So don't live in darkness. Get rid of your evil deeds. Shed them like dirty clothes. Clothe yourselves with the armor of right living, as those who live in the light. (Romans 13:12)

We should be decent and true in everything we do, so that everyone can approve of our behavior. Don't participate in wild parties and getting drunk, or in adultery and immoral living, or in fighting and jealousy. But let the Lord Jesus Christ take control of you, and don't think of ways to indulge your evil desires. (Romans 13:13-14)

Accept Christians who are weak in faith, and don't argue with them about what they think is right or wrong. (Romans 14:1)

In the same way, some think one day is more holy than another day, while others think every day is alike. Each person should have a personal conviction about this matter. (Romans 14:5)

While we live, we live to please the Lord. And when we die, we go to be with the Lord. So in life and in death, we belong to the Lord. (Romans 14:8)

Yes, each of us will have to give a personal account to God. (Romans 14:12)

So don't condemn each other anymore. Decide instead to live in such a way that you will not put an obstacle in another Christian's path. (Romans 14:13)

So then, let us aim for harmony in the church and try to build each other up. (Romans 14:19)

We may know that these things make no difference, but we cannot just go ahead and do them to please ourselves. We must be considerate of the doubts and fears of those who think these things are wrong. We should please others. If we do what helps them, we will build them up in the Lord. (Romans 15:1-2)

May God, who gives this patience and encouragement, help you live in complete harmony with each other—each with the attitude of Christ Jesus toward the other. Then all of you can join together with one voice, giving praise and glory to God, the Father of our Lord Jesus Christ. (Romans 15:5-6)

So accept each other just as Christ has accepted you; then God will be glorified. (Romans 15:7)

And now I make one more appeal, my dear brothers and sisters. Watch out for people who cause divisions and upset people's faith by teaching things that are contrary to what you have been taught. Stay away from them. (Romans 16:17)

We who have the Spirit understand these things, but others can't understand us at all. (1 Corinthians 2:15)

You are still controlled by your own sinful desires. You are jealous of one another and quarrel with each other. Doesn't

that prove you are controlled by your own desires? You are acting like people who don't belong to the Lord. (1 Corinthians 3:3)

Now anyone who builds on that foundation may use gold, silver, jewels, wood, hay, or straw. But there is going to come a time of testing at the judgment day to see what kind of work each builder has done. Everyone's work will be put through the fire to see whether or not it keeps its value. If the work survives the fire, that builder will receive a reward. But if the work is burned up, the builder will suffer great loss. The builders themselves will be saved, but like someone escaping through a wall of flames. (1 Corinthians 3:12-15)

Don't you realize that all of you together are the temple of God and that the Spirit of God lives in you? God will bring ruin upon anyone who ruins this temple. For God's temple is holy, and you Christians are that temple. (1 Corinthians 3:16-17)

Stop fooling yourselves. If you think you are wise by this world's standards, you will have to become a fool so you can become wise by God's standards. For the wisdom of this world is foolishness to God. As the Scriptures say, "God catches those who think they are wise in their own cleverness." (1 Corinthians 3:18-19)

So be careful not to jump to conclusions before the Lord returns as to whether or not someone is faithful. When the Lord comes, he will bring our deepest secrets to light and will reveal our private motives. And then God will give to everyone whatever praise is due. (1 Corinthians 4:5)

How terrible that you should boast about your spirituality, and yet you let this sort of thing go on. Don't you realize that if even one person is allowed to go on sinning, soon all will be affected? Remove this wicked person from among you so that you can stay pure. Christ, our Passover Lamb, has been sacrificed for us. (1 Corinthians 5:6-7)

What I meant was that you are not to associate with anyone who claims to be a Christian yet indulges in sexual sin, or is greedy, or worships idols, or is abusive, or a drunkard, or a

swindler. Don't even eat with such people. (1 Corinthians 5:11)

Don't you know that someday we Christians are going to judge the world? And since you are going to judge the world, can't you decide these little things among yourselves? Don't you realize that we Christians will judge angels? So you should surely be able to resolve ordinary disagreements here on earth. (1 Corinthians 6:2-3)

You may say, "I am allowed to do anything." But I reply, "Not everything is good for you." And even though "I am allowed to do anything," I must not become a slave to anything. (1 Corinthians 6:12)

Run away from sexual sin! No other sin so clearly affects the body as this one does. For sexual immorality is a sin against your own body. Or don't you know that your body is the temple of the Holy Spirit, who lives in you and was given to you by God? You do not belong to yourself, for God bought you with a high price. So you must honor God with your body. (1 Corinthians 6:18-20)

But because there is so much sexual immorality, each man should have his own wife, and each woman should have her own husband. The husband should not deprive his wife of sexual intimacy, which is her right as a married woman, nor should the wife deprive her husband. The wife gives authority over her body to her husband, and the husband also gives authority over his body to his wife. So do not deprive each other of sexual relations. The only exception to this rule would be the agreement of both husband and wife to refrain from sexual intimacy for a limited time, so they can give themselves more completely to prayer. Afterward they should come together again so that Satan won't be able to tempt them because of their lack of self-control. (1 Corinthians 7:2-5)

It's true that we can't win God's approval by what we eat. We don't miss out on anything if we don't eat it, and we don't gain anything if we do. But you must be careful with this freedom of yours. Do not cause a brother or sister with a weaker conscience to stumble. (1 Corinthians 8:8-9)

Nor should we put Christ to the test, as some of them did and then died from snakebites. And don't grumble as some of them did, for that is why God sent his angel of death to destroy them. (1 Corinthians 10:9-10)

If you think you are standing strong, be careful, for you, too, may fall into the same sin. But remember that the temptations that come into your life are no different from what others experience. And God is faithful. He will keep the temptation from becoming so strong that you can't stand up against it. When you are tempted, he will show you a way out so that you will not give in to it. (1 Corinthians 10:12-13)

You say, "I am allowed to do anything"—but not everything is helpful. You say, "I am allowed to do anything"—but not everything is beneficial. Don't think only of your own good. Think of other Christians and what is best for them. (1 Corinthians 10:23-24)

Whatever you eat or drink or whatever you do, you must do all for the glory of God. (1 Corinthians 10:31)

So if anyone eats this bread or drinks this cup of the Lord unworthily, that person is guilty of sinning against the body and the blood of the Lord. That is why you should examine yourself before eating the bread and drinking from the cup. (1 Corinthians 11:27-28)

If I could speak in any language in heaven or on earth but didn't love others, I would only be making meaningless noise like a loud gong or a clanging cymbal. If I had the gift of prophecy, and if I knew all the mysteries of the future and knew everything about everything, but didn't love others, what good would I be? And if I had the gift of faith so that I could speak to a mountain and make it move, without love I would be no good to anybody. If I gave everything I have to the poor and even sacrificed my body, I could boast about it; but if I didn't love others, I would be of no value whatsoever. (1 Corinthians 13:1-3)

Dear brothers and sisters, don't be childish in your understanding of these things. Be innocent as babies when it

comes to evil, but be mature and wise in understanding matters of this kind. (1 Corinthians 14:20)

Be on guard. Stand true to what you believe. Be courageous. Be strong. And everything you do must be done with love. (1 Corinthians 16:13-14)

That is why we never give up. Though our bodies are dying, our spirits are being renewed every day. For our present troubles are quite small and won't last very long. Yet they produce for us an immeasurably great glory that will last forever! So we don't look at the troubles we can see right now; rather, we look forward to what we have not yet seen. For the troubles we see will soon be over, but the joys to come will last forever. (2 Corinthians 4:16-18)

So we are always confident, even though we know that as long as we live in these bodies we are not at home with the Lord. That is why we live by believing and not by seeing. Yes, we are fully confident, and we would rather be away from these bodies, for then we will be at home with the Lord. So our aim is to please him always, whether we are here in this body or away from this body. (2 Corinthians 5:6-9)

So we have stopped evaluating others by what the world thinks about them. Once I mistakenly thought of Christ that way, as though he were merely a human being. How differently I think about him now! What this means is that those who become Christians become new persons. They are not the same anymore, for the old life is gone. A new life has begun! (2 Corinthians 5:16-17)

We are Christ's ambassadors, and God is using us to speak to you. We urge you, as though Christ himself were here pleading with you, "Be reconciled to God!" (2 Corinthians 5:20)

Don't team up with those who are unbelievers. How can goodness be a partner with wickedness? How can light live with darkness? (2 Corinthians 6:14)

Therefore, come out from them and separate yourselves from them, says the Lord. Don't touch their filthy things, and I will welcome you. (2 Corinthians 6:17)

Because we have these promises, dear friends, let us cleanse ourselves from everything that can defile our body or spirit. And let us work toward complete purity because we fear God. (2 Corinthians 7:1)

Remember this—a farmer who plants only a few seeds will get a small crop. But the one who plants generously will get a generous crop. You must each make up your own mind as to how much you should give. Don't give reluctantly or in response to pressure. For God loves the person who gives cheerfully. And God will generously provide all you need. Then you will always have everything you need and plenty left over to share with others. (2 Corinthians 9:6-8)

For God is the one who gives seed to the farmer and then bread to eat. In the same way, he will give you many opportunities to do good, and he will produce a great harvest of generosity in you. (2 Corinthians 9:10)

We use God's mighty weapons, not mere worldly weapons, to knock down the Devil's strongholds. With these weapons we break down every proud argument that keeps people from knowing God. With these weapons we conquer their rebellious ideas, and we teach them to obey Christ. (2 Corinthians 10:4-5)

As the Scriptures say, "The person who wishes to boast should boast only of what the Lord has done." (2 Corinthians 10:17)

Since I know it is all for Christ's good, I am quite content with my weaknesses and with insults, hardships, persecutions, and calamities. For when I am weak, then I am strong. (2 Corinthians 12:10)

Examine yourselves to see if your faith is really genuine. Test yourselves. If you cannot tell that Jesus Christ is among you, it means you have failed the test. I hope you recognize that we have passed the test and are approved by God. (2 Corinthians 13:5-6)

So Christ has really set us free. Now make sure that you stay free, and don't get tied up again in slavery to the law. (Galatians 5:1)

But we who live by the Spirit eagerly wait to receive everything promised to us who are right with God through faith. (Galatians 5:5)

So I advise you to live according to your new life in the Holy Spirit. Then you won't be doing what your sinful nature craves. The old sinful nature loves to do evil, which is just opposite from what the Holy Spirit wants. And the Spirit gives us desires that are opposite from what the sinful nature desires. These two forces are constantly fighting each other, and your choices are never free from this conflict. But when you are directed by the Holy Spirit, you are no longer subject to the law. (Galatians 5:16-18)

When you follow the desires of your sinful nature, your lives will produce these evil results: sexual immorality, impure thoughts, eagerness for lustful pleasure, idolatry, participation in demonic activities, hostility, quarreling, jealousy, outbursts of anger, selfish ambition, divisions, the feeling that everyone is wrong except those in your own little group, envy, drunkenness, wild parties, and other kinds of sin. Let me tell you again, as I have before, that anyone living that sort of life will not inherit the Kingdom of God. (Galatians 5:19-21)

But when the Holy Spirit controls our lives, he will produce this kind of fruit in us: love, joy, peace, patience, kindness, goodness, faithfulness, gentleness, and self-control. Here there is no conflict with the law. Those who belong to Christ Jesus have nailed the passions and desires of their sinful nature to his cross and crucified them there. (Galatians 5:22-24)

Dear brothers and sisters, if another Christian is overcome by some sin, you who are godly should gently and humbly help that person back onto the right path. And be careful not to fall into the same temptation yourself. Share each other's troubles and problems, and in this way obey the law of Christ. If you think you are too important to help

someone in need, you are only fooling yourself. You are really a nobody. Be sure to do what you should, for then you will enjoy the personal satisfaction of having done your work well, and you won't need to compare yourself to anyone else. For we are each responsible for our own conduct. (Galatians 6:1-5)

Those who are taught the word of God should help their teachers by paying them. (Galatians 6:6)

Don't be misled. Remember that you can't ignore God and get away with it. You will always reap what you sow! Those who live only to satisfy their own sinful desires will harvest the consequences of decay and death. But those who live to please the Spirit will harvest everlasting life from the Spirit. (Galatians 6:7-8)

So don't get tired of doing what is good. Don't get discouraged and give up, for we will reap a harvest of blessing at the appropriate time. Whenever we have the opportunity, we should do good to everyone, especially to our Christian brothers and sisters. (Galatians 6:9-10)

I have never stopped thanking God for you. I pray for you constantly, asking God, the glorious Father of our Lord Jesus Christ, to give you spiritual wisdom and understanding, so that you might grow in your knowledge of God. I pray that your hearts will be flooded with light so that you can understand the wonderful future he has promised to those he called. I want you to realize what a rich and glorious inheritance he has given to his people. (Ephesians 1:16-18)

So now you Gentiles are no longer strangers and foreigners. You are citizens along with all of God's holy people. You are members of God's family. We are his house, built on the foundation of the apostles and the prophets. And the cornerstone is Christ Jesus himself. (Ephesians 2:19-20)

Because of Christ and our faith in him, we can now come fearlessly into God's presence, assured of his glad welcome. (Ephesians 3:12)

And I pray that Christ will be more and more at home in your hearts as you trust in him. May your roots go down

deep into the soil of God's marvelous love. And may you have the power to understand, as all God's people should, how wide, how long, how high, and how deep his love really is. May you experience the love of Christ, though it is so great you will never fully understand it. Then you will be filled with the fullness of life and power that comes from God. (Ephesians 3:17-19)

With the Lord's authority let me say this: Live no longer as the ungodly do, for they are hopelessly confused. Their closed minds are full of darkness; they are far away from the life of God because they have shut their minds and hardened their hearts against him. They don't care anymore about right and wrong, and they have given themselves over to immoral ways. Their lives are filled with all kinds of impurity and greed. (Ephesians 4:17-19)

Throw off your old evil nature and your former way of life, which is rotten through and through, full of lust and deception. Instead, there must be a spiritual renewal of your thoughts and attitudes. (Ephesians 4:22-23)

Put away all falsehood and "tell your neighbor the truth" because we belong to each other. (Ephesians 4:25)

Don't sin by letting anger gain control over you. Don't let the sun go down while you are still angry, for anger gives a mighty foothold to the Devil. (Ephesians 4:26-27)

If you are a thief, stop stealing. Begin using your hands for honest work, and then give generously to others in need. (Ephesians 4:28)

Don't use foul or abusive language. Let everything you say be good and helpful, so that your words will be an encouragement to those who hear them. And do not bring sorrow to God's Holy Spirit by the way you live. Remember, he is the one who has identified you as his own, guaranteeing that you will be saved on the day of redemption. (Ephesians 4:29-30)

Get rid of all bitterness, rage, anger, harsh words, and slander, as well as all types of malicious behavior. Instead, be kind to each other, tenderhearted, forgiving one another, just

as God through Christ has forgiven you. (Ephesians 4:31-32)

Follow God's example in everything you do, because you are his dear children. Live a life filled with love for others, following the example of Christ, who loved you and gave himself as a sacrifice to take away your sins. And God was pleased, because that sacrifice was like sweet perfume to him. (Ephesians 5:1-2)

Let there be no sexual immorality, impurity, or greed among you. Such sins have no place among God's people. Obscene stories, foolish talk, and coarse jokes—these are not for you. Instead, let there be thankfulness to God. (Ephesians 5:3-4)

You can be sure that no immoral, impure, or greedy person will inherit the Kingdom of Christ and of God. For a greedy person is really an idolater who worships the things of this world. (Ephesians 5:5)

Though your hearts were once full of darkness, now you are full of light from the Lord, and your behavior should show it! For this light within you produces only what is good and right and true. Try to find out what is pleasing to the Lord. (Ephesians 5:8-10)

Take no part in the worthless deeds of evil and darkness; instead, rebuke and expose them. It is shameful even to talk about the things that ungodly people do in secret. But when the light shines on them, it becomes clear how evil these things are. (Ephesians 5:11-13)

Don't be drunk with wine, because that will ruin your life. Instead, let the Holy Spirit fill and control you. Then you will sing psalms and hymns and spiritual songs among yourselves, making music to the Lord in your hearts. And you will always give thanks for everything to God the Father in the name of our Lord Jesus Christ. (Ephesians 5:18-20)

You will submit to one another out of reverence for Christ. (Ephesians 5:21)

You wives will submit to your husbands as you do to the Lord. For a husband is the head of his wife as Christ is the head of his body, the church; he gave his life to be her

Savior. As the church submits to Christ, so you wives must submit to your husbands in everything. (Ephesians 5:22-24)

You husbands must love your wives with the same love Christ showed the church. He gave up his life for her to make her holy and clean, washed by baptism and God's word. (Ephesians 5:25-26)

Children, obey your parents because you belong to the Lord, for this is the right thing to do. "Honor your father and mother." This is the first of the Ten Commandments that ends with a promise. And this is the promise: If you honor your father and mother, "you will live a long life, full of blessing." (Ephesians 6:1-3)

Now a word to you fathers. Don't make your children angry by the way you treat them. Rather, bring them up with the discipline and instruction approved by the Lord. (Ephesians 6:4)

Work with enthusiasm, as though you were working for the Lord rather than for people. Remember that the Lord will reward each one of us for the good we do, whether we are slaves or free. (Ephesians 6:7-8)

A final word: Be strong with the Lord's mighty power. Put on all of God's armor so that you will be able to stand firm against all strategies and tricks of the Devil. For we are not fighting against people made of flesh and blood, but against the evil rulers and authorities of the unseen world, against those mighty powers of darkness who rule this world, and against wicked spirits in the heavenly realms. (Ephesians 6:10-12)

Stand your ground, putting on the sturdy belt of truth and the body armor of God's righteousness. For shoes, put on the peace that comes from the Good News, so that you will be fully prepared. In every battle you will need faith as your shield to stop the fiery arrows aimed at you by Satan. Put on salvation as your helmet, and take the sword of the Spirit, which is the word of God. Pray at all times and on every occasion in the power of the Holy Spirit. Stay alert and be persistent in your prayers for all Christians every-where. (Ephesians 6:14-18)

I pray that your love for each other will overflow more and more, and that you will keep on growing in your knowledge and understanding. For I want you to understand what really matters, so that you may live pure and blameless lives until Christ returns. May you always be filled with the fruit of your salvation —those good things that are produced in your life by Jesus Christ—for this will bring much glory and praise to God. (Philippians 1:9-11)

Is there any encouragement from belonging to Christ? Any comfort from his love? Any fellowship together in the Spirit? Are your hearts tender and sympathetic? Then make me truly happy by agreeing wholeheartedly with each other, loving one another, and working together with one heart and purpose. Don't be selfish; don't live to make a good impression on others. Be humble, thinking of others as better than yourself. Don't think only about your own affairs, but be interested in others, too, and what they are doing. (Philippians 2:1-4)

Dearest friends, you were always so careful to follow my instructions when I was with you. And now that I am away you must be even more careful to put into action God's saving work in your lives, obeying God with deep reverence and fear. For God is working in you, giving you the desire to obey him and the power to do what pleases him. (Philippians 2:12-13)

In everything you do, stay away from complaining and arguing, so that no one can speak a word of blame against you. You are to live clean, innocent lives as children of God in a dark world full of crooked and perverse people. Let your lives shine brightly before them. Hold tightly to the word of life, so that when Christ returns, I will be proud that I did not lose the race and that my work was not useless. (Philippians 2:14-16)

Whatever happens, dear brothers and sisters, may the Lord give you joy. I never get tired of telling you this. I am doing this for your own good. (Philippians 3:1)

I once thought all these things were so very important, but now I consider them worthless because of what Christ has

done. Yes, everything else is worthless when compared with the priceless gain of knowing Christ Jesus my Lord. I have discarded everything else, counting it all as garbage, so that I may have Christ and become one with him. I no longer count on my own goodness or my ability to obey God's law, but I trust Christ to save me. For God's way of making us right with himself depends on faith. (Philippians 3:7-9)

I don't mean to say that I have already achieved these things or that I have already reached perfection! But I keep working toward that day when I will finally be all that Christ Jesus saved me for and wants me to be. No, dear brothers and sisters, I am still not all I should be, but I am focusing all my energies on this one thing: Forgetting the past and looking forward to what lies ahead, I strain to reach the end of the race and receive the prize for which God, through Christ Jesus, is calling us up to heaven. (Philippians 3:12-14)

Let everyone see that you are considerate in all you do. Remember, the Lord is coming soon. Don't worry about anything; instead, pray about everything. Tell God what you need, and thank him for all he has done. If you do this, you will experience God's peace, which is far more wonderful than the human mind can understand. His peace will guard your hearts and minds as you live in Christ Jesus. (Philippians 4:5-7)

Now, dear brothers and sisters, let me say one more thing as I close this letter. Fix your thoughts on what is true and honorable and right. Think about things that are pure and lovely and admirable. Think about things that are excellent and worthy of praise. Keep putting into practice all you learned from me and heard from me and saw me doing, and the God of peace will be with you. (Philippians 4:8-9)

I know how to live on almost nothing or with everything. I have learned the secret of living in every situation, whether it is with a full stomach or empty, with plenty or little. For I can do everything with the help of Christ who gives me the strength I need. (Philippians 4:12-13)

Then the way you live will always honor and please the Lord, and you will continually do good, kind things for

others. All the while, you will learn to know God better and better. We also pray that you will be strengthened with his glorious power so that you will have all the patience and endurance you need. May you be filled with joy, always thanking the Father, who has enabled you to share the inheritance that belongs to God's holy people, who live in the light. (Colossians 1:10-12)

Since you have been raised to new life with Christ, set your sights on the realities of heaven, where Christ sits at God's right hand in the place of honor and power. Let heaven fill your thoughts. Do not think only about things down here on earth. For you died when Christ died, and your real life is hidden with Christ in God. (Colossians 3:1-3)

Put to death the sinful, earthly things lurking within you. Have nothing to do with sexual sin, impurity, lust, and shameful desires. Don't be greedy for the good things of this life, for that is idolatry. God's terrible anger will come upon those who do such things. You used to do them when your life was still part of this world. But now is the time to get rid of anger, rage, malicious behavior, slander, and dirty language. (Colossians 3:5-8)

Don't lie to each other, for you have stripped off your old evil nature and all its wicked deeds. In its place you have clothed yourselves with a brand-new nature that is continually being renewed as you learn more and more about Christ, who created this new nature within you. (Colossians 3:9-10)

Since God chose you to be the holy people whom he loves, you must clothe yourselves with tenderhearted mercy, kindness, humility, gentleness, and patience. You must make allowance for each other's faults and forgive the person who offends you. Remember, the Lord forgave you, so you must forgive others. And the most important piece of clothing you must wear is love. Love is what binds us all together in perfect harmony. (Colossians 3:12-14)

Let the peace that comes from Christ rule in your hearts. For as members of one body you are all called to live in peace. And always be thankful. Let the words of Christ, in all their richness, live in your hearts and make you wise. Use his

words to teach and counsel each other. Sing psalms and hymns and spiritual songs to God with thankful hearts. And whatever you do or say, let it be as a representative of the Lord Jesus, all the while giving thanks through him to God the Father. (Colossians 3:15-17)

You wives must submit to your husbands, as is fitting for those who belong to the Lord. And you husbands must love your wives and never treat them harshly. You children must always obey your parents, for this is what pleases the Lord. Fathers, don't aggravate your children. If you do, they will become discouraged and quit trying. (Colossians 3:18-21)

Devote yourselves to prayer with an alert mind and a thankful heart. Don't forget to pray for us, too, that God will give us many opportunities to preach about his secret plan—that Christ is also for you Gentiles. That is why I am here in chains. (Colossians 4:2-3)

Live wisely among those who are not Christians, and make the most of every opportunity. Let your conversation be gracious and effective so that you will have the right answer for everyone. (Colossians 4:5-6)

As we talk to our God and Father about you, we think of your faithful work, your loving deeds, and your continual anticipation of the return of our Lord Jesus Christ. (1 Thessalonians 1:3)

May the Lord make your love grow and overflow to each other and to everyone else, just as our love overflows toward you. As a result, Christ will make your hearts strong, blameless, and holy when you stand before God our Father on that day when our Lord Jesus comes with all those who belong to him. (1 Thessalonians 3:12-13)

I don't need to write to you about the Christian love that should be shown among God's people. For God himself has taught you to love one another. (1 Thessalonians 4:9)

This should be your ambition: to live a quiet life, minding your own business and working with your hands, just as we commanded you before. As a result, people who are not Christians will respect the way you live, and you will not

*need to depend on others to meet your financial needs.
(1 Thessalonians 4:11-12)*

Let us who live in the light think clearly, protected by the body armor of faith and love, and wearing as our helmet the confidence of our salvation. For God decided to save us through our Lord Jesus Christ, not to pour out his anger on us. (1 Thessalonians 5:8-9)

Encourage each other and build each other up, just as you are already doing. (1 Thessalonians 5:11)

*Think highly of them and give them your wholehearted love because of their work. And remember to live peaceably with each other. Brothers and sisters, we urge you to warn those who are lazy. Encourage those who are timid. Take tender care of those who are weak. Be patient with everyone.
(1 Thessalonians 5:13-14)*

See that no one pays back evil for evil, but always try to do good to each other and to everyone else. (1 Thessalonians 5:15)

Always be joyful. Keep on praying. No matter what happens, always be thankful, for this is God's will for you who belong to Christ Jesus. (1 Thessalonians 5:16-18)

*Do not stifle the Holy Spirit. Do not scoff at prophecies, but test everything that is said. Hold on to what is good.
(1 Thessalonians 5:19-21)*

With all these things in mind, dear brothers and sisters, stand firm and keep a strong grip on everything we taught you both in person and by letter. (2 Thessalonians 2:15)

May our Lord Jesus Christ and God our Father, who loved us and in his special favor gave us everlasting comfort and good hope, comfort your hearts and give you strength in every good thing you do and say. (2 Thessalonians 2:16-17)

Now, dear brothers and sisters, we give you this command with the authority of our Lord Jesus Christ: Stay away from any Christian who lives in idleness and doesn't follow the tradition of hard work we gave you. (2 Thessalonians 3:6)

I urge you, first of all, to pray for all people. As you make your requests, plead for God's mercy upon them, and give thanks. Pray this way for kings and all others who are in authority, so that we can live in peace and quietness, in godliness and dignity. (1 Timothy 2:1-2)

I want women to be modest in their appearance. They should wear decent and appropriate clothing and not draw attention to themselves by the way they fix their hair or by wearing gold or pearls or expensive clothes. (1 Timothy 2:9)

It is a true saying that if someone wants to be an elder, he desires an honorable responsibility. For an elder must be a man whose life cannot be spoken against. He must be faithful to his wife. He must exhibit self-control, live wisely, and have a good reputation. He must enjoy having guests in his home and must be able to teach. He must not be a heavy drinker or be violent. He must be gentle, peace loving, and not one who loves money. He must manage his own family well, with children who respect and obey him. (1 Timothy 3:1-4)

Be careful then, dear brothers and sisters. Make sure that your own hearts are not evil and unbelieving, turning you away from the living God. You must warn each other every day, as long as it is called "today," so that none of you will be deceived by sin and hardened against God. For if we are faithful to the end, trusting God just as firmly as when we first believed, we will share in all that belongs to Christ. (Hebrews 3:12-14)

That is why we have a great High Priest who has gone to heaven, Jesus the Son of God. Let us cling to him and never stop trusting him. This High Priest of ours understands our weaknesses, for he faced all of the same temptations we do, yet he did not sin. So let us come boldly to the throne of our gracious God. There we will receive his mercy, and we will find grace to help us when we need it. (Hebrews 4:14-16)

It is impossible to restore to repentance those who were once enlightened—those who have experienced the good things of heaven and shared in the Holy Spirit, who have tasted the goodness of the word of God and the power of the age to

come—and who then turn away from God. It is impossible to bring such people to repentance again because they are nailing the Son of God to the cross again by rejecting him, holding him up to public shame. (Hebrews 6:4-6)

Our great desire is that you will keep right on loving others as long as life lasts, in order to make certain that what you hope for will come true. Then you will not become spiritually dull and indifferent. Instead, you will follow the example of those who are going to inherit God's promises because of their faith and patience. (Hebrews 6:11-12)

Let us go right into the presence of God, with true hearts fully trusting him. For our evil consciences have been sprinkled with Christ's blood to make us clean, and our bodies have been washed with pure water. Without wavering, let us hold tightly to the hope we say we have, for God can be trusted to keep his promise. Think of ways to encourage one another to outbursts of love and good deeds. (Hebrews 10:22-24)

And let us not neglect our meeting together, as some people do, but encourage and warn each other, especially now that the day of his coming back again is drawing near. (Hebrews 10:25)

Dear friends, if we deliberately continue sinning after we have received a full knowledge of the truth, there is no other sacrifice that will cover these sins. (Hebrews 10:26)

Do not throw away this confident trust in the Lord, no matter what happens. Remember the great reward it brings you! Patient endurance is what you need now, so you will continue to do God's will. Then you will receive all that he has promised. (Hebrews 10:35-36)

As you endure this divine discipline, remember that God is treating you as his own children. Whoever heard of a child who was never disciplined? If God doesn't discipline you as he does all of his children, it means that you are illegitimate and are not really his children after all. (Hebrews 12:7-8)

Try to live in peace with everyone, and seek to live a clean and holy life, for those who are not holy will not see the

Lord. Look after each other so that none of you will miss out on the special favor of God. Watch out that no bitter root of unbelief rises up among you, for whenever it springs up, many are corrupted by its poison. (Hebrews 12:14-15)

See to it that you obey God, the one who is speaking to you. For if the people of Israel did not escape when they refused to listen to Moses, the earthly messenger, how terrible our danger if we reject the One who speaks to us from heaven! (Hebrews 12:25)

Since we are receiving a Kingdom that cannot be destroyed, let us be thankful and please God by worshiping him with holy fear and awe. For our God is a consuming fire. (Hebrews 12:28-29)

Continue to love each other with true Christian love. Don't forget to show hospitality to strangers, for some who have done this have entertained angels without realizing it! (Hebrews 13:1-2)

Don't forget about those in prison. Suffer with them as though you were there yourself. Share the sorrow of those being mistreated, as though you feel their pain in your own bodies. (Hebrews 13:3)

Give honor to marriage, and remain faithful to one another in marriage. God will surely judge people who are immoral and those who commit adultery. (Hebrews 13:4)

Stay away from the love of money; be satisfied with what you have. For God has said, "I will never fail you. I will never forsake you." (Hebrews 13:5)

Remember your leaders who first taught you the word of God. Think of all the good that has come from their lives, and trust the Lord as they do. (Hebrews 13:7)

So do not be attracted by strange, new ideas. Your spiritual strength comes from God's special favor, not from ceremonial rules about food, which don't help those who follow them. (Hebrews 13:9)

With Jesus' help, let us continually offer our sacrifice of praise to God by proclaiming the glory of his name. Don't

forget to do good and to share what you have with those in need, for such sacrifices are very pleasing to God. (Hebrews 13:15-16)

Obey your spiritual leaders and do what they say. Their work is to watch over your souls, and they know they are accountable to God. Give them reason to do this joyfully and not with sorrow. That would certainly not be for your benefit. (Hebrews 13:17)

Dear brothers and sisters, whenever trouble comes your way, let it be an opportunity for joy. For when your faith is tested, your endurance has a chance to grow. So let it grow, for when your endurance is fully developed, you will be strong in character and ready for anything. (James 1:2-4)

If you need wisdom—if you want to know what God wants you to do—ask him, and he will gladly tell you. He will not resent your asking. But when you ask him, be sure that you really expect him to answer, for a doubtful mind is as unsettled as a wave of the sea that is driven and tossed by the wind. People like that should not expect to receive anything from the Lord. (James 1:5-7)

Christians who are poor should be glad, for God has honored them. And those who are rich should be glad, for God has humbled them. They will fade away like a flower in the field. The hot sun rises and dries up the grass; the flower withers, and its beauty fades away. So also, wealthy people will fade away with all of their achievements. (James 1:9-11)

God blesses the people who patiently endure testing. Afterward they will receive the crown of life that God has promised to those who love him. (James 1:12)

Remember, no one who wants to do wrong should ever say, "God is tempting me." God is never tempted to do wrong, and he never tempts anyone else either. Temptation comes from the lure of our own evil desires. These evil desires lead to evil actions, and evil actions lead to death. (James 1:13-15)

My dear brothers and sisters, be quick to listen, slow to speak, and slow to get angry. Your anger can never make things right in God's sight. (James 1:19-20)

If you just listen and don't obey, it is like looking at your face in a mirror but doing nothing to improve your appearance. You see yourself, walk away, and forget what you look like. But if you keep looking steadily into God's perfect law—the law that sets you free—and if you do what it says and don't forget what you heard, then God will bless you for doing it. (James 1:23-25)

If you claim to be religious but don't control your tongue, you are just fooling yourself, and your religion is worthless. Pure and lasting religion in the sight of God our Father means that we must care for orphans and widows in their troubles, and refuse to let the world corrupt us. (James 1:26-27)

Yes indeed, it is good when you truly obey our Lord's royal command found in the Scriptures: "Love your neighbor as yourself." But if you pay special attention to the rich, you are committing a sin, for you are guilty of breaking that law. And the person who keeps all of the laws except one is as guilty as the person who has broken all of God's laws. For the same God who said, "Do not commit adultery," also said, "Do not murder." So if you murder someone, you have broken the entire law, even if you do not commit adultery. (James 2:8-11)

So whenever you speak, or whatever you do, remember that you will be judged by the law of love, the law that set you free. For there will be no mercy for you if you have not been merciful to others. But if you have been merciful, then God's mercy toward you will win out over his judgment against you. (James 2:12-13)

Dear brothers and sisters, what's the use of saying you have faith if you don't prove it by your actions? That kind of faith can't save anyone. Suppose you see a brother or sister who needs food or clothing, and you say, "Well, good-bye and God bless you; stay warm and eat well"—but then you don't give that person any food or clothing. What good does that do? So you see, it isn't enough just to have faith. Faith that doesn't show itself by good deeds is no faith at all—it is dead and useless. (James 2:14-17)

If you are wise and understand God's ways, live a life of steady goodness so that only good deeds will pour forth. And if you don't brag about the good you do, then you will be truly wise! But if you are bitterly jealous and there is selfish ambition in your hearts, don't brag about being wise. That is the worst kind of lie. For jealousy and selfishness are not God's kind of wisdom. Such things are earthly, unspiritual, and motivated by the Devil. (James 3:13-15)

Even when you do ask, you don't get it because your whole motive is wrong—you want only what will give you pleasure. You adulterers! Don't you realize that friendship with this world makes you an enemy of God? I say it again, that if your aim is to enjoy this world, you can't be a friend of God. (James 4:3-4)

Humble yourselves before God. Resist the Devil, and he will flee from you. Draw close to God, and God will draw close to you. Wash your hands, you sinners; purify your hearts, you hypocrites. Let there be tears for the wrong things you have done. Let there be sorrow and deep grief. Let there be sadness instead of laughter, and gloom instead of joy. When you bow down before the Lord and admit your dependence on him, he will lift you up and give you honor. (James 4:7-10)

Don't speak evil against each other, my dear brothers and sisters. If you criticize each other and condemn each other, then you are criticizing and condemning God's law. But you are not a judge who can decide whether the law is right or wrong. Your job is to obey it. God alone, who made the law, can rightly judge among us. He alone has the power to save or to destroy. So what right do you have to condemn your neighbor? (James 4:11-12)

What you ought to say is, "If the Lord wants us to, we will live and do this or that." Otherwise you will be boasting about your own plans, and all such boasting is evil. Remember, it is sin to know what you ought to do and then not do it. (James 4:15-17)

Dear brothers and sisters, you must be patient as you wait for the Lord's return. Consider the farmers who eagerly look

for the rains in the fall and in the spring. They patiently wait for the precious harvest to ripen. You, too, must be patient. And take courage, for the coming of the Lord is near. (James 5:7-8)

Don't grumble about each other, my brothers and sisters, or God will judge you. For look! The great Judge is coming. He is standing at the door! (James 5:9)

Most of all, my brothers and sisters, never take an oath, by heaven or earth or anything else. Just say a simple yes or no, so that you will not sin and be condemned for it. (James 5:12)

Are any among you suffering? They should keep on praying about it. And those who have reason to be thankful should continually sing praises to the Lord. Are any among you sick? They should call for the elders of the church and have them pray over them, anointing them with oil in the name of the Lord. And their prayer offered in faith will heal the sick, and the Lord will make them well. And anyone who has committed sins will be forgiven. (James 5:13-15)

Confess your sins to each other and pray for each other so that you may be healed. The earnest prayer of a righteous person has great power and wonderful results. (James 5:16)

My dear brothers and sisters, if anyone among you wanders away from the truth and is brought back again, you can be sure that the one who brings that person back will save that sinner from death and bring about the forgiveness of many sins. (James 5:19-20)

So think clearly and exercise self-control. Look forward to the special blessings that will come to you at the return of Jesus Christ. Obey God because you are his children. Don't slip back into your old ways of doing evil; you didn't know any better then. But now you must be holy in everything you do, just as God—who chose you to be his children—is holy. For he himself has said, "You must be holy because I am holy." (1 Peter 1:13-16)

Remember that the heavenly Father to whom you pray has no favorites when he judges. He will judge or reward you

285

according to what you do. So you must live in reverent fear of him during your time as foreigners here on earth. For you know that God paid a ransom to save you from the empty life you inherited from your ancestors. And the ransom he paid was not mere gold or silver. (1 Peter 1:17-18)

Now you can have sincere love for each other as brothers and sisters because you were cleansed from your sins when you accepted the truth of the Good News. So see to it that you really do love each other intensely with all your hearts. (1 Peter 1:22)

So get rid of all malicious behavior and deceit. Don't just pretend to be good! Be done with hypocrisy and jealousy and backstabbing. You must crave pure spiritual milk so that you can grow into the fullness of your salvation. Cry out for this nourishment as a baby cries for milk, now that you have had a taste of the Lord's kindness. (1 Peter 2:1-3)

Dear brothers and sisters, you are foreigners and aliens here. So I warn you to keep away from evil desires because they fight against your very souls. Be careful how you live among your unbelieving neighbors. Even if they accuse you of doing wrong, they will see your honorable behavior, and they will believe and give honor to God when he comes to judge the world. (1 Peter 2:11-12)

For the Lord's sake, accept all authority—the king as head of state, and the officials he has appointed. For the king has sent them to punish all who do wrong and to honor those who do right. It is God's will that your good lives should silence those who make foolish accusations against you. You are not slaves; you are free. But your freedom is not an excuse to do evil. You are free to live as God's slaves. (1 Peter 2:13-16)

Show respect for everyone. Love your Christian brothers and sisters. Fear God. Show respect for the king. (1 Peter 2:17)

Finally, all of you should be of one mind, full of sympathy toward each other, loving one another with tender hearts and humble minds. Don't repay evil for evil. Don't retaliate when people say unkind things about you. Instead, pay them

back with a blessing. That is what God wants you to do, and he will bless you for it. (1 Peter 3:8-9)

Even if you suffer for doing what is right, God will reward you for it. So don't be afraid and don't worry. Instead, you must worship Christ as Lord of your life. And if you are asked about your Christian hope, always be ready to explain it. But you must do this in a gentle and respectful way. Keep your conscience clear. Then if people speak evil against you, they will be ashamed when they see what a good life you live because you belong to Christ. (1 Peter 3:14-16)

Remember, it is better to suffer for doing good, if that is what God wants, than to suffer for doing wrong! Christ also suffered when he died for our sins once for all time. He never sinned, but he died for sinners that he might bring us safely home to God. He suffered physical death, but he was raised to life in the Spirit. (1 Peter 3:17-18)

The end of the world is coming soon. Therefore, be earnest and disciplined in your prayers. Most important of all, continue to show deep love for each other, for love covers a multitude of sins. (1 Peter 4:7-8)

Cheerfully share your home with those who need a meal or a place to stay. God has given gifts to each of you from his great variety of spiritual gifts. Manage them well so that God's generosity can flow through you. (1 Peter 4:9-10)

Are you called to be a speaker? Then speak as though God himself were speaking through you. Are you called to help others? Do it with all the strength and energy that God supplies. Then God will be given glory in everything through Jesus Christ. All glory and power belong to him forever and ever. Amen. (1 Peter 4:11)

Instead, be very glad—because these trials will make you partners with Christ in his suffering, and afterward you will have the wonderful joy of sharing his glory when it is displayed to all the world. Be happy if you are insulted for being a Christian, for then the glorious Spirit of God will come upon you. (1 Peter 4:13-14)

So humble yourselves under the mighty power of God, and in his good time he will honor you. (1 Peter 5:6)

Give all your worries and cares to God, for he cares about what happens to you. (1 Peter 5:7)

Be careful! Watch out for attacks from the Devil, your great enemy. He prowls around like a roaring lion, looking for some victim to devour. Take a firm stand against him, and be strong in your faith. Remember that your Christian brothers and sisters all over the world are going through the same kind of suffering you are. (1 Peter 5:8-9)

So make every effort to apply the benefits of these promises to your life. Then your faith will produce a life of moral excellence. A life of moral excellence leads to knowing God better. Knowing God leads to self-control. Self-control leads to patient endurance, and patient endurance leads to godliness. Godliness leads to love for other Christians, and finally you will grow to have genuine love for everyone. The more you grow like this, the more you will become productive and useful in your knowledge of our Lord Jesus Christ. (2 Peter 1:5-8)

Since everything around us is going to melt away, what holy, godly lives you should be living! You should look forward to that day and hurry it along—the day when God will set the heavens on fire and the elements will melt away in the flames. (2 Peter 3:11-12)

Dear friends, while you are waiting for these things to happen, make every effort to live a pure and blameless life. And be at peace with God. And remember, the Lord is waiting so that people have time to be saved. This is just as our beloved brother Paul wrote to you with the wisdom God gave him. (2 Peter 3:14-15)

Grow in the special favor and knowledge of our Lord and Savior Jesus Christ. To him be all glory and honor, both now and forevermore. Amen. (2 Peter 3:18)

If we are living in the light of God's presence, just as Christ is, then we have fellowship with each other, and the blood of Jesus, his Son, cleanses us from every sin. If we say we

have no sin, we are only fooling ourselves and refusing to accept the truth. But if we confess our sins to him, he is faithful and just to forgive us and to cleanse us from every wrong. If we claim we have not sinned, we are calling God a liar and showing that his word has no place in our hearts. (1 John 1:7-10)

If someone says, "I belong to God," but doesn't obey God's commandments, that person is a liar and does not live in the truth. But those who obey God's word really do love him. That is the way to know whether or not we live in him. Those who say they live in God should live their lives as Christ did. (1 John 2:4-6)

If anyone says, "I am living in the light," but hates a Christian brother or sister, that person is still living in darkness. Anyone who loves other Christians is living in the light and does not cause anyone to stumble. (1 John 2:9-10)

Stop loving this evil world and all that it offers you, for when you love the world, you show that you do not have the love of the Father in you. For the world offers only the lust for physical pleasure, the lust for everything we see, and pride in our possessions. These are not from the Father. They are from this evil world. And this world is fading away, along with everything it craves. But if you do the will of God, you will live forever. (1 John 2:15-17)

Anyone who denies the Son doesn't have the Father either. But anyone who confesses the Son has the Father also. (1 John 2:23)

Dear children, don't let anyone deceive you about this: When people do what is right, it is because they are righteous, even as Christ is righteous. But when people keep on sinning, it shows they belong to the Devil, who has been sinning since the beginning. But the Son of God came to destroy these works of the Devil. Those who have been born into God's family do not sin, because God's life is in them. So they can't keep on sinning, because they have been born of God. (1 John 3:7-9)

If anyone has enough money to live well and sees a brother or sister in need and refuses to help—how can God's love be

in that person? Dear children, let us stop just saying we love each other; let us really show it by our actions. (1 John 3:17-18)

We will receive whatever we request because we obey him and do the things that please him. And this is his commandment: We must believe in the name of his Son, Jesus Christ, and love one another, just as he commanded us. Those who obey God's commandments live in fellowship with him, and he with them. And we know he lives in us because the Holy Spirit lives in us. (1 John 3:22-24)

Dear friends, let us continue to love one another, for love comes from God. Anyone who loves is born of God and knows God. But anyone who does not love does not know God—for God is love. (1 John 4:7-8)

If someone says, "I love God," but hates a Christian brother or sister, that person is a liar; for if we don't love people we can see, how can we love God, whom we have not seen? And God himself has commanded that we must love not only him but our Christian brothers and sisters, too. (1 John 4:20-21)

If you see a Christian brother or sister sinning in a way that does not lead to death, you should pray, and God will give that person life. But there is a sin that leads to death, and I am not saying you should pray for those who commit it. (1 John 5:16)

You, dear friends, must continue to build your lives on the foundation of your holy faith. And continue to pray as you are directed by the Holy Spirit. Live in such a way that God's love can bless you as you wait for the eternal life that our Lord Jesus Christ in his mercy is going to give you. (Jude 1:20-21)

Show mercy to those whose faith is wavering. Rescue others by snatching them from the flames of judgment. There are still others to whom you need to show mercy, but be careful that you aren't contaminated by their sins. (Jude 1:22-23)

Look, I am coming quickly. Hold on to what you have, so that no one will take away your crown. All who are victori-

ous will become pillars in the Temple of my God, and they will never have to leave it. And I will write my God's name on them, and they will be citizens in the city of my God—the new Jerusalem that comes down from heaven from my God. And they will have my new name inscribed upon them. (Revelation 3:11-12)

I advise you to buy gold from me—gold that has been purified by fire. Then you will be rich. And also buy white garments so you will not be shamed by your nakedness. And buy ointment for your eyes so you will be able to see. I am the one who corrects and disciplines everyone I love. Be diligent and turn from your indifference. (Revelation 3:18-19)

Blessed are those who wash their robes so they can enter through the gates of the city and eat the fruit from the tree of life. (Revelation 22:14)